The Official SpinRite™ II and Hard Disk Companion

How Hard Disks Work and Why They Die

By John M. Goodman, Ph.D

With special introduction by
Steve Gibson
President, Gibson Research
Makers of SpinRite

IDG Books Worldwide, Inc.
San Mateo, California 94402

The Official SpinRite II and Hard Disk Companion
Michael McCarthy, Editor-in-Chief
Jeremy Jusdon, Associate Editor
Lana Olson, Production Manager
Edited by Elizabeth Eva
Technical Edit by Susan McBride and Steve Gibson
Interior design by Mark Houts and Hartman Publishing
Production by Hartman Publishing

Published by
IDG Books Worldwide, Inc.
155 Bovet Road, Suite 730
San Mateo, CA 94402
(415) 358-1250

Library of Congress Catalog Card No.: 90-84497

ISBN 1-878058-08-8

Printed in the United States of America

10 9 8 7 6 5 4 3 2

Distributed in the United States by IDG Books Worldwide.
Distributed in Canada by Macmillan of Canada, a Division of Canada Publishing Corporation.

For information on translations and availability in other countries, contact IDG Books Worldwide.
For sales inquiries and special prices for bulk quantities, write to the address above or call IDG Books Worldwide at (415) 358-1250.

Dedication

I dedicate this book to my parents, who set me on the right track in the first place and realigned me to it as necessary. In particular, I have learned from my father a passion for how things work and for stating ideas with precision, clarity, and accuracy.

Acknowledgements

This book would not have been at all the same without the generous cooperation of many people. Foremost among them is Steve Gibson.

SpinRite is his program and Gibson Research is his company. Both are very personally his. In an industry where paranoia is legend and nearly all entrepreneurs hide what they think of as their competitive advantages, Steve Gibson has been uncommonly forthcoming. He answered my questions with candor. He studied my drafts carefully, picking out everything from simple typographic errors to the most subtle errors of reasoning or fact. Thank you Steve!

I have also been fortunate to have had a number of other readers whose attention to detail and wealth of knowledge helped keep me from a host of minor pitfalls. These include Steve Donegan, engineer at Western Digital; Daniel Likins, PC custom hardware designer extraordinaire; and Barry Workman, of Workman and Associates.

Susan McBride read some of the early chapters. I benefited greatly from her relative lack of technical knowledge and her willingness to share with me the points in my writing that confused her. My wife, Pauline Merry, played a similar role.

I must also thank my copy editor, Liz Eva of InfoWorld, for adding polish while reducing length. Finally, I thank Michael McCarthy,

Editor-in-Chief at IDG Books, for believing in me and in this project. It has been a pleasure working with both of you.

Naturally, all the responsibility for the final text is mine. Still, I sleep a lot more soundly knowing I have had knowledgeable, careful, and meticulous readers going over everything I wrote.

I would be remiss if I did not also thank other who helped me.

Brad Kingsbury, the project chief for Calibrate at Peter Norton Computing, met with me for several hours. We went over that product's features and the company's design goals in great detail. He further enlightened me about some of the fundamentals of hard disk operation and various DOS arcana.

I would also like to acknowledge the help of Norman Ivans, President of Prime Solutions; Mark Kolad, President of Kolad Research; Dave Bushong, author of IAU; and Bart Dangerfield, Marketing Director for Gazelle Systems.

Richard Evins shared his knowledge of the industry and introduced me to some helpful people and interesting products. Johnny Tseng at UltraStor helped me understand their fine disk controllers. Howard Chan at Wyse Technologies helped me to understand some special features of his company's products.

I prepared the text using *Microsoft Word*, Version 5.0, and I used *Corel Draw*, Version 1.21, and *Ventura Publisher for Windows*, Version 3.0, to prepare the figures.

I wish to thank Microsoft for including me in the beta testing of Word and later on giving me a copy of the final version. Fiona Rochester at Corel Systems was instrumental in getting me a copy of their fine product. Marie Trafficanda at Hill & Knowlton arranged for me to get a copy of the latest version of *Ventura Publisher*. Without the help of all of them, this project would have been much harder to do, especially on time.

The Official *SpinRite*™ *II* and Hard Disk Companion

TABLE OF CONTENTS

PART I

GUIDE TO SPINRITE

A concise description of both the old and the new ways to reinterleave your hard disk. This chapter introduces one of the main values of SpinRite. It closes with a brief indication of the other benefits that such a program can have, details of which are covered in the next chapter.

This chapter explains the traditional factory analog disk surface analysis and contrasts it with the testing done by SpinRite and similar programs. After detailing how SpinRite does its tests, we conclude with some recommendations for when to rely on defect information provided by the disk manufacturer and when it may safely be ignored.

In this chapter we go "under the hood" to explain in detail the algorithms that SpinRite uses to accomplish its wonders.

A guided tour to the use of the software in both interactive
and batch modes. This chapter begins with a comparison
of this version with earlier ones, and gives a
recommendation regarding upgrades. The reader will

learn much more about how to interpret the information presented by SpinRite on screen and in its log files than is given in the product literature.

This chapter also details the need for head parking utilities and describes some that are safe and some that are dangerous.

It concludes with some hints and tips for achieving greater data safety and easier operation of SpinRite.

PART II

HOW HARD DISKS WORK AND WHY THEY SOMETIMES DIE

This chapter covers the fundamentals of magnetic storage technologies. Starting with a discussion of the lowest level of data storage, with bits and flux reversals, it describes in detail several different data encoding technologies as well as error correction and error detection strategies. The fundamentals section ends with a discussion of the important, but little understood, topics of sector interleaving and head skewing for better disk drive performance.

This chapter also introduces each of the popular standards for hard disk interfaces in personal computers. It also explains the physical construction of drives and how this affects their performance, describes "recalibration" and other funny sounds that disk drives make, and ends with a discussion of disk caching.

Disk drives on PCs do not operate in a vacuum. Most PCs run the MS-DOS or PC-DOS operating system. This provides some important limits on how any computer program can access data on the drives. This chapter details the fundamentals of how MS-DOS defines and uses hard disk drives. It points out both the limits that are built into the operating system and some ways innovative manufacturers have evaded those limits. It ends with a discussion of error messages from the disk controller, the BIOS, and from DOS, telling both what makes them happen and what you need to do about them when they occur.

7. Preparing a Hard Disk to Store Information 203

A disk drive fresh from the manufacturer is useless for
data storage. This chapter details the three steps necessary
to prepare the drive for use and tells of some strange
methods used by certain manufacturers to accomplish
these steps.

8. How Hard Disks Die 237

In this chapter the reader learns all the failure modes of disk drives. For some of them lost data can be recovered. In other cases you can even reverse the damage by the use of SpinRite. Other options are also mentioned for dealing with the rest of the failures.

Preface

by Steve Gibson

Hi!

Although I've developed other commercially successful products in my time, no one ever wrote a book about one of them. Needless to say, I'm delighted and flattered. My role in this project as an information source and the book's technical editor has been interesting and rewarding. I think you'll find that John Goodman's straightforward writing style moves with just the right mixture of speed and detail. Since the result is both manageable and worthwhile, the book fills a void in a market that currently overflows with rehashed owner's manuals and ghost-written hearsay. A quick look through the Table of Contents reveals that this book is something different. If you have even a passing interest in the mechanisms of modern hard disk storage on IBM compatible PCs, this book is for you.

Hard disk drive reliability has been a casualty of extreme pricing pressure. The hard disk is the only complex mechanical component in the typical PC. As such, it has not been nearly as amenable to manufacturing economies of scale as mass-produced, solid-state electronics. Many sharp engineering pencils have been dulled by the job of making hard disk drives cheaper. Unfortunately, as engineers succeeded in reducing the cost of manufacturing hard disks, they also cheapened the quality.

The sad fact is that contemporary PC hard disk drives are not as reliable as they need to be to deliver years of error-free operation. In the name of ever-cheaper PCs, manufacturers have sacrificed building in the engineering tolerances that create margins for error. *SpinRite*'s surprising success in the marketplace testifies to the fact that hard disks die daily.

Whether you're reading John's book casually for background information, or from a need to resolve a recent hard-disk disaster, I'm sure you'll find that he presents the information clearly and accurately.

Here's to a future of long-term hard disk health through simple periodic maintenance and understanding.

Steve Gibson, President
Gibson Research Corporation
October 1990

Introduction

Nearly all personal computers sold today have hard disks. We use them because they provide a very effective means of storing information and accessing it quickly and easily. Most of us expect them to work perfectly. We do so because it usually seems as if they are perfect. This is far from the truth, though. Only the most exquisite feats of hardware design and programming allow them to appear as perfect as they do.

In this book a "personal computer," or PC, will mean any IBM-PC, XT, AT, PS/2 or compatible personal computer—that is, any computer capable of running the MS-DOS operating system. A "hard disk" will refer to any non-removeable magnetic storage device, sometimes also called a "Winchester drive" or a "Fixed Direct Access Storage Device" (Fixed DASD). Some of the discussion will also apply to certain removeable media disk drives, but only if they appear to the computer to be virtually the same as a fixed disk drive.

In the first part of this book you will learn about a marvelous new category of utility software which has the potential for vastly increasing your hard disk's performance. Even more important, these utilities can often extend greatly the time before your hard disk's inevitable death.I tell you how they work, how SpinRite works, how to use it, what all those menus mean, and what SpinRite is *really* doing when you set it going.

In the second part of this book you will learn all the gory, interesting details of how hard disks work. This includes those near-miracles of design that let them mask their imperfections. You also will learn all the ways in which they can and do eventually "die." (That often means merely that they are finally revealing their underlying imperfection.) If you really want to understand hard disk storage, in English, here's where you'll find enough detail to keep you going for years.

A suggestion

You may have bought this book to learn how to get the most out of your copy of *SpinRite*. You may have bought this book because you want to learn all you can about how your hard disk works. The second type of reader needs a lot of details which the first type of reader may neither need nor want. The book has been written with both kinds of reader in mind; hence this suggestion.

If you find some sections contain more information than you want to know about that topic, feel free to skip ahead to the next topic — or the next chapter. Most of the topics and the chapters stand on their own, so you can benefit from reading them even if you have not read all the sections that come before. And I refer you to other chapters if you need to check out some passing detail.

To make it easier, I've flagged the *really* technical discussions (which *I'm* most interested in) by marking those paragraphs with an icon and vertical bar — that way, if you're *not* that interested, you can skip over it easily. On the other hand, if you're already pretty knowledgeable and technical detail is what you love most, you can head straight for those parts.

A Warning

All hard disks do eventually die. You must have a procedure for doing regular backups of your valuable data from the hard disk to some other medium and you must use it. To do otherwise is simply folly.

If you have been foolish, though, and have allowed your disk to die with important data on it for which you have no backup copies, it *may* be possible to resurrect those data. Maybe. (The details are in Chapter 8.) But please don't count on it. Make backups regularly.

Part
– I –

Guide to Spinrite

Chapter 1

Reinterleaving Software: A New Category of Utility Program

In 1987, personal computers were not nearly so efficient as they are now. Among other things, we now have some revolutionary new utility software, the focus of this book. Steve Gibson was bothered by the effort one had to go through to adjust precisely an arcane hard disk parameter called the *sector interleave*. He knew that getting the right value meant that his PC would work *much* faster. Pained by how hard it was to set the sector interleave using the methods available, Gibson was shocked to discover that almost no PCs then in use had it set right.

Gibson devised a better method to set the interleave, from which came the product *SpinRite*. What he did not foresee was the revolutionary effect that program would have as the beginning of a new category of utility software for PCs.

To understand this revolution, you must first know what things were like back "in the good old days" before *SpinRite*.

1 The Old Method

Disks on PCs store information in chunks called *sectors* (usually with 512 bytes per sector). The sectors are arranged around the disk in rings called *tracks*. As the disk turns, the read/write head passes over the track reading or writing information (see Figure 1-1). (For a more detailed description of each of these ideas, see Chapter 5.)

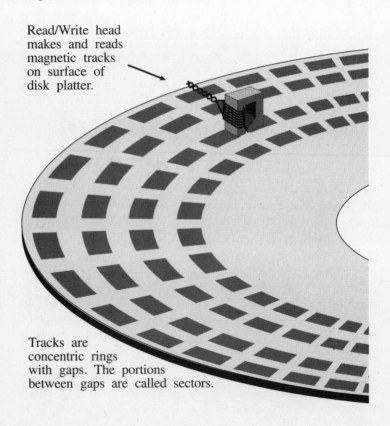

Read/Write head makes and reads magnetic tracks on surface of disk platter.

Tracks are concentric rings with gaps. The portions between gaps are called sectors.

Figure 1-1 Tracks and Sectors on a hard disk

Any useful collection of information, called a *file*, is stored in one or more sectors. If you have a file that takes up several sectors, it might seem, naively, that the sensible way to store it would be in successive sectors along a track. Then the pieces could be put down in order and picked up in order.

Though fine in theory, this method often fails in execution, because your PC may not be able to write or read one sector immediately after it has written or read another one. There is some minimum "digestion time" that must pass between reading (or writing) one sector and the next. Often it will turn out that while the PC is waiting for that digestion time to go by, the next sector, or even more than one sector, also will go past the read/write head.

If that happens, then you must wait till the disk turns around the rest of that revolution before the sector you want comes into view again. This drastically reduces the speed at which a file may be read or written, since you only read or write one sector on each revolution of the disk.

A clever solution to this problem is to arrange the sectors of information around the track in a more sophisticated manner. Instead of having sector number 2 placed right after sector number 1, it may be put several sectors farther down the track. If you do it just right, the added time it takes for sector 2 to come into view under the read/write head after the PC has finished with sector 1 will be just a bit more than the "digestion time." Then when the PC is ready for sector 2, voila! There it is. (See Figure 1-2 and the discussion in Chapter 5 in the section "Improving Hard Disk Performance by Sector Interleaving and Head Skewing.") Though the idea of sector interleave proves simple enough, setting it correctly before the advent of *SpinRite* was no mean feat.

Testing to find the right value

There are three major steps to preparing a new hard disk for use in a PC. (See Chapter 7 for details.) The system assembler must conduct the first of these, the low-level format, after connecting the drive to the controller in the PC. Until recently, no one ever repeated this format after this first time.

The system interleave gets established at the time of that low-level format. You can't change the interleave without going back to that

Figure 1-2 Three examples of different Sector Interleave values. An example showing the problem with reinterleaving without testing for data safety.

step. Before *SpinRite* existed, most PCs users never considered doing that, even if they knew what that step was all about (and most users did not). On the other hand, until all three steps are complete, DOS cannot use the hard disk. So one cannot easily test to see whether you have the sector interleave correct until after the last of these steps.

A lengthy process: Thus to get the interleave set correctly, using only the tools included in DOS, you had to do the low-level formatting, the partitioning, and then the high-level formatting of the disk, after which you could test to see if you had the interleave set correctly. A wrong interleave meant you had to repeat the entire tedious process, which only the most perfectionistic of PC users ever bothered to do.

An early attempt to make it easy: A fellow named Mark Kolad created a collection of programs to help those perfectionistic PC users. His HOPTIMUM program allowed one to check a hard disk and find the optimum value for its sector interleave. His HFORMAT program then made it possible to redo the low-level interleave, and in the process to set the sector interleave to the optimum value. A third program in his collection, HTEST, could test the ability of your hard disk to store and retrieve data reliably.

> **TECHNICAL NOTE** HOPTIMUM dramatically shortens the process of finding the optimum interleave value. Instead of redoing the low-level format on the entire disk, it simply directs the hard disk controller to redo the low-level format on one or a few tracks with some specified sector interleave value. Then it tests how rapidly it can read or write data to that track. It repeats this process for several other sector interleave values. Finally, HOPTIMUM shows you which interleave value yields the highest average data transfer rate (the number of bytes per second you can read or write).
>
> Since these tests can be done somewhere past the first few cylinders of the disk, they can be done without destroying the partitioning and high-level format information. They will destroy any data you may have stored on the cylinders you use, though. The programs did not make you do the tests on a safely empty cylinder, but they allowed you to do so if you knew where one was, and if you remembered to tell it to use that empty cylinder. This capability and the use of only one or a few cylinders for the tests made it possible to choose the optimum sector interleave value in only a few minutes, instead of the few hours that typically were needed before.

These programs contained the kernel of what was needed, but they required that you know a lot about how your PC worked, and they did their work in a "destructive" fashion, destroying any data that resided on the track being tested or reformatted. (HTEST did have a non-destructive, read-only test, but it didn't report nearly as much about the integrity of the disk.)

One of Steve Gibson's key insights was how to do this work without destroying data on the hard disk. In fact, using his new approach, you could do these steps without losing even one byte of it. Further, he realized the importance of making his program do all this

1

very technically sophisticated work without requiring a matching sophistication in its users.

A Better Way

What was Gibson's key insight? In retrospect it is simplicity itself: First read all the data on a single track and store it someplace safe. Test that one track and redo its low-level format. When you are through, put the data back.

That is it, in its essence. Of course, reality has a way of complicating things a bit.

A few pitfalls along the way

Gibson's original plan was simply to read a track's data, redo its low-level interleave, and then put the data back. Doing just that is not safe, though. It is essential to do at least some testing as you go.

If a sector on the track has a bad spot as a result of a pinhole defect in the magnetic coating on the platter, then that sector will still be bad after redoing the low-level interleave. If you change the sector interleave value, this sector will no longer have the same sector number. If you simply restore the data to each sector according to its sector number, the bad sector may get some important data put in it (see Figure 1-3).

If you noticed that the sector was marked as bad, you could simply avoid placing any data in it. That might work, but since errors have a way of creeping in when you least expect them, it would be, at best, an imprudent way to do things.

The only safe way to proceed is by following these four steps.

1. Read and save the data for a given track.
2. Redo the low-level format for that track with the optimal sector interleave value.
3. Test every sector in that track very carefully.
4. If the sectors are all perfect, put the data back. If one or more of the sectors are flawed, store their data somewhere else and make whatever other adjustments are needed to let DOS find those data when it wants them.

Before: The Sector Interleave was set to 3:1. Also, there was (and still is) a defect in the sector that was numbered 14. Since we knew that, none of our valuable data was stored there.

After: Sector Interleave is now set to 1:1. The disk sure works faster. But, oops! The valuable data that was in the sector numbered 6 has now been put into the defective one. Ouch!

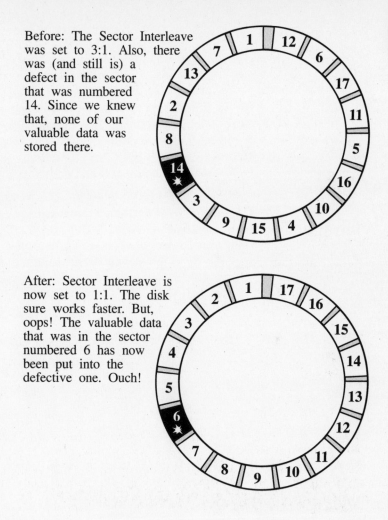

Figure 1-3: The problem with reinterleaving without testing

As the development of *SpinRite* progressed, Gibson realized that his task was much more complicated than he had first imagined. He began with the intention of making a program to allow easy, safe resetting of the sector interleave value. In the end he was *forced* to make a program that is at least as useful for data recovery and for ensuring the integrity of future data storage.

1 Side Benefits

Gibson tested hard drives thoroughly to learn all the many ways they can fail, to make sure his new program would not trip up on any of them and cause an accidental data loss. He was flabbergasted to find out just how many different ways hard disks can fail. The subtleties of the interactions between all the different brands and types of hard disks and hard disk controllers with the many different brands of IBM-PC compatible computers were mind-boggling. Developing *SpinRite* took a lot longer than he had expected.

After all that research, *SpinRite* emerged a much more capable program than the one Gibson initially envisioned. The additional benefits fall into three categories: refreshing sector header information; recovering unreadable data; and moving data to safety.

Refreshing the sector headers

A scary error message to get from your PC is "Sector Not Found." You know your data is out there, but your PC simply cannot find it.

Before DOS can read or write any data, it must find the right sector in which to place or look for those data. It does this by reading the sector headers (see Figure 1-4).

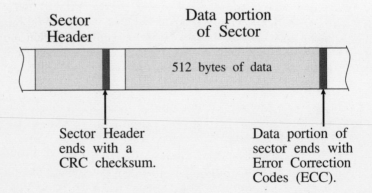

Figure 1-4 Anatomy of a hard disk sector.

1

Naturally, it must first move the head assembly to the right cylinder and activate the correct head. Then it reads the header on each sector of that track till it finds the one it is looking for, or until the entire track has gone past the head. The sector headers contain all three address numbers: cylinder, head, and physical sector number. Thus, if it sees all three right numbers, the controller can be sure it has positioned the head assembly correctly and switched on the right head and that it has found the right sector around the track.

There are three things that can make a sector header unreadable: a physical defect in the magnetic coating in that part of the disk surface; a data accident that may have damaged the data stored in the sector header, but not have done any damage to the magnetic coating; or the head assembly may have drifted slightly to one side, so that it no longer tracks over the sector header enough to read it accurately. Let's look at each of these possibilities.

If the magnetic coating is damaged where the sector header information should be stored, it will be impossible to record data there. Most such coating defects are on the drive from the day it is manufactured, but new ones can occur, such as if something jars the disk enough to make the head bounce on the surface hard enough to gouge out a bit of the magnetic coating.

The controller reads all the information in a sector header and then checks to see if what it read was valid. It uses a cyclical redundancy checksum (CRC) strategy to do this validation. (See Chapter 6 under "A Problem of Imperfection and Some Solutions" for more on CRC.) If the CRC value it read from the header does not agree with the value it computes, it will reject that sector as unreadable.

A data accident may also render a sector header unreadable. If anything changes even one bit of the information stored in the header, the controller will reject that sector as unreadable. Such an accident may occur if the head comes to rest over that sector header when you turn off power to your PC. When you turn on your PC again, the head may jerk around a bit before the platter starts turning. Further, a brief surge of current may pass through the head winding, causing a magnetic field that might reverse some bits recorded in the sector header. Even the residual magnetization of the head might be enough to alter those bits, even without a current surge.

1

A misalignment may also cause the sector header to become un-readable, simply because it is too far to one side of the path that the read head is currently following (see Figure 1-5).

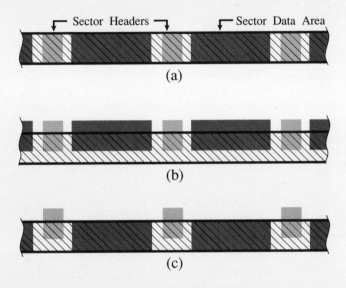

Sector Headers   Sector Data Area

(a)

(b)

(c)

Figure 1-5 Head Drift and Read Errors. The path of the read/write head is indicated by the shaded region between the two heavy lines.
(a) At first the sector headers and data sections are created by the head under its path.
(b) Later on the head path may drift to one side enough to make reading data difficult.
(c) Rewriting the data puts them on track, but the sector headers remain dangerously to one side. Using SpinRite one can redo the low-level format and get the sector headers into line, as in (a).

You can solve each of these problems by having *SpinRite* refresh the low-level format, which is the only way to rewrite the sector head-ers. The rewriting realigns the sector headers under the present head path and repairs any changes induced by a data accident. Only physical damage to the surface cannot be repaired this way, but *SpinRite* can detect it and relocate data to some safer spot.

Recovering unreadable data

1

Another horrible error message is "Read fault," which means that DOS cannot read some sector. It may give you a portion of your file, or it may refuse to give you any of your file, even though the error only affects a minute part of a single sector.

Sometimes DOS or the BIOS will force the controller to attempt to reread the sector several or even many times, but eventually they will give up. *SpinRite* is both more persistent and more clever in how it rereads a sector, and so it can often succeed where DOS and the BIOS have failed.

It can very often read the whole file accurately. If it cannot, at least it will give you back all but the very few bytes that actually were damaged. Chapter 3 includes a description of just how *SpinRite* performs this sort of "magic."

Moving data to safety

The third category of side benefits a program like *SpinRite* provides is moving data to safety. When your disk develops weak places, *SpinRite* will relocate the data. *SpinRite* looks for indications of problems that DOS normally hides from us.

The controller will tell the BIOS any time it has difficulty reading a sector, in particular whenever it needs to use the ECC stored in the sector with the data. (When it cannot read all the data accurately, the controller uses the ECC [error correction codes] to deduce what the sector data used to be; see Chapter 5 in the section "A Better Solution: Error Correction," for details on how ECC works.) It also will report any sector that it is unable to read or reconstruct.

If the controller says it has successfully reconstructed the data using ECC, DOS accepts the data as reported without informing us of any difficulties. Though you may receive the right data this time, you may not be so lucky the next time.

SpinRite goes through incredible gyrations trying to get an accurate reading of the data in the sector without using ECC. If ever it gets one perfect reading of those data, it will use them. If it must

1

use ECC to correct them it will, finally, accept that solution, but it will move the data to prevent possible future data loss.

SpinRite's persistence in reading data despite great difficulties, and its insistence on relocating data from suspicious sectors are what makes it so good at keeping your data safe.

In the next chapter, you will learn more about the preventable slow deaths of hard disks, and what role *SpinRite* and other similar programs play in preventing those failures.

Chapter 2

Preventing the Slow Death of Your Hard Drive

All hard disks die, eventually. Programs like *SpinRite* strive to postpone that eventuality as long as possible.

Catching Problems Before They Become Problems

Hard disk calamities can strike instantaneously, such as if an earthquake or a clumsy colleague knocks your PC on the floor, or if your hard disk controller suffers a violent electronic breakdown. Other, less dramatic problems build up over time until they finally show themselves by preventing your hard disk from working. The only defense against the swift, sudden death of your hard disk is to have good backups. You can often catch the problems that creep up on you, though, before they become disasters. In this chapter, we will focus on some slow death mechanisms and how *SpinRite* can help *forestall* those deaths. (See Chapter 5 for a detailed explanation of how hard disks are built and how they work. In Chapter 8, we go into a lot of detail about ways disks die and how to recover them.)

2

A common misconception

A commonly held misconception purports that our hard disks store data digitally. Though this would be wonderful, it is not actually the case. Digital data (bits of information, that is to say, a whole lot of ones and zeros) is sent from and returned to the computer in digital form, but the drives store the data as analog signals in the form of magnetic field patterns, which vary from place to place on the disk continuously.

The advantage that digital data has over analog is that in digital form, noise is usually ignored. (Noise means any deviation from the ideal pattern.) As long as the noise is not "too loud," it will not overwhelm the data, allowing us to reconstruct the digital information with complete reliability. Errors creep in when the noise exceeds a critical level.

Some complex electronics called the write circuitry create the magnetic field patterns that represent our data. The read circuitry, some other electronics that are as least as fancy, detect the patterns. The read/write heads lay the patterns down and pick them up. The head-positioning assembly positions these heads over the spinning platters. (See Chapter 5 for details.)

Some of these aspects may change temporarily, impairing the disk's capability to read data without affecting its storage capability. The head-positioning assembly may not always return the heads to precisely the same places, or the motor that turns the platters, bringing the magnetic field patterns under the heads, may not always turn at the same speed.

Other alterations have a more permanent effect. The magnetic field patterns may weaken or may get rearranged a bit, causing the data they represent to become harder and harder to read.

The notion of magnetic field patterns "weakening" over time on a hard disk has become a controversial one. Some people have noted that permanent magnets are just that. For all practical purposes, they keep their magnetization forever. So, they say, data patterns once recorded on the disk platter surface should stay there, full strength, until new data are recorded over them. Mostly that is true. Experience suggests that sometimes something happens to the patterns to make them appear to be weaker. What might that be?

As the read-write head sweeps over the platter surface, it records a swath of data called a track. Later it will again sweep over that part of the platter surface to detect those data. The band of magnetized surface is as wide as the head. It is possible for the magnetic field to get reversed for a portion of that width, which means that when the head sweeps along the track reading data, it will find a weaker signal in that region. This is just one way the recorded data patterns can effectively get weaker.

While some of these problems reflect an underlying defect in the disk, others are merely alterations of the data stored there. If your disk is damaged, you must retrieve your data somehow and store them elsewhere. If your data were merely altered, you again must retrieve the data, but you may then put them back where they came from, only without the errors.

Benefits of Rewriting the Data

You can deal with some problems decisively and easily. If the magnetic signals representing your data become weakened or have some "confusing dirt" signals mixed in, you may be able to repair the damage by rewriting the data. If the sector happens to reside on a damaged part of the disk surface, then you must move the data.

TECHNICAL NOTE If the signals representing the data are all correctly placed, but simply a bit weaker than normal, then rewriting will return them to full strength. If a few of the magnetic field transitions have been altered, the pattern of transitions will represent some slightly altered bits of information. This means you must solve the problem of reading the data before you rewrite them.

There are two very different cases of altered data patterns. If altered data lies in the sector header, we can detect the problem by using the cyclical redundancy checksum (CRC) number stored in that header. If the altered data lies in the data portion of the sector, we will catch the error by use of the error correction codes (ECC) stored with the data. (Both are discussed in Chapter 5.)

The CRC allows us to catch problems with the sector header information. If we find that the data we have read are not consistent with the CRC, however, we know only that an error exists. All we can do is try reading that sector header again and again, hoping to

2

get it right. Worse, when we rewrite the data in that sector, the sector header will not be rewritten, so its defect will remain.

It is easier to cope with an error in the data section. The ECC numbers stored with the data not only allow detection of errors, they can often be used to reconstruct the original information.

Once you have recovered the data, you can replace them without error, provided the sector is not physically damaged. This rewriting of the data will completely remove most of the problems that commonly occur. You can deal with the other problems by moving those data to some other sector that does not have any physical damage.

Another advantage of rewriting the data is that the process cures at least part of the problem of head misalignment. If the head positioning mechanism has drifted, rewriting the data will align the data under the new position of the head, making them easier to read. Rewriting data will not realign the sector header, though. That requires the aid of a program like *SpinRite*, which will move data from a flawed sector in addition to rewriting all your data. (Chapter 8 explains why sector heads are special.)

Benefits of refreshing the low-level format

A head alignment problem, or a data glitch in the sector header, requires more than simply rewriting the data portion of the sectors. Otherwise the sector header information will continue to be difficult or impossible to read reliably.

The sector headers get written only during a low-level format, even though we must read each of them every time we access the data in that sector. If you can read the data in a bad sector even once, then you can move them to a safer place. Even better, if you can rewrite the sector header, you may remove any damage entirely, making the location a safe place for your data once more.

On most disk controller and drive combinations, running *SpinRite* will also redo the low-level format, thereby rewriting all the sector headers. The program's extensive testing of the disk before restoring the data will catch all the residual problems caused by defects in the disk surface.

TECHNICAL NOTE `0110 0110`   Neither *SpinRite* nor the other programs like it can do a low-level reformat on all drive and controller combinations. Mostly the problem is with controllers that "lie" about the dimensions of the drive. *SpinRite* must know the real number of heads, cylinders, and sectors per cylinder to do low-level reformatting safely.

Some controllers must lie about these numbers (and some others may do so). They "translate" or "map" real locations on the drive to equivalent locations on a fictitious drive with some other dimensions. We call these controllers "translating controllers." We explain this in more detail in "Sector Mapping" in Chapter 6.

Any drive/controller combination that uses sector mapping to translate sectors will prohibit all programs from redoing their low-level format. Still, *SpinRite* can do a lot for these drives by its testing and refreshing of the data portions of the sectors.

Just how *SpinRite* does its testing is an interesting story. Understanding this story will make it clear why you are better off relying on *SpinRite* than on the table of defects the manufacturer may have pasted on the drive.

Surface Analysis

Disk manufacturers routinely run a surface analysis once on every hard disk, testing to see if the disk platter can store data reliably. Using *SpinRite*, you can perform your own surface analysis whenever you wish. *SpinRite's* tests differ from the manufacturers'; for your purposes, they are better.

Bad Tracks, Sectors, and Clusters

It is impossible for drive manufacturers to make a large hard drive that is completely free of flaws. Small drives (up to 30-MB capacity) may be perfect, but larger ones may have up to 0.1% of the disk surface flawed. Of course, that means they are more than 99.9% perfect. That sounds pretty good—and it is. Still, they are not perfect. Most of the flaws consist of tiny pinholes in the magnetic coating on the disk platters — places where the coating is thinner than usual. These areas simply don't have enough magnetic mate-

2

rial to hold the field patterns reliably, making them an unsafe place
to store data.

The manufacturers test each drive before shipping it and include a
label or a slip of paper that lists any defects they found. Years ago
the conventional wisdom was that one should not use any portion
of a track that contained a defect. This policy might make sense if
the defect were a micro-boulder sticking up out of the surface.
Then positioning the head over that track would mean it would
have to bounce over that micro-boulder with each revolution of the
disk, possibly damaging the head and further ruining the disk
surface when the head crashed down on the other side of the
boulder.

Fortunately, such defects are exceedingly rare. Today's conventional wisdom says it is okay to use any of the disk surface except the
immediate neighborhood of each defect. The former approach led
to the term "bad track," meaning any track with at least one bad
spot on it. Now we instead use the term "bad sector," meaning the
portion of that track that holds the defect.

> **TECHNICAL NOTE** If you really thought you had micro-boulders to contend
> with, you should declare "bad cylinders," not just bad tracks,
> since the head positioner puts the heads over all the tracks
> of a cylinder at once. (That is the definition of which tracks make up
> a given cylinder.) Even the most conservative experts have not
> seriously proposed doing this. The actual reason for marking whole
> tracks as bad more likely has to do with some limitations on the way
> disks are tested by the manufacturers. We discuss these limitations
> in the section "Why This Is Less Helpful Than It Appears" later in
> this chapter.
>
> Older-style XT controllers have two commands to low-level format
> a track. One sets up the interleave you specify and marks all the
> sectors as good (INT 13, Function 5). The other formats all the
> sectors the same, but marks every one of them bad (INT 13,
> Function 6).
>
> More modern disk controllers allow you to tell them which sectors
> in a track to mark good and which to mark bad. They also support
> a more flexible approach to sector numbering. Instead of telling
> them simply an interleave factor, you give them a table of sector
> numbers (and associated good or bad sector flags), which lets you
> number the sectors in any fashion you may wish.

The command used is INT 13, Function 5. This is the same as the "format a track that is good" command for an XT. The difference is that for AT and PS/2 computers, the ES:BX register points to a 512-byte buffer. The entries in this buffer are pairs of bytes, one pair for each sector around the track. The first number in each pair is 0 if the sector is good, and 80H if that sector is bad. The second byte in each pair gives the physical sector number (see Figure 2-1).

Since DOS manages the disk in terms of a unit larger than the sector (the "cluster" or "allocation unit"), this also gives us the term "bad cluster," meaning a cluster with one or more bad sectors in it. (Chapter 7 gives details on clusters and the file allocation table used to keep track of them.)

What the Factory Tells You

Drive manufacturers carefully test their drives just after finishing the drive construction, before attaching the drive electronics board.

How they test

In the first step of their test, manufactureres attach a drive electronics board designed specifically for testing, which they will swap for the regular board before shipping the drive. This special test board carries a duplicate of the electronics that will ultimately control the spindle motor and the head-positioning mechanism, but it also has some very different read/write circuitry.

The test board records a special constant-strength analog signal on the drive surface. The voltage picked up from the read head goes to a distortion analyzer. (This process is much like that for testing an audio magnetic recording tape.) The test equipment looks for any spots on the disk where the voltage varies from the norm. The manufacturer considers these anomalous spots to be defects.

How they report defects

Notice that this test circuit does not record data bits. It is not even specific to the kind of data encoding technology that will later be used with the drive. (See Chapter 5 for a discussion of data encoding.) This means that the manufacturer cannot tell you in which sectors these defects will appear, only the cylinder and head (i.e.,

2

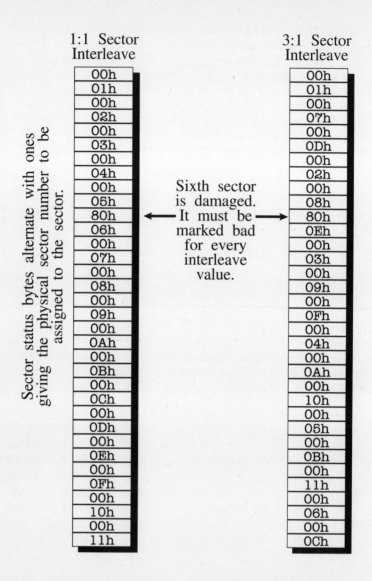

1:1 Sector
Interleave

3:1 Sector
Interleave

Sector status bytes alternate with ones
giving the physical sector number to be
assigned to the sector.

Sixth sector
is damaged.
◄— It must be —►
marked bad
for every
interleave
value.

Figure 2-1 Sample of the table of bytes that is used to tell an AT-style (16-bit) hard disk controller both how to interleave a track and which sectors on that track are to be marked as bad.

the track) and how far around the track each defect is from an index position. By making some assumptions about how data are going to be encoded (usually by assuming either MFM or 2,7 RLL), you can translate the angle from the index into an assumed number of *bytes from index*.

The manufacturer reports the defects in this manner, either pasting on a label or including a list with the drive that shows numbers for the cylinder, head, and bytes from index of each defect. You need to know the drive-model number, and what that suggests about the data-encoding technology being assumed, to derive any meaning from these numbers. Of course, if all you want to do is mark bad tracks, you can just use the numbers for the cylinder and head at which the defects were found and ignore the bytes-from-index values.

Why this is less helpful than it appears

If the drive's final electronics board has identical circuits for positioning the heads and for turning the spindle, the defects will appear to be where the manufacturer said they were. If the spindle motor turns just a tad slower with the final board than with the test board, all the defects will appear to be a bit farther along each track than the manufacturer said.

Even that assumes that the clock rate at which the data encoder turns data bits into magnetic field transitions is exactly the same as that assumed by the tester. Not only do individual clocks tend to vary, some controllers will intentionally alter their clock rates in certain circumstances. For instance, they speed up their clocks when they are asked (by the drive assembler) to produce a spare sector at the end of each track. This is another reason not to count on those bytes-from-index numbers.

To make matters worse, if the head positioner functions differently, the tracks on the drive with its final electronics board will not lie exactly where the tester assumed they would, in which case even the bad track information will be wrong.

Before it was possible to do a thorough digital test, one had to rely on the manufacturer's analog test results. With *SpinRite*, you no longer need to rely on these dubious results, which many system assemblers were ignoring anyway.

Digital Surface Testing

What makes a digital test good? Exactly how does it work? Are digital tests as sensitive as analog ones? These are some of the questions we will answer in the rest of this chapter.

SpinRite performs meticulous digital testing. *SpinRite* checks the disk's ability to store every conceivable data pattern and then reports which sectors contain the defects it finds. It expedites these tasks without requiring much sophistication on the part of its user.

Worst-case paradigm

Considering that there are an astronomical number of possible magnetic-field-transition patterns that could be recorded on your hard disk, programs like *SpinRite* test only the "worst-case" scenarios. The program designers deduce which test patterns will give your disk sub-system the toughest workout, and then use them.

What makes a case "worst"

Look at the pattern of magnetic field transitions in Figure 2-2(a). The data are encoded by where the transitions occur and where they do not. When the disk turns, the pattern moves under the read head. Voltage pulses are generated each time a field transition goes under the head (see Figure 2-2(b)).

If a microscopic weakness in the disk coating exists at certain places on the disk (as in Figure 2-2(c), you will notice it because a signal you otherwise would see will be missing (see Figure 2-2(d) and (e)). But if the weakness occurs in places where there normally wouldn't be a pulse anyway, you might not detect the flaw.

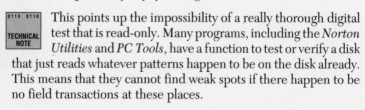 This points up the impossibility of a really thorough digital test that is read-only. Many programs, including the *Norton Utilities* and *PC Tools*, have a function to test or verify a disk that just reads whatever patterns happen to be on the disk already. This means that they cannot find weak spots if there happen to be no field transactions at these places.

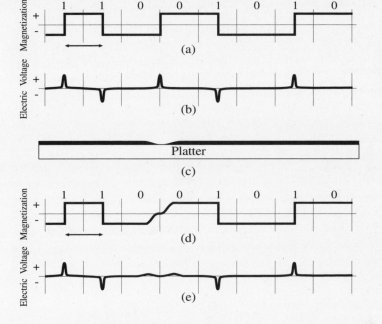

Figure 2-2 How a thin spot (or similar defect) in platter coating can obliter-ate a magnetic field transition, thus causing a data error.
(a) Normal MFM pattern to record 11001010.
(b) Resulting voltage pulses as pattern passes under read head.
(c) A thin spot in platter coating.
(d) If this defect is where a field transition should go it will make the sharp field change into a blurry one.
(e) The resulting voltage pulse is smeared and reduced in size so far it cannot be read.

If the defect lies just to one side of one of these special spots, the write head might be able to record any data pattern in which there is a transition on either side of the spot, but not a pattern in which there are transitions on both sides of the spot. Depending on how the write and read electronics function, other data patterns may also be particularly hard to record and read back reliably.

2

Testing the disk surface

We can test the disk surface for these microscopic defects by making sure that the patterns we put down and attempt to read back will reveal their presence — our worst-case patterns. Later in this chapter, we describe the specific patterns *SpinRite* uses, and how it uses them to reveal even the most subtle defects.

An important first step

Before testing the disk-surface integrity, you must ascertain that every other aspect of the drive is functioning properly. This includes testing some parts of the PC outside the disk sub-system, to verify that the defects you find on the surface don't stem from a general system problem. For example, you may have a flaky head positioner or read or write circuitry, or even an intermittent problem with some of your computer's main memory. Before it embarks on its surface analysis, *SpinRite* tests extensively all parts of the PC that it will be using.

How the Encoding Technology Affects the Choice of Worst-Case Patterns

The first key to good digital surface analysis is to put down the magnetic-field transitions in every possible place on the disk. Next, a program should put down combinations of adjacent transitions that stress the write and read circuitry to the fullest.

Figure 5-6 (in Chapter 5) shows four different ways to encode the same byte of data. Notice that the places where the magnetic field changes from plus to minus or from minus to plus form a very different pattern in each of these four cases. In order to test the surface thoroughly, you need to choose different data for each kind of data-encoding schemes. These different schemes in turn place different demands on the data-decoding circuitry. If the drive uses MFM data-encoding, the pulses come with only two possible spacings. When the drive uses 2,7 RLL, six possible pulse spacings exist. Thus we need two different groups of test patterns: one for MFM and one for RLL.

What about SCSI, ESDI, and IDE? Rather than types of data recording, they are specifications for the interface between drive and computer. Most SCSI, ESDI, and IDE drives use 2,7 RLL as their data encoding technique. A few use MFM, while some others use a variation of RLL called, variously, ARLL or ERLL (which stand for advanced or enhanced RLL). Chapter 5 briefly describes these alternate forms of data encoding. For all such drives, either *SpinRite's* MFM or its RLL test patterns work just fine.

2

SpinRite's Digital Tests

For this book, Steve Gibson has flung open the door to reveal his hither to hidden algorithms, to detail for us exactly how *SpinRite* tests your hard disk. In this and in later chapters, you'll learn more about how *SpinRite* works than you can currently learn about any other commercial program's testing procedure. That Gibson has agreed to share his methodology is a measure of his faith in how well chosen it is. It also allows you to examine his procedures and assure yourself that indeed he does know what he is doing.

Things get pretty technical from this point. If I lose you on some detail, just plow through—you'll find background on everything in Part Two of this book.

The test patterns

To test the disk, *SpinRite* uses five basic patterns of data, which it breaks into two groups: one for MFM drives, and one for RLL drives. Before it begins pattern testing, *SpinRite* figures out which kind of data encoding your drive uses.

Figure 2-3 shows all ten patterns. The first line for each test pattern is the byte string *SpinRite* sends to DOS. The program repeats this pattern as many times as is necessary to fill one whole track. Below that the figure shows this pattern expressed as the sequence of bits (ones and zeros) that gets sent to the disk.

 For the very simplest patterns, it is easy to see how the bit sequence follows from the byte string. Each pair of hexadecimal symbols represents one byte (8 bits) of data. If the test pattern repeats every byte, you need merely write those bytes in bit form to get the bit sequence.

2

Once you reach the fourth test pattern, things get more interesting. To get from that byte string to its bit sequence, you must know that DOS stores a string of bytes on the disk in pairs, called words (16-bits). It puts the "least significant byte" of each word first. Thus DBB6 will get stored with the B6 byte before the DB byte.

The pattern of magnetic field transitions, rather than the byte string or its corresponding bit sequence, is what matters. Below each bit sequence we show a graph of the magnetic field transitions that will be stored on the disk.

> **TECHNICAL NOTE** You can verify these patterns by applying the rules for MFM and RLL encoding given in Chapter 5 in the section on data encoding. In particular, see Figures 5-6 and 5-8. You will find that in a few cases, your pattern may differ from that in Figure 2-3 for the first few bits. This is because the encoding depends partly on the bit or bits that came just before the ones you are encoding. The patterns shown in the figure are what you would find in the middle of the track as the test pattern repeats itself over and over.

Finally notice that for each test pattern, Figure 2-3 shows a "number of shifted repetitions" to be used. We explain this in the section "Using the Patterns" later in this chapter.

Why these patterns were chosen

Applying test data patterns to the hard disk surface and reading them back can reveal much more than defective spots on the disk surface. If the program designer chose the patterns appropriately, they also will reveal any problems the disk or controller may have, such as problems with the head-positioning mechanism, the circuitry used to keep the disk turning at a constant speed, the clock-data separator, or the write precompensation circuits. (We describe these parts in Chapter 5, in the sections "Messy Physical Details" and "How Big is a Bit?")

After consulting with hard disk drive and controller design engineers and other experts, Steve Gibson chose these patterns, then tested them extensively to be sure they really were doing the job.

Low-Frequency Test: The first test for either MFM or RLL drives is a data pattern that produces magnetic field transitions, spaced as widely apart as possible. This procedure measures the disk drive's constancy of rotation and the ability of the read circuitry to find data bits in the presence of whatever speed drift or flutter may occur.

High-Frequency Test: Next, *SpinRite* uses a data pattern that produces magnetic field transitions spaced as closely together as possible, a good way to test the entire system's ability to work at top speed. This pattern also tests the effectiveness of the write-precompensation circuits.

MFM Mixed-Frequency Test: For MFM drives, the third test mixes regions of maximum and minimum frequency in order to measure the capability of certain circuits to follow changes. (These circuits track the rate at which the voltage pulses emerge from the head.) Since some of those circuits help keep the disk turning at a constant speed, it also tests that aspect of the drive.

Rapid Low-High Alteration Test: The fourth MFM test resembles the mixed-frequency test, differing only in the length of each region of high or low frequency. It tests the same aspects of the drive, but in slightly different ways.

Scrambled Bits Test: Steve Gibson named the final MFM test "scrambled bits." It consists of a pseudo-random pattern of transitions, which means that the pattern is the same every time you run it, but it contains lots of variety. (A truly random pattern would be different each time, but not in a dependable way, which means it would vary in its capability to detect problems.)

Isolated Ones Test: Silence is hard to hear. Likewise, recording a pattern of almost all zeros is often challenging for a hard drive, particularly for an RLL drive. (See the discussion of data encoding in Chapter 5 for more on this point.) After conducting a low-frequency and a high-frequency test, *SpinRite* imposes this important test on RLL drives.

RLL Narrow-Band and Wide-Band Mixed-Frequency Tests: The last two RLL test patterns are long; they do not repeat for 80 bits. Through these chaotic signals, *SpinRite* measures the capability of the read-write amplifiers to follow rapid fluctuations.

How the patterns are used

All the test patterns repeat after some length. The MFM and RLL high-frequency bit sequences are all ones and all zeros respec-

2

tively, which means these patterns repeat every bit. The MFM low-frequency bit sequence alternates ones with zeros, which means it repeats every 2 bits. The RLL low-frequency bit sequence repeats every 4 bits. The rest of the patterns repeat every 8 bits, except the last two RLL tests, which only repeat every 80 bits.

For each pattern, *SpinRite* first fills the entire track with repetitions of that pattern. It then reads back the pattern. It has found a defect if even a single bit differs from what was written. *SpinRite* will accept only data that were read correctly without the aid of ECC.

Applying all five tests gives a good workout to the read and write circuitry and catches some surface defects. To catch all the defects, *SpinRite* must reapply the patterns in all possible locations. If you choose the deepest level of pattern testing in *SpinRite* (Depth 4), the program will apply each pattern more than once, shifting the pattern by one bit position between each application. The number of shifts used varies with the pattern (see Figure 2-3).

> **TECHNICAL NOTE** The number of shifts used for each pattern depends on a couple of things. The patterns that repeat every few bytes are shifted at least enough bits so that they return to where they started. The two patterns that do not repeat for 80 bits are shifted only 32 times. Since these patterns were chosen mostly to test the read/write circuitry, more shifts don't help.

Pattern testing at Depth 3 works similarly but uses about half as many shifted versions of each pattern. Though this level of testing is not thorough enough to catch all defects, it takes only half as long to run as Depth 4. When you allow *SpinRite* to test at its maximum depth (using all the patterns a maximum number of times), it will catch all data-affecting defects and will detect any dysfunction that could affect your data in any other aspect of the disk drive and controller's operation. Though *SpinRite* cannot guarantee that your disk is truly perfect, the disk should act as if it is. For most of us, that is good enough.

Which Way Is Best?

Advocates of relying on the manufacturer's analog surface testing often point out that analog testing is inherently more sensitive than digital testing. After all, the digital circuitry on the drive, which

SpinRite or any program running in your PC has to use in its digital testing, is built to discard noise. The analog test circuits sense noise-like variations in signal strength as their means of seeing anomalous spots on the disk surface. Though this is true, but irrelevant, PC users don't care what the precise "signal-to-noise" ratio is for the head signals. They want to know that they can rely on their disk drives to work without any loss of data.

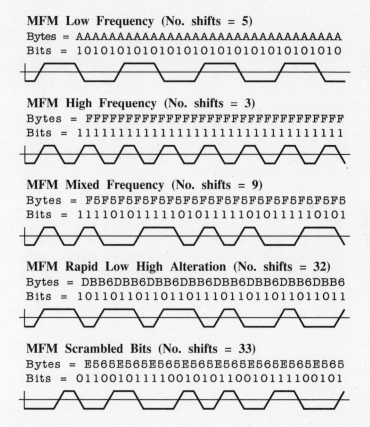

MFM Low Frequency (No. shifts = 5)
Bytes = AAAAAAAAAAAAAAAAAAAAAAAAAAAAAAAAAAAAAAAA
Bits = 1010101010101010101010101010101010

MFM High Frequency (No. shifts = 3)
Bytes = FFFFFFFFFFFFFFFFFFFFFFFFFFFFFFFFFFFFFFFF
Bits = 1111111111111111111111111111111111

MFM Mixed Frequency (No. shifts = 9)
Bytes = F5F5F5F5F5F5F5F5F5F5F5F5F5F5F5F5F5F5F5F5
Bits = 1111010111110101111010111110101

MFM Rapid Low High Alteration (No. shifts = 32)
Bytes = DBB6DBB6DBB6DBB6DBB6DBB6DBB6DBB6
Bits = 10110110110110110110110110110110 11011

MFM Scrambled Bits (No. shifts = 33)
Bytes = E565E565E565E565E565E565E565E565
Bits = 01100101110010101100101111001 0 1

Figure 2-3(a) The SpinRite data test patterns for MFM drives. Each test pattern is shown in full in the "Bytes =" line. There are many more bits and field transitions than can fit here, but these samples give a good feel for the patterns.

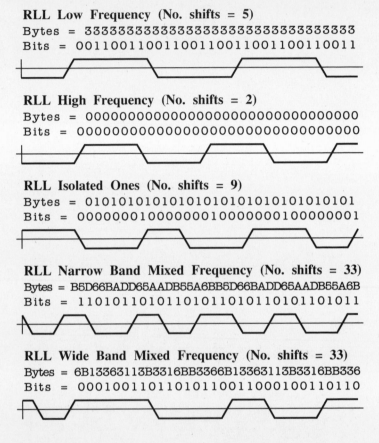

Figure 2-3(b) The SpinRite data test patterns for RLL drives. The last two cases have a byte pattern that does not repeat for a full 10 bytes (80 bits). All the others repeat much more often. Again, this figure shows only a tiny, but typical sample of the full pattern of field transitions.

You may be overreacting if you mark spots on your disk as bad simply because the manufacturer said they were. Just because you can measure something doesn't mean it's important. You wouldn't declare yourself sick just because your temperature is a tenth of a degree off normal. Analog test data has its own limitations, as we discussed in the section "Why This Is Less Helpful Than It Appears," earlier in this chapter. By testing the drive with actual digital data patterns, *SpinRite* can report and pinpoint the location of any defect that affects data-storage integrity. Data-context error reporting is one of *SpinRite*'s greatest strengths.

Another of *SpinRite*'s great strengths is its ability to discover and return to service once-defective sectors that are no longer flawed. This is one way it is unique among programs that perform non-destructive low-level reformatting.

 Some people shy away from storing data in a once-defective area. Although Steve Gibson believes that this is not a proper concern, *SpinRite* will allow you to disable that feature if you wish.

2

Chapter 3

Details of *SpinRite*'s Operation

This chapter reveals the secrets behind *SpinRite*'s magic and how the program decides whether it can safely perform its tricks on your PC.

Getting Ready to Work

To avoid making any mistakes, *SpinRite* runs a comprehensive check before it does anything to the data on your hard disk.

SpinRite checks its own health

SpinRite first checks to see that it has not been tampered with or damaged in any way—a surprisingly uncommon precaution among PC programs. The program comes on the disk in a compressed form and contains its own decompressing program. *SpinRite* runs a checksum test on the original, compressed program. If it does not come up with the right value, it will refuse to operate. After *SpinRite* decompresses itself into your PC's main system memory, it again executes a checksum test, which also must provide the correct value for the program to run.

These tests will catch a number of problems. The first test assures you that the program on your disk is not damaged. Passing the second checksum test assures you, and *SpinRite*, that your PC's system RAM (its main memory) is working correctly, at least in that part of RAM where the program resides. Finally, it ensures that no "computer virus" has attached itself to *SpinRite*; it would be close to impossible for a virus to attach itself in a way that would not produce an error in one or the other of the checksum tests.

Choosing what to do and where

Once *SpinRite* is sure it is in good shape, it displays its main menu. From here you can choose which test to do, and set various options for how *SpinRite* will function. After completing a test, *SpinRite* returns you here so that you can generate a report, either on your printer or in a disk file.

 If you interrupt a *SpinRite* operation, your first option is to resume that operation. We discuss the details of how *SpinRite* does this in the last section of this chapter.

The first main menu option, "Quick Surface Scan," is a good place to start. It checks out the disk sub-system and shows you the readability of your data. As its name implies, it doesn't take a long time. Most of the time you will use the second option, "Begin SpinRite Analysis," in order to test your disk thoroughly.

After choosing a test, you must next indicate which disk, or actually which DOS partition, *SpinRite* should examine. (If you are unsure about the difference between a disk and a DOS partition, see the section "Partitioning" in Chapter 7.) *SpinRite* then assures itself that the rest of your PC is functioning properly before proceeding with a surface scan or a deeper disk analysis.

Making sure the system memory is good enough

SpinRite uses more of your PC's system memory than simply the area in which its program code resides. Unlike some programs, it has no regions of zeros within its code that are later used for buffers. (This helps keep it safe from viral infection.) Consequently, *SpinRite* must allocate several regions in the PC's system memory as temporary storage places for data. It then tests those regions very carefully to be sure of their integrity.

3

SpinRite's **scratch pads:** *SpinRite's* buffers, or scratch-pad areas, serve several purposes. One of two track buffers serves to hold the data read from the track, while the other provides an area for the program to construct test data patterns. *SpinRite* writes these patterns to the track and then compares what it reads back against them. As it finishes testing sectors, the program assembles full clusters of data in another buffer area, returning the data to the disk when the buffer is full. The buffer's size depends on how large the clusters are on your hard disk.

SpinRite also keeps a status byte for each sector in the current track, plus one for any sectors that may have been left in the cluster buffer when it finished the previous track. These status bytes tell *SpinRite* where it should put the sectors (back where they came from or elsewhere) and which messages to put in the detailed Technical Log file.

A two-sector (1,024-byte) area serves double duty. When *SpinRite* needs to work with information from the file allocation table (FAT), it reads two consecutive sectors from the first FAT into this buffer. (See the File Allocation Table section under "High-Level Formatting" in Chapter 7 for an explanation of what a FAT is.)

> **TECHNICAL NOTE** The reason for keeping two sectors in *SpinRite's* buffer is that if the FAT has 12-bit entries, then one of those entries could overlap a sector boundary. Smaller hard disk partitions or those formatted by earlier versions of DOS typically have FATs with 12-bit entries. Having both of the sectors in the buffer makes it easier to work with that information.

At other points in its operation, *SpinRite* uses this 1,024-byte buffer as a place to receive "raw data" from the disk. When the controller reports difficulty reading a sector, *SpinRite* can request that it pass on all the information it was able to read, including both the data and the ECC bytes.

> **TECHNICAL NOTE** Naturally, to store data plus ECC requires a buffer at least a little bit larger than is needed to hold just the standard 512 bytes of data. Having an entire extra sector is far more than is needed; that is okay. Different controllers use different numbers of ECC bytes, but none use nearly 512 of them.

In addition, the program maintains an *interleave buffer* and a system stack. Before each track is reformatted, *SpinRite* prepares a table of sector status and sector numbers in the interleave buffer (see Figure 2-1). It uses the system stack to keep track of various pointers and other numbers it needs to do its work.

Checking the scratch pads: Once it has allocated these different memory areas, *SpinRite* checks them. The power-on self test (POST) routine in the BIOS of most (but not all) computers has already tested this system memory, a process that occurs when you see those memory numbers counting up on your screen as your PC is first booting. Though the POST catches most memory errors, Gibson had *SpinRite* take the test much further, so you can be sure that at least one portion of your system RAM is in the absolute pink of health.

Testing the hard disk controller

As the gateway between your hard disk and your PC's main memory, the hard disk controller is an essential element in your system. Before messing with the data on your hard disk, *SpinRite* tries to assure itself that the controller is working perfectly. Since controllers vary so much, the most *SpinRite* can feasibly do is command the controller to run its own built-in diagnostic routines. Then *SpinRite* asks the controller to check the health of the scratch pad RAM that it has on itself. Only if the controller reports no errors in either of these tests will *SpinRite* proceed to work with your hard disk.

Catching active caching

Disk caching can greatly increase the speed with which you can get data on and off your hard disk, but it can also prevent a program from knowing just how long it takes the disk to do anything. In order to run its precise timing tests, *SpinRite* must be sure that no caching software or hardware will get in the way. (For more details on a variety of caching programs and hardware and how they work, see the section "Disk Caching" near the end of Chapter 5.)

> The test for this is simple. *SpinRite* first reads sector A on the disk. Then it reads sector B, located far away from A. Finally it goes back and reads sector A again. Any caching program worth its salt will have kept a copy of A, so the time delay between reading B and rereading A will appear to be almost zero. This is a sure sign of disk caching.

Earlier versions of *SpinRite* were totally blocked by any active caching scheme. Version 1.1 of *SpinRite II* can turn off hardware caching for some controllers. Version 1.1A is able to get behind almost any caching scheme, so it can do all its work. (The next chapter has more details on this.)

SpinRite will notify you if you are using disk caching, and (depending on the version) it will refuse to do any low-level reformatting of your disk. Fortunately, it can still deliver its other major benefits, data integrity testing and data recovery. If you can, you should always turn off disk caching before running *SpinRite*. If you installed some disk speed-up program through a line in your CONFIG.SYS or AUTOEXEC.BAT file, boot off a "clean" DOS floppy and then run *SpinRite*. (See the section "The 'Clean' Boot Disk Approach" in the next chapter for more details.)

Watching for device driver weirdness

DOS at its highest levels thinks of your hard disk as simply a long string of sectors in which to store data. The BIOS level, which must use a more physically accurate picture, specifies the location of data three-dimensionally, using three separate numbers for the cylinder, head, and physical sector.

A built-in part of DOS that translates from logical addresses to physical ones and back is called the block device driver. You may install a replacement block device driver. For example, if you use *Disk Manager* from On Track, or *SpeedStor* from Storage Dimensions, you are replacing the DOS-resident block device with their special one. (See the section "Physical Size Limits Under DOS" in Chapter 6 for more details on installable block devices and why you might be using them.)

In order to assure itself that your controller's block device operates in a standard mode, *SpinRite* first asks the BIOS what the drive's dimensions are. Then it sends several "read logical sector" requests to the device driver and watches the "read physical sector" commands into which they get translated. If the translations agree with what *SpinRite* thinks they should be, it knows the device driver is doing its job in the standard manner.

 The drive dimensions, according to the BIOS, are easy to get. Just ask it, using INT 13, Function 8. What you get back may not be the real, physical dimensions of the drive, but

3

they are what the BIOS believes and what the device driver must assume. Later, *SpinRite* will check to see if these dimensions are the same as the real, physical ones.

SpinRite hooks INT 13 so that it can see all commands that are sent to the BIOS that way. Then it uses INT 25 to request sector reads. It asks for many different sectors, each 100 logical sectors apart. From watching what the device driver asks for from the BIOS (through INT 13), *SpinRite* can easily tell if the driver is using a strange translation algorithm.

If your system's device driver produces a "funny" translation, then *SpinRite* cannot do low-level reformatting, though it still can and will do data testing and data recovery. (Actually, Gibson says he has never seen a device driver of this sort. He included this test for completeness. He says if he finds it is never needed, he may remove it from later versions of the program.)

When passed, these tests satisfy *SpinRite* that it can safely proceed with a surface scan. If you had selected the deeper disk analysis, *SpinRite* would have some additional tests.

The Quick Surface Scan

The Quick Surface Scan is a read-only test; *SpinRite* doesn't write or move information on your disk. This test verifies the readability of your disk, or confirms that the unreadable portions are safely locked out and marked as bad clusters in the FAT, so that DOS won't use them.

During a Quick Surface Scan, *SpinRite* reads every track in the DOS partition. If it cannot get an entire track's data correctly in one step, it reads each sector individually, comparing its findings with what the FAT says about the disk's condition. The program reports on-screen and in the detailed Technical Log file the details about every bad sector in the partition.

 The difference between full track reads and single sector reads is dramatic. You will notice three things if you look and listen carefully. First, you will notice that *SpinRite* dwells on the bad locations much longer. Second, you may notice that the head is constantly being repositioned as *SpinRite* attempts to read a difficult sector. This partially explains why it can successfully read data when other programs give up.

Finally, you may notice a funny chunk-chunk sound every few tracks. That is when *SpinRite* goes back to the start of the partition to read another couple of sectors from the FAT.

You can examine the Quick Surface Scan results on the Track Map, a screen display that graphically represents the entire DOS partition, showing a symbol for every few tracks. Initially, the symbols are blank, with a question mark showing where *SpinRite* is currently working. A period on the Track Map represents one or more tracks that were tested and deemed perfect, as far as this test could tell. Deeper pattern testing might reveal problems, but for now you may consider that a safe place for your data.

The letter "B" indicates a sector with part of a cluster already marked as bad in the FAT. No data is stored there now, and without a lot more testing first it wouldn't be safe to store any there in the future.

Any other letter marks a place that the controller reported some difficulty reading the data. The letter "C" means a sector that could not be read, but for which the ECC sufficed to deduce the sector's contents. The letter "U" indicates *SpinRite* couldn't read the sector, even with the help of the ECC. This means some data was lost. An uppercase letter signals that one of your files was using the sector in question. A lowercase letter indicates that none of your data lies in the sector yet.

Upon completing the Quick Surface Scan, *SpinRite* allows you to return to the main menu, where you can create a report in a file or on your printer.

Further Testing Before Doing Anything Serious

If you choose "Begin SpinRite Analysis," *SpinRite* will conduct more tests, in addition to performing the system diagnostics described above.

Seek and maybe you'll find a problem

SpinRite first checks to be sure the head-positioning assembly is working correctly, by measuring four numbers to determine the *seek performance* of your drive.

TECHNICAL NOTE

Seeking means moving the heads to the right cylinder. Before the drive can do this, the BIOS has to compose and deliver the appropriate command. That takes a little bit of time. It is not much, but if you are going to be as fussy as Steve Gibson, you will want to measure this "BIOS overhead."

SpinRite measures the BIOS overhead by asking the controller to tell the drive to seek to the same cylinder many times. Since it has nothing to do, the controller will immediately return from each such command with a message saying it is done. The time taken to do these commands must, therefore, be the time it took the BIOS to compose and deliver them.

Next, *SpinRite* checks to see how quickly the drive can move the heads from one track to the adjacent one. This is followed by testing the time it takes to move the heads from the outermost cylinder to the innermost one (a "full stroke" seek). Finally, it checks the average time to do many seeks to "randomly" chosen cylinders.

In these last two tests, *SpinRite* uses the full range of cylinders for that physical hard drive. Some other programs only test seek times within the DOS partition. If you want to compare the results with those published by manufacturers of hard drives, you must test the full range of head motion, because when manufacturers conduct their tests, the drives don't have partitions.

After each time *SpinRite* commands the drive to seek to some cylinder, it checks to see if that is where the heads actually went. If the drive seeks over a thousand times without error, *SpinRite* is assured that it can position the heads where it needs to, every time.

If your drive passes this test many times without incident, you may wish to turn off this aspect of *SpinRite*'s testing (as explained in the next chapter).

Scoping Out the Drive

In Chapter 2, we pointed out that *SpinRite* or any similar program chooses a set of test data patterns based on the drive's data-encoding scheme. *SpinRite* deduces whether your drive is MFM or RLL by performing exquisitely accurate timing tests, which also reveal your drive's sector-interleave value, data transfer rate, and several other important numbers.

It's all a matter of timing

To produce these measurements, *SpinRite* looks at the time between reading one sector and another. Since the program depends
on these numbers to base its decision on how to handle the drive,
they must be precise.

Checking RPM: How and what *SpinRite* times is an interesting
story. First, it measures the average time the controller takes to go
from reading sector number 1 on a certain track to reading that
same sector again. This gives it the disk's RPM.

Getting the inter-sector times right: Next, *SpinRite* measures
the interval between reading sector #1 and reaching each other
sector on the track, a process more complicated than you might
think.

 Many things can corrupt or bias the times that one measures. For example, there may be occasional misreads of a
sector. The controller will automatically try to read that
sector again. If it succeeds, it will give back the data without com-
ment, but it will have taken longer than normal by at least one full
revolution time for the disk.

Interruptions by the PC's "timer tick" can also produce timing
errors. Approximately 18 times each second, DOS triggers a special
interrupt. Any process that needs to be sure to do its job in a timely
manner may hook that interrupt. Then it will get a chance to have
the PC do its work 18 times each second. DOS uses these opportu-
nities to update its time-of-day counter.

Depending on what other programs you have hooking that interrupt and what they do when they get control of the PC, the
intersector times reported to *SpinRite* may be anywhere from a
little bit to wildly wrong. This is yet another a reason you should use
SpinRite only in a "clean" system.

Since any single timing measurement is suspect, *SpinRite* uses many
of them for each number it wishes to find. It does not simply
average those many measurements, however; it is far more clever
than that.

SpinRite measures time in multiples of some arbitrary, small time.
That internal unit of time, which we will call one "click," is about 1.5
microseconds. It takes about 11,000 "clicks" for the disk to turn one
full revolution.

3

That full revolution time is measured by asking repeatedly for sector #1 of the same track. The average of all plausible values it reads becomes a second important unit of time for *SpinRite*. (A sector misread would at least double the value. Clearly that time should not be averaged in with the others.)

Next comes the interval between reading one sector to reading any other sector on that same track. Here is where *SpinRite* gets very fancy, in order to be sure to reject all the instances of a timing measurement that are somehow messed up.

The BIOS told *SpinRite* how many sectors there were on a track. Since this may not be the real number, we assume it is correct at first, but *SpinRite* will shortly test and find out what the truth really is.

For every sector number from 1 to whatever the BIOS said was the maximum number of sectors per track, *SpinRite* measures an intersector time. That is, it reads sector #1 then sector #N, and it notes the time between those two operations.

For each sector pair (#1 and #N), *SpinRite* begins by getting 16 measurements of the intersector time. Many of these are pretty good values, but some may be wildly wrong. *SpinRite* picks the four measurements in the middle of the pack. (That is, it ignores six smaller times and six larger times.) It averages those four times and then sets up a "measurement window" around that average time.

For any drive, the maximum time between sectors will be about the same as the full revolution time. For drives turning at 3,600 revolutions per minute, that is about 16 milliseconds. In *SpinRite*'s units this is about 11,000 clicks. The minimum intersector time will occur between adjacent sectors on a drive with the largest number of sectors. If the drive has no more than 55 sectors, that time will be at least 300 microseconds, which is about 200 clicks.

SpinRite assumes that all valid measurements of an intersector time must lie within 200 clicks of the average it computed from that first set of measurements. This is the measurement window it uses to validate the intersector times for that particular sector number. Now it measures that intersector time repeatedly until it gets 16 measurements that are valid by that criterion. The average of these 16 measurements is a really good estimate of the true intersector time.

This whole process is repeated for every value of sector number, N, from 2 to the maximum sector number according to the BIOS. Armed with these very accurate intersector timings, *SpinRite* is ready to identify a couple of important facts about the drive.

Once it has completed these intersector timing measurements, *SpinRite* uses them to deduce the data-encoding technique. It also uses them to get the actual, physical drive dimensions, the sector-interleave value, and the data-transfer rate for this drive.

> **TECHNICAL NOTE** *SpinRite* sets up a table of all possible differences between these numbers. It looks for the time difference that corresponds to adjacent sectors. If all the sectors really were on one track, that would be the smallest time difference in the table. Since the controller may be doing sector translation, *SpinRite* cannot depend on such a simple strategy.

> Whatever the true adjacent sector time is, it will show up many times in the table. Also, multiples of two, three, and four times that number will show up. *SpinRite* looks for a number that satisfies both these tests.

Breaking the code: Once we know how long it takes for the disk to turn from one sector to the adjacent one, we can get the true number of sectors per track by dividing that adjacent sector time into the time for a full revolution.

> **TECHNICAL NOTE** Notice that if the controller created a spare sector at the end of the track or if the end-of-track gap is unusually large, the computed number may come out a bit higher than the BIOS-reported number, though not by much. If the two numbers agree to within plus or minus 2, *SpinRite* will accept the controller as non-translating. Then it can do low-level reformatting.

If the true number of sectors per track is 17, you have an MFM controller and drive. Twenty-six sectors per track means you have an RLL controller and drive. At 54, *SpinRite* classes it as an ERLL controller and drive.

> **TECHNICAL NOTE** *SpinRite* assumes the encoding is MFM if the number of sectors is less than 22. For 22 through 30 sectors, it reports RLL. Any more than that and it reports ERLL.

What's your interleave?: We can similarly compute the current sector interleave value. Just divide the time to go from sector #1 to sector #2 by the adjacent sector time.

3

SpinRite makes all of these measurements on a track near the center of the DOS partition. This explains something that has puzzled some *SpinRite* users. Suppose you had run *SpinRite* previously and asked it to change your sector interleave. Suppose you had interrupted it in the middle of its work. What interleave would it report when you next started it?

That depends on whether you had interrupted it before or after the halfway point. If you had interrupted it early, the central track would still have its sector interleave set to the old value, which is what *SpinRite* would measure and report. If you had interrupted it a bit later, *SpinRite* would see and report the new value.

Other calculations: Finally *SpinRite* measures the time to read a full track's worth of sectors (using the number of sectors on a logical track, as reported by the BIOS). From this, it calculates the maximum data-transfer rate your disk will support with its present setting of sector interleave.

It also reports the number of revolutions required to transfer a full (logical) track of data. If your controller is doing sector translation, this latter number may be misleading.

For example, suppose you have an actual sector interleave of 1:1 and an actual sector count of 54. Further suppose your controller says to the BIOS it has 63 sectors per track. You can read a physical track in a single revolution, but it will take more than one revolution to read all 63 sectors of a logical track.

SpinRite's Disk Analysis

Having assured itself that your PC's system memory, disk controller, and disk-head-positioning mechanisms are working perfectly, *SpinRite* can proceed to the serious work for which it was designed, knowing what data-encoding technology is in use and whether the controller is doing any sector translating. If its tests say it is safe to proceed, *SpinRite* will now attempt to read every byte of data in your DOS partition, test every sector, and replace the data. It may also, if you wish (and if it can do so safely), redo the low-level format for each track, thus curing the maximum possible number of disk errors and setting the sector interleave to whatever value you choose.

Getting the interleave

Well, there is one more test to do. Though *SpinRite* knows the current sector-interleave value, it still must find out what impact changing that number would have. It will then be able to recommend the optimum value and let you choose the value you want. The program skips this test only if you have told it you don't want low-level reformatting, or if your drive or controller will not permit *SpinRite* to do that operation.

SpinRite discovers the impact of different sector-interleave values by reformatting, eight times, a track in the diagnostic cylinder, which resides outside any disk partition. (See Chapter 7 for a description of this cylinder.)

 In order for these tests to be meaningful, the track being tested must have no defects. *SpinRite* first tests the track at Head 0 of the diagnostic cylinder. If it is perfect, and if *SpinRite* can get stable timings for reading that track, it will use it.

If the first track won't do, it tries Head 1. It keeps this up till it finds a perfect track to use. If none of the tracks in the diagnostic cylinder are perfect, then *SpinRite* will do the same thing it would do if there were no diagnostic cylinder: It will refuse to do any low-level reformatting.

Once *SpinRite* has found a suitable track, it reformats it with a 1:1 sector interleave. It reads all the sectors on the track in sector number order several times. From the time it takes, *SpinRite* computes a maximum data-transfer rate for this interleave setting. This process is repeated for sector-interleave values from 2:1 to 8:1.

SpinRite displays the results of the interleave tests, highlighting the optimum interleave (the one leading to the highest data-transfer rate). While *SpinRite* recommends that interleave setting, the user is free to choose another.

Setting the interleave

Once the user has chosen the desired interleave, *SpinRite* reads a track, reformats it with the new sector-interleave value, tests it, and then restores the data. If it finds any bad sectors in the testing step, it repeats the reformatting, marking those sectors as bad in their headers before putting back the data.

The user may select one of four levels of testing. *SpinRite* can reformat the disk without performing any tests, but you should do this only if you are not changing the interleave. In the next chapter, we discuss how to choose the appropriate level of pattern testing.

When *SpinRite* can't reformat your drive

To recap, *SpinRite* cannot safely redo the low-level format on your drive if your controller has buffering that cannot be turned off or gotten around, if the controller "lies" about the drive dimensions (does sector translation), or if there is no diagnostic cylinder (or all the diagnostic cylinder tracks are flawed). You also can tell *SpinRite* that you don't want it to do any low-level reformatting by selecting an option on the "Alter *SpinRite*'s Operation" submenu.

Data Integrity Testing and Data Recovery

Even if *SpinRite* does not redo the low-level format, you can still use the program to recover data that are unreadable by normal means and to move those data to safety. It also can discover defects in the disk before any data are rendered unreadable and again move them out of harm's way.

Reading the data

SpinRite is exceptionally good at reading data. When the going test tough, *SpinRite* gets very clever. At the point where most programs give up, *SpinRite* is just getting going.

When it's easy: The BIOS accepts commands to read a string of consecutive sectors, and when it can, *SpinRite* uses this fast and easy technique.

When it's hard: When this technique doesn't work, the controller will inform the BIOS of its difficulty. To whatever program issued the request, the BIOS in turn either presents the data but reports to DOS that the controller had to use ECC to reconstruct what the data probably were (a correctable error); or it reports an uncorrectable error, which means that even with the ECC, the controller could not deduce what should have been read.

> 0110 0110
> **TECHNICAL
> NOTE**
> There is a small chance when the ECC are used that the correction will be wrong. If the error in the data was confined to a few adjacent bits, the ECC will suffice to correct it perfectly. If there are some wrong bits in two or more regions of the sector, the ECC will suggest an erroneous "fix." This does not occur as often as the truly correctable errors. That it can ever occur is another reason for *SpinRite* to pay very close attention to all uses of ECC and, whenever it can, refuse to accept data obtained that way.

Any program that uses DOS to read from the disk will not learn about correctable errors, because DOS hides them from the application, reporting only uncorrectable errors. When an uncorrectable error occurs (and then giving back no data), most programs either give up or try again exactly as they tried before. Neither approach is likely to produce the data.

When the BIOS reports any error, correctable or not, *SpinRite* immediately begins to read the track a sector at a time. Though it may get most of the sectors this way with little effort, at least one sector is likely to present a problem.

When DOS or almost any other program reads a sector, it simply sends the heads to the correct cylinder, switches on the right head, and then waits for the sector it wants to come into view. *SpinRite* knows better. Since a misalignment of the heads often causes misreads, the capability to align the heads just slightly off the track to one side or the other often helps a lot. Some older, very expensive disk drives and some of the latest servo-controlled ESDI and SCSI drives support commands to do just that. Typical PC hard disks do not.

To get around this limitation, *SpinRite* takes advantage of a property shared by all mechanical systems, which is that any positioning mechanism will not go to exactly the same place if it approaches that place in a different way each time. We call that *backlash* or *hysteresis*. *SpinRite* uses this technique to achieve slightly off-track head alignments.

Each time before it asks the BIOS to read a recalcitrant sector, *SpinRite* will request that it move the heads to a cylinder one side or the other from the one it wants, then back again. By varying the off-track direction or distance, *SpinRite* can induce various off-track alignments when the heads return, after which it again tries to read the sector. This method often works.

If the controller still cannot read the sector perfectly, but the use of the ECC will allow the data to be reconstructed, *SpinRite* will accept that. If the sector has an uncorrectable error, *SpinRite* can still command the controller to forget about trying to correct the data and just turn over what it found, errors and all. Most uncorrectable errors affect only a few bits of data. Out of 4,096 bits, maybe as few as 12 (less than two bytes) are messed up. Most people would prefer to get back all but two bytes of a file, rather than lose it entirely. In addition, *SpinRite* will point out which sector of which file was flawed, so you can more easily repair the damage.

Low-level reformatting

Once *SpinRite* has safely stowed your data in one of its track buffers, it is ready to reformat the track. Amazingly, this step often repairs all its defects, restoring a previously flawed track to full health. In its next step, *SpinRite* tests to see if this happened.

Pattern testing

We described *SpinRite*'s pattern testing in Chapter 2. Depending on the level of testing you have chosen, it will apply 82 test patterns, or 43, or 5, or it may skip pattern testing altogether. The deeper the level of pattern testing you choose, the more thoroughly *SpinRite* examines your disk to catch all surface defects and drive dysfunctions. The level of testing you choose is important. Any is better than none, more is even better. The trade-off is that each level takes progressively longer to complete. But, only with the deepest level can you be completely sure to catch all surface defects and all drive dysfunctions.

If it gets a correctable error even once while pattern testing, *SpinRite* will declare the sector in question a bad place to store data. But the many times and clever ways it tries to read your original data means they almost always can be recovered. That *SpinRite* has no tolerance for even a correctable error during pattern testing means your data is will not be put in jeopardy after testing is completed.

Recording problems

SpinRite informs you of every problem it encounters, reporting bad sectors in three ways.

On the screen and in the report: The first way in which *SpinRite* reports bad sectors is via the Track Map display, which will show one of the symbols described above if it found an error reading your original data or if the FAT shows those clusters marked as bad, or it will display a number if it found one or more defect during pattern testing.

 For all but the smallest drives, the Track Map is not big enough to show a different symbol for each track. One symbol often shows the status of four or more tracks. What if those tracks deserve different symbols? The order of precedence reflects the seriousness of the problems detected.

The worst problems are difficulties reading your original data. Next most serious are difficulties reading sectors that happen not to have any data you care about (but which soon might). Defects that show up in pattern testing come next. Of lowest precedence is showing where there are clusters marked as bad in the FAT.

Every sector on each track for a given Track Map symbol "earns" a symbol. These are **U** or **u** for uncorrectable errors (**U** if that sector is part of a file and **u** if not). Correctable errors get a **C** or a **c**, again depending on whether that sector is currently in use. A sector that proves defective upon pattern testing gets a **1**. Sectors that are part of a marked bad cluster get a **B**.

We combine the symbols for all those sectors to derive the symbol for the Track Map. A **U** beats a **C** beats a **u** beats a **c**. If the worst sector has a **1**, the Track Map will show a number (**1** to **9**) telling how many sectors there were with a **1** in those tracks. If a **B** is the worst sector's symbol, that is what will show.

When testing is complete, you can ask *SpinRite* to create a report, either a printed copy or a disk file, showing everything that appeared on the screen during its operation.

In the detailed technical log: The symbols give a good overview of the health of your drive but don't provide you with all the details you might wish to know. The Detailed Technical Log, a new feature with *SpinRite II*, records those details.

While it is running, *SpinRite* always makes available the last 1,000 lines of the Detailed Technical Log. You can review them by using your cursor pad keys (HOME, END, and the arrow keys). If you don't tell it otherwise, *SpinRite* will write the same information to a file named SPINRITE.LOG in the root directory of the partition it is testing.

In the sector: Finally, for all but 8-bit XT-class hard disk controllers, which don't allow it, *SpinRite* makes sure that any sector it finds bad is marked as such in its sector header. (See Figure 2-1 for an example of how this is done.)

TECHNICAL NOTE

If a controller board has only one "tongue" on the slot that plugs into the PC's bus, it is an 8-bit controller. If it has two tongues, it is a 16-bit controller. The former can be used in any PC. They are not able to transfer data as rapidly as the latter. Only PCs with the full ISA bus, like the AT, can accept the 16-bit controllers. Since those controllers are faster, almost all ISA PCs use them.

With few exceptions, the 8-bit controllers do not allow marking individual sectors bad. All the 16-bit controllers do.

Since *SpinRite* moves sector headers by performing a second low-level reformatting of the track, it can't do this if a low-level reformatting has been suppressed, either by user request or hardware limitations.

Putting the data back

In the final step, *SpinRite* restores your data. If the entire track has received a clean bill of health, which is usually the case, *SpinRite* places the data back where it came from.

Moving data to safety

DOS keeps track of data on a hard disk only in clusters, so if *SpinRite* detects that a sector is bad, it must move the data from all the sectors of that cluster.

TECHNICAL NOTE

SpinRite keeps track of the status of each sector on the track. It puts each sector's data into the cluster buffer and updates the status of that group of sectors. When the cluster buffer is full, *SpinRite* either puts those data back where they came from or moves them, depending on the status of the group of sectors.

One exception is if the data are a part of a "hidden" or "system" file, possibly signalling a copy-protected file, in which case *SpinRite* will not move those data. Instead, it will report its findings in the Detailed Technical Log and recommend that you move that file if you can safely do so.

Where should it go?: When *SpinRite* must move a cluster of data, it scans the FAT for the first available cluster, starting at the beginning. This maximizes the chance that it will find one where it has already finished testing.

3

How will DOS find it?: Besides copying the data to the new location, *SpinRite* makes sure DOS can find it by adjusting the pointers in the FAT appropriately (see Figure 3-1).

 If the cluster in question contains data from the middle of a file, all one has to do is update FAT pointers. If the cluster is the first one of a file, then one must also update the directory entry for that file. The worst case is when one must relocate a cluster containing a subdirectory, which requires adjusting many directory entries.

This does fragment the file a bit. (See the discussion in the section "File Fragmentation" in Chapter 8.) You could remedy this if you wish by running a disk unfragmenter after running *SpinRite*, but it is not usually worth the effort.

Telling the user: Naturally, *SpinRite* records these actions in the Detailed Technical Log, alerting the user to where the defect was found, where *SpinRite* relocated the data, and the name of the affected file. Knowing which file got fragmented may help one decide if it is worth unfragmenting.

When bad becomes good

Mostly we think of *SpinRite* as a program that finds defects and moves data out of harm's way. But it can also turn this trick inside out. Sometimes a sector marked as bad will test out on as flawless. This is a case of a "bad" place spontaneously becoming "good" and fully usable. Yes, it happens!

3

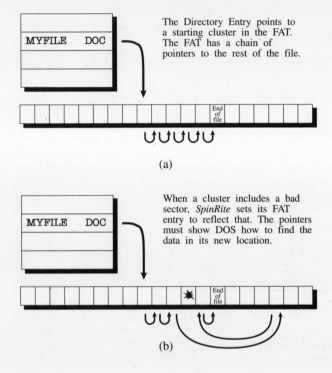

(a)

(b)

Figure 3-1 When SpinRite detects a bad sector it will mark the corresponding cluster as bad in the FAT. If it was in use, the data stored there must be put elsewhere. There are three cases:
(1) If the cluster is in the middle of a file the data are moved and the FAT pointers adjusted.
(2) If the cluster is the first of a file then the directory entry pointing to it must also be adjusted.

If *SpinRite* proves the full health of a formerly defective sector, it can return that sector to use for storing data. To be certain, it must use the deepest level of pattern testing. This feature is unique to *SpinRite*. Like most of its features, it may be turned off.

Interrupting *SpinRite*

In order to carry out a task as Herculean as a deepest-level pattern test of a 300-MB drive, *SpinRite* might require more than a day.

The fact that it involves moving some 50,000 megabytes of data on and off the disk should give you an idea of why. Gibson realized that few PC users would want to interrupt their work that long, even for so important a task, so he made it easy to interrupt *SpinRite*.

What gets stored and where

To allow for these interruptions, *SpinRite* retains in the diagnostic cylinder some data about what it was doing when it was interrupted.

 A caution: If your controller did not create a diagnostic cylinder on your drive, *SpinRite* will be unable to store the information it needs to resume.

Unfortunately you will not get a reminder when you interrupt *SpinRite*'s operation. You simply will not be given the option of resuming that operation when you next run *SpinRite*.

All but a few PC hard disk controllers create a diagnostic cylinder. Some AT clones, however, have a motherboard BIOS that does not. Be attentive when *SpinRite* is first testing your system. If your system lacks a diagnostic cylinder, you'll get this message: "ATTENTION! SpinRite utilizes and requires the pre-defined auxiliary last track which is found on all true IBM compatible hard drives. This drive does not have the required last track. Consequently, *SpinRite* will be surpressing its low-level formatting of this drive." If you get this message, you will not want to interrupt *SpinRite* quite so freely.

When you press the Escape key, *SpinRite* first finishes with the track on which it is working before it reacts to your request to stop. It stores on every track of the diagnostic cylinder a record of what operation it was doing (for example, Quick Surface Scan or Low-Level Format with Depth 4 Pattern Testing), on which partition, and where it was in that process.

It also stores everything it has displayed on the screen since the program session began. This means that when you resume the interrupted operation, the Track Map will reappear just as it was right before the interruption. When *SpinRite* finally finishes its work, you can create a report file that contains all the information it would have if the job had been done in a single session, including any disk seek performance details or bad sectors found in an earlier session. Since the Detailed Technical Log entries are written to the disk file \SPINRITE.LOG as they are generated, they are not also stored in the diagnostic cylinder.

The information that gets stored on the diagnostic cylinder takes up less than one track. *SpinRite* places a copy of it on each track in that cylinder, along with a checksum and a record of the version of *SpinRite* used. Thus you can resume an interrupted operation only if you run the same version of *SpinRite*. Further, if one copy of the stored information is corrupted, the checksum will reveal this fact and *SpinRite* will use another copy in its stead.

3

When you resume

When you first start *SpinRite*, it checks the diagnostic cylinder of each physical drive, just in case you interrupted an operation on it. There can be only one such record there, so you can suspend and resume work on only one partition of each physical drive. If it finds a valid interruption record created by the same version of *SpinRite*, it will display a menu offering to resume the interrupted operation. Before picking up where it left off, *SpinRite* will first run through the system diagnostics to be sure your PC's system memory and controller are still working adequately.

Upon resuming, the only discernible difference will be a notation in the Detailed Technical Log window showing the date on which you resumed. That entry will be added to the end of the Technical Log file, SPINRITE.LOG. If there is no such file (for example, if you renamed or moved it between *SpinRite* sessions), then it will create the file.

This concludes our rundown on how *SpinRite* performs its magic. We hope this look under the hood makes you feel more confident in *SpinRite*'s abilities. Besides, wasn't that interesting?

Chapter 4

Advanced User's Guide to *SpinRite II*

4

Some of you may be reading this book to learn all you can about how hard disks work and why they die. This chapter, on the other hand, is geared toward those of you who want to learn everything you can to make *SpinRite* dance and sing. As the chapter head promises, here are your dancing and singing lessons.

A Short History of *SpinRite*

See Appendix A if you want to learn how Steve Gibson came to write *SpinRite*. This chapter focuses on how to get the optimum value from the program. To do that, you must first determine which version of the product you own.

Various versions

Steve Gibson introduced the original *SpinRite* in March 1987. A significantly enhanced product, *SpinRite II*, debuted in October 1989. In all, Gibson Research has marketed eight distinct versions of *SpinRite*, three of which were versions of *SpinRite II*. The following sections describe each of those versions and how they differ from one another, which may help you decide whether you wish to upgrade your version. Also, knowing the limitations and problems others have encountered with earlier versions may help you avoid trouble.

SpinRite, **Version 1.0:** Version 1.0 was the initial release of the program. Already a fully developed, essentially bug-free program, *SpinRite* 1.0 did the job for which it was designed, unlike some new releases of software today. Still, it was created by a mere human being, not an omniscient god. Before releasing it, Gibson had many people test it on a wide variety of PC systems, but he couldn't come close to testing it on the variety of machines on which end users ran the program. Given this variety, not surprisingly some incompatibilities surfaced.

SpinRite, **Version 1.1:** Though PC users initially reacted to *SpinRite* with enthusiasm, that reaction was tempered in some quarters by the discovery of some special situations in which the program could cause catastrophic data loss. Naturally, once Gibson heard about these situations, he reacted quickly.

He released Version 1.1 of *SpinRite* just a few weeks after Version 1.0. Establishing the Gibson Research upgrade policy, Gibson announced that since this upgrade corrected a potentially serious oversight, he would ship a copy to all registered users. This upgrade was not only free, it came to the users without their having to request it. Gibson's goal was to "rid the world" of the potentially dangerous version.

The problem that Version 1.1 solved stemmed from *SpinRite*'s interaction with certain unusual disk controllers that Gibson had not anticipated. Some early DTC autoconfiguring hard disk controllers save the drive dimensions in a special sector. The problem arises with where the controller places that sector and how it creates it. Under their brand name, Seagate marketed a version of this controller that had the same problem.

These controllers put the drive dimensions into a sector with only 64 bytes of data (one-eighth the normal amount). That sector is given the number 63 (the maximum legal value) and it is put on the very first track of the drive after all the normal sectors. That is, its location is cylinder 0, head 0, sector 63.

When the controller is asked by the BIOS to redo the low-level format on that track, it does *not* automatically recreate that extra sector. No program other than the special disk initialization program in the controller's ROM can make it do so. All programs that attempted to control low-level formatting of a disk attached to such a controller encountered a serious problem. They could do the low-level format just fine, but the next time you restarted your computer, the controller had no idea how big your drive was. You were unable to do anything useful with it.

This was a nuisance for people who were initially preparing a disk for use. It could be a disaster if they were trying to optimize its performance with *SpinRite* and had the disk full of valuable programs and data (especially if they did not have a good set of backups).

> **TECHNICAL NOTE** Programs that have difficulties with this controller include the current (mid-1990) *Disk Manager* and *SpeedStor*. These programs can safely be used to create partitions on a drive after the controller has done the low-level format. But if you use these programs in their normal manner, they will attempt to manage the whole initialization process and will fail dramatically.

4

The original *SpinRite* would redo the low-level format on every track in the DOS partition. It also would redo the low-level format on the track containing the Master Boot Record (which is at cylinder 0, head 0, sector 0). The new version solved the problem with these controllers by simply omitting the reformatting of the Master Boot Record's track. All versions of *SpinRite* since then have not attempted to redo the low-level format on cylinder 0, head 0.

> **TECHNICAL NOTE** If your disk was formatted with DOS 3.0 or a later version, it does not use that initial track for anything but the Master Boot Record. There is no speedup to be gained from resetting the sector interleave value for that one track. Thus giving this up is no great sacrifice. Even if you are using DOS 2.x, for which the rest of the track is used, the loss in efficiency will be minor.

Certain disk performance-testing programs, including Steve Gibson's own SPINTEST.COM and the Norton SI program, use that initial track very heavily in measuring the disk's data transfer rate. If that track has a different sector interleave value than the rest of the disk, these programs will report a data transfer rate that is not a fair measure of how the disk will work in normal use.

The *Norton Utilities* Calibrate program (in its initial release) avoids low-level reformatting of the Master Boot Record track. However, if the disk was formatted using DOS 2.x, it will attempt to low-level format the first track of the DOS partition. That is the same track.

So if Calibrate is used on a controller that creates this special sector in the first track and the disk was formatted with DOS 2.x, it will very likely have the same problem as the initial release of *SpinRite*.

Gibson wanted to help any *SpinRite* user who had lost data because of this problem. He contacted DTC, who told him there was no way to recover data from a disk after redoing the low-level format on its first track. Upon exploring their controller's ROM code, Gibson found a part of it that would allow one to recreate that special sector, complete with the drive dimensions. He shared his discovery with the DTC technical support department.

Gibson Research does not now assist its users directly with this problem. If you have a DTC controller and lose your data using the original *SpinRite*, DTC should be able to help you. Of course, it would be better to upgrade your copy of *SpinRite* before that happens.

Version 1.1 also incorporated a few other minor changes. For example, the original program did a test for compatibility between the drive and controller. Since this test turned out to be completely unnecessary, Gibson Research removed it from all later versions of the product.

***SpinRite*, Version 1.2, 1.2A, and 1.2B:** The other versions of the original *SpinRite* contained the usual assortment of minor improvements. Version 1.2 addressed one more discovery of a controller incompatibility: It turned out that Omti made some auto-configuring controllers that stored their drive dimensions in a special, hidden place, similar to what DTC had done.

> **TECHNICAL NOTE** These controllers also do something else in an unusual and interesting way — they automatically remap bad tracks. That means that if your drive has a defect on, say, cylinder 12, head 5, and you tell the controller it is a bad track, then Omti will substitute some track out near the end of the drive. Thus whenever the BIOS asks the controller to put some information into a sector at cylinder 12, head 5, it actually will go to the remapped track.

This is nice in that it makes your drive look as if it does not have any bad tracks. It is definitely not nice in that every time you try to access one of the tracks that was bad, the controller will have to send the drive searching way off to the end of the disk for its replacement. Even files that are unfragmented, according to DOS, may get scattered very widely on the disk.

Omti used this capability to do their hiding of the disk dimensions. Whenever one of these controllers is in an autoconfiguring mode, it will take the track at head 0 of cylinder 100 for this purpose. It marks that track as one that is to be remapped. Then whenever the BIOS thinks it is reading or writing that track, it actually will be reading or writing the remapped track out near the end of the drive. Unfortunately, when you ask the controller to redo the low-level format on that track, it will comply. That actual physical track gets reformatted, not the remapped one.

Starting with Version 1.2, *SpinRite* knows enough to detect Omti controllers. It even can learn which model and revision-level controller it is dealing with, and whether that controller is in an autoconfiguring mode. (If the controller is not in autoconfiguring mode, it is not dangerous, no matter what the model.) When *SpinRite* is running on a system with one of the dangerous controllers, it will avoid redoing the low-level format on that special track.

Since these upgrades were of no significance to most users, Gibson Research offered them, without cost, only to those users who requested them.

SpinRite II, Version 1.0: This version saw the dawn of a new generation of *SpinRite*. Significantly enhanced, the product retained its basic purpose and operation, but it augmented these with six major and several minor new features. In recognition of these changes, Gibson changed the name to *SpinRite II*.

The most delightful new feature, from a user perspective, is that one no longer has to "configure" *SpinRite* for your PC. This makes it much easier to use.

 DOS hides many things. Its purpose is to make life easy for application programs, but not necessarily for application programmers. Without benefit of some special knowledge, it is not possible to make an application program talk directly to the hard disk controller.

The original *SpinRite* got around this in a clever way. You were asked to boot your computer from a DISKCOPY of the original *SpinRite* diskette that used a special "operating system" to get a view of your PC without DOS. It stored what it learned inside SPINRITE.COM.

4

Later, after you had rebooted your computer with DOS, *SpinRite* still would know how to access the hardware directly. The difficulty with this approach was that whenever you changed your PC's configuration, even if you just changed the video card, you had to "reconfigure" *SpinRite* before it would operate.

Gibson made *SpinRite* so sensitive to your computer's configuration for a very good reason. He was concerned that you might move the program to a new computer without "telling it" what you had done. Then it might make some mistakes, thinking it could access the new hardware the same way it had learned to do for the old. Thus, while it was an inconvenience, reconfiguring *SpinRite* any time any part of your PC was changed provided a significant level of added protection.

By the time he created *SpinRite II*, Gibson had acquired considerable knowledge about undocumented DOS and BIOS features. He used that knowledge to make *SpinRite II* know how to find the routines it needs in the BIOS and the hardware despite the attempts of DOS at obfuscation. The earlier clever idea of booting off the *SpinRite* disk was no longer necessary.

The benefits of this improvement are two-fold. First, you can make a backup copy of the *SpinRite II* files with the regular DOS COPY command. You no longer have to use DISKCOPY. Second, you can merely run SPINRITE.COM. You don't have to be concerned if you have changed some aspect of your PC. *SpinRite II* will detect those changes and accommodate them automatically.

The second major new feature was *SpinRite II*'s ability to work with DOS partitions of any size. Up till this version, it could operate only on 32-megabyte or smaller partitions. The new program understands large partitions created by PC-DOS or MS-DOS version 4.0 or later, by Compaq's DOS 3.31, and by the various third-party disk partitioning programs such as *Disk Manager* and *SpeedStor*.

> **TECHNICAL NOTE** Earlier versions of DOS limited partitions to 32 megabytes. (The reasons for this are discussed in Chapter 6 in the section "Logical Size Limits." Some popular ways to get around this limitation are discussed in the section "Evading the Logical Limits" in that same chapter.)

Essentially, the limit comes from restricting the number of sectors to 65,536 (64K), with a fixed sector size of 512 bytes. Multiply these out and you get 32 megabytes (or 33,554,432 bytes). *SpinRite II* can accommodate many more sectors, as well as sectors of most any size.

Third, *SpinRite II* reports substantially more about what it finds and what it does with those findings. Some of the new information can be extremely useful.

SpinRite was designed to be a "no-brainer." That is, anyone can use it with little effort. Already in the first versions, it reported some things the user did not need to know. Still, the amount it told was intentionally limited to avoid intimidating users.

Many users wanted to be told more. Even more important, sometimes they needed to know more.

If *SpinRite* encounters an uncorrectable error while reading data from the disk, at least a couple of bytes of your data will inevitably be lost. With the earlier program, you could not easily find out which file had been damaged, let alone where in the file the damage could be found. The new *SpinRite II* Detailed Technical Log gives that information very explicitly. Armed with that knowledge, it is easy to repair the damage or replace the damaged file.

Fourth, while users of the original *SpinRite* were advised to remove any copy-protected programs before running *SpinRite*, that is no longer necessary with *SpinRite II*. Again, this makes *SpinRite* much more convenient to use.

When it discovers a disk defect, *SpinRite* moves the data from that sector to some safer place. To some copy-protected programs, such a change looks the same as an unauthorized copy. They will refuse to operate.

Most such copy-protected programs are concerned only with the location of certain special files. These files are typically marked with the DOS file attributes "hidden" or "system," or both. *SpinRite II* checks the file attributes before moving any data. It will not move a sector if it is part of a hidden or system file, even if it finds a defect there. It will, of course, tell the user about the problem. The user can then solve it another way.

4

If *SpinRite II* tells you that it found a defect but did not move the data because it was part of a hidden file, you should then remove the copy-protected program and rerun *SpinRite*. This time it will mark the defective sector bad. Then, when you reinstall the copy protected program, it will not be put back in the defective sector. (If you have more than one copy-protected program, you may have to investigate a bit to find out which one's hidden file is occupying the defective sector.)

The fifth major new feature was the introduction of a hypertext on-line help system. Sixth, *SpinRite II* now marks defective sectors as bad in their sector headers. All versions of *SpinRite* mark the FAT to show which clusters contain flawed sectors. That prevents DOS from using them. Still this was not enough for some users, so when working with a 16-bit hard disk controller, the new *SpinRite* also records sector defects in their headers. Unfortunately, this improvement included a bug that necessitated creating *SpinRite II*, Version 1.1, just a few months later.

> 0110 0110
> **TECHNICAL NOTE**
> One cannot selectively mark sectors bad in their headers on XT-class hard disk controllers. One can only mark an entire track as bad or good. Selective sector marking can only be done on AT-style (16-bit bus interface) controllers. We describe how sectors get marked bad in the section "Bad Tracks, Sectors, and Clusters" in Chapter 2; the process is illustrated in Figure 2-1. The original *SpinRite* was written to treat all disks equally, so it simply marked all sector headers as if the sectors were good.

> To mark individual sectors bad requires an extra step. The original *SpinRite* would go through four steps for each track. First it read the original data and saved them. Next it reformatted the track (marking all sectors as good). Third it tested the track, and finally it restored the original data.

> *SpinRite II* adds to this. After testing, before replacing the original data, it again reformats the track. This is the only way it can insert the bad sector marks into the sector headers.

Finally, *SpinRite II* has been improved in a number of other minor ways. These include cosmetic improvements to the screens and some internal changes of no interest to users.

SpinRite II, Version 1.1: As soon as Gibson heard of a problem with *SpinRite II*, Version 1.0, he got to work finding and fixing it.

Again he mailed the fix, which was Version 1.1, to all registered users free of charge. (His commitment to supporting his users in this fashion has cost Gibson more than $50,000, but he says he regards it as money well spent.)

> **TECHNICAL NOTE** The bug in *SpinRite II*, Version 1.0, only showed up when one had a disk with a defective next-to-last sector on some track whose last sector was not defective. In that case, it marked the last sector as defective also. Further, it mistakenly set the sector number of that last sector to 0, rendering it inaccessible.
>
> *SpinRite* next tried to put the original data back into that last sector. Since the sector number had been changed to zero, *SpinRite* could not find it. The program at that point simply locked up. The problem was simple enough to fix, once its cause was found. Finding that required running the program on enough machines to happen to encounter a disk with that special combination of problems.
>
> This did not happen often, and when it did, not much data was likely to be lost (at most a couple of sectors). Still, it was enough to prevent *SpinRite* from working further on that disk. Furthermore, Gibson says, any data loss is too much.

Version 1.1 includes a number of other improvements to the program, such as extending the range of controllers that it can work with, increasing its ability to recover "unreadable" data, and speeding the program when dealing with massively defective drives. The hypertext help program was completely overhauled, and there were the usual number of minor tweaks to the screen displays and internal workings.

> **TECHNICAL NOTE** Some controllers contain track buffers. That feature can greatly speed their operation. It also totally frustrated earlier versions of *SpinRite*. Those versions noted the buffering and declined to do anything with the drives attached to those controllers.
>
> Version 1.1 knows how to turn off track buffering on many of those controllers. This makes it possible for *SpinRite* to work with them, often doing all of its functions for drives attached to those controllers. If those controllers also were doing sector translation, *SpinRite* still could not do any low-level reformatting, but it now could do all the data-integrity testing.

Data recovery was much enhanced by the addition of "head jiggling" during reading of the original data. This is discussed in the section "Reading the Data: When It's Hard" in Chapter 3. The program also now tries twice as many times before giving up on an unreadable sector.

Version 1.1 more than makes up for the extra time these steps take by some added efficiencies. If a cluster is marked bad in the FAT, there should be no valuable data stored there. Earlier versions of *SpinRite* ignored this fact and attempted to read data from these sectors anyway. Version 1.1 notes this and doesn't bother trying to read what is probably one or more badly flawed sectors. After it redoes the low-level format, it will test those sectors, since they may have been repaired by the reformatting.

Another time saver is that *SpinRite* now stops pattern testing of a sector at the earliest possible moment. No longer does it try its full repertoire of tests even if it has already found a defect.

***SpinRite II*, Version 2.0:** With the release of *SpinRite II*, Version 1.1, Gibson Research claimed it could do defect analysis on "anything that spins." While they never intended this to mean it would test Frisbees and phonograph records, they seriously intended it to be true for all PC hard drives.

Because the world of PCs is incredibly diverse, some weird combinations of PC, controller, and drive still caused *SpinRite* problems. Version 2.0 is able to work with all of those weird systems that Gibson Research is aware of.

> ![0110 0110] **TECHNICAL NOTE** There is still one limit to this ability. *SpinRite* only works with drives that are accessed through INT 13h BIOS calls. Some drives, such as the Bernoulli Boxes made by the Iomega Corporation, use their own device drivers and do not go through INT 13h. *SpinRite* still cannot do anything at all for them.

Version 2.0 also incorporates a major new technological breakthrough. It now is able to do all of its functions, including both data-integrity testing and low-level reformatting, on most systems with disk caching.

> ![0110 0110] **TECHNICAL NOTE** In particular, it can do so with most hard disk controllers that contain a hardware cache. The one exception is any controller that implements a "deferred write" caching strategy and which does not allow its cache to be turned off. (See

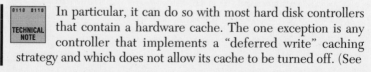

the discussion of disk caching in Chapter 5 for an explanation of what this means.) Fortunately such controllers are rare to nonexistent. *SpinRite* also is able to "get behind" most software disk caching schemes. When it can, it will no longer report that caching is active, and it will do all its work with complete safety. When it cannot get behind software disk caching, Version 2.0 will at least do all its data recovery and testing work.

You might think this means you need not disable your disk cache before running *SpinRite*. Though you might get away with that with Version 2.0, Gibson doesn't recommend it.

In line with their earlier upgrade policy, this version is available free of charge to any registered user of *SpinRite II* upon request. If you find *SpinRite II* won't do low-level reformatting or defect analysis, or if it has any other problem working with your PC, call Gibson Research's technical support line and describe your system and your problem. Their solution may be to send you Version 1.1A.

Should I upgrade?

All versions of *SpinRite* perform the same basic jobs. The later versions simply do them better, for more drives and controllers. If you have an early version and are happy with it, you need not upgrade. If you think you might run into one of the problems described above, though, perhaps you should.

From its inception, Gibson Research has had a policy of offering free upgrades within a given product generation. It even ships the upgrades free of charge, without waiting to be asked by users if the upgrade repairs some major bug. So users can upgrade from Version 1.0 to Version 1.1 automatically, at no cost. Owners of all other versions of *SpinRite* can upgrade for $25.

Since a major reason for owning and using *SpinRite* is to protect your data, most users have decided that upgrading is well worth the small amount of money. This way, if ever any of their data becomes unreadable, they will have the very best chance of getting it back.

Become a *SpinRite* Power User

Now that you know how the versions differ, let's get down to the meat of this chapter — how to make the latest version do all it can for you.

The "clean" boot disk approach

The most important single thing you can do to help *SpinRite* help you is let it have the machine to itself. Of course you must have DOS running, but you don't *need* that nifty pop-up appointment calendar. In fact, you had better *not* have that pop-up calendar or any other non-essential resident software active while *SpinRite* is working.

You can copy SPINRITE.COM to your hard disk and then run it from there. If you do so, please remember to rename your CONFIG.SYS and AUTOEXEC.BAT files and reboot your computer before you run *SpinRite*.

4

If your CONFIG.SYS file loads some disk partitioning software, like DMDRVR.BIN, SSTOR.SYS, or HARDRIVE.SYS, then you will have to create a special CONFIG.SYS file that loads only that driver and use it each time you run *SpinRite*.

> **0110 0110**
> **TECHNICAL NOTE**
> If your disk was partitioned using *Disk Manager* or *SpeedStor* or a similar product, then their special device driver is required in order to get at all but the first partition (C:). If you fail to place a reference to it in your CONFIG.SYS file on the boot disk, you will find that D: and any other partitions on that drive will be unrecognized by DOS. ("Losing" a disk partition in this way is a common problem. Fortunately, recovering from that problem is easy once you realize what happened.)

> If you are using DOS 3.3 or a later version, you probably do not need to continue using such a third-party disk partitioning program. To stop using it, you will need to backup all your data, reformat the drive, and reinstall your data. See the section on using third-party disk partitioning software under "Filling in the Partition Table" in Chapter 7 for details.

There is an easier way to run *SpinRite*. Create a special boot disk for the purpose. Since this floppy disk will load DOS and any essential disk access drivers, but it will not load anything extraneous, we call this the "Clean Boot Disk Approach."

> **0110 0110**
> **TECHNICAL NOTE**
> First, boot your system as usual. Put a blank floppy disk in your A drive. Use the DOS command FORMAT A: /S /V. This will both format the diskette and put the essential DOS files on it. Next copy SPINRITE.COM and PARK.COM from the *SpinRite* disk to that floppy.

Examine your CONFIG.SYS file. See if it has a line that says DEVICE= followed by DMDRVR.BIN or possibly SSTOR.SYS or HARDRIVE.SYS. There might be a path shown in front of the device driver name. For example, the line might read DEVICE=C:\DRIVERS\SSTOR.SYS.

If you have such a line in your C drive's CONFIG.SYS file, then you must create a CONFIG.SYS file for your floppy boot disk. Use your favorite text editor. (If you use a word processor, be sure to save your work as a "pure ASCII" text file. If you are not sure you have done so, you can check your work by using the DOS command TYPE A:CONFIG.SYS when you finish. If you can read what it shows you and there are no extraneous "garbage" symbols, then you have a pure ASCII file.)

Put the DEVICE= line in the CONFIG.SYS file on the floppy, but leave out the directory path—so it reads, for example, DEVICE=SSTOR.SYS. Also remember to copy the device driver itself (the DMDRVR.BIN file, for example) to the floppy disk.

An optional enhancement would be to add AUTOEXEC.BAT file that will run *SpinRite* with your own options automatically (the command-line options for *SpinRite* are described later in this chapter).

Now try booting your computer from the floppy boot disk (by putting the disk in the drive and restarting the machine). You should get an A> prompt (or whatever your AUTOEXEC.BAT file on the floppy specified for the prompt). Try changing to each of your DOS partitions. Do a DIR listing on each. If that works, then you are set. Write-protect the floppy boot disk so it cannot easily have its files altered. Boot from it whenever you wish to run *SpinRite*.

You can also use the Clean *SpinRite* Boot Disk Approach to semi-automate running *SpinRite* in different ways for different purposes. In the next section, you will learn how to use the program interactively, after which we will tell you how to use it from a batch file. On your bootable, "clean" *SpinRite* diskette, you could have a menu and several *SpinRite* batch files, which would make it simple to command *SpinRite* to do whichever task you wished.

Using DOS's CHKDSK First

SpinRite works with your hard disk on several levels. Sometimes, at the lowest level, it gets down and dirty with the bits, looking behind ECC to see what really can be read. At other times, it views your disk at much higher level, above the organization imposed on those data by DOS. Here it cares about the grouping of sectors into clusters and clusters into files, and here it must also find and sometimes change directory entries.

To give *SpinRite* the best chance of doing wonderful things for you, it is important that you run the DOS program CHKDSK first.

4

Why it is needed: Despite its name, CHKDSK, which stands for "CHecKDiSK," does not really test your disk. Its job is to check on the consistency of the DOS organization of the files in a DOS partition.

When you create a file on your disk, DOS must perform two independent functions — create a directory entry for that file, and allocate space for it. It accomplishes the latter task by putting special markers in the file allocation table (FAT).

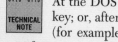 The section "High Level Formatting" in Chapter 7 gives many more details about this process. The section "How Clusters Become 'Lost'" describes one way that it can go awry.

CHKDSK primarily looks to see if the information about files contained in the directories is consistent with that in the FAT. You can also use it to check for file fragmentation. If CHKDSK finds a problem, you probably should fix it before you run *SpinRite*.

What it can tell you: There are several ways you can run CHKDSK. Depending on which method you choose, you may get different messages from it. The ones we are most concerned with are those you get when you run the program "straight," without any command-line parameters.

At the DOS prompt, type CHKDSK and press the Enter key; or, after the name, you can add a partition designator (for example: CHKDSK D:). This will tell CHKDSK to perform its most basic tests for consistency between the FAT and the directories.

The optional parameters are /V and /F. If you add /V to the end of the command line, CHKDSK will list all the files on the disk and tell you about any that are fragmented. If you add /F, it will attempt to fix anything it finds that it thinks is wrong. You don't need the first parameter, while the second one can sometimes be positively dangerous, since not all its "fixes" are right.

The most common message says CHKDSK found some number of "lost clusters" in some number of chains. The next most common tells about "cross-linked chains." Various others tell of less common but potentially more serious problems.

What it might do to you: CHKDSK is pretty good at spotting certain problems with the file structure of your disk. It is much less capable at fixing most of them. About all it is safe to let CHKDSK do is fix lost chains of clusters. If CHKDSK reports many cross-linked chains, unreadable subdirectories or FAT, or any of several other messages, you would be well advised to seek a second opinion. Run some other utility program that excels at disk file-structure analysis, such as *Norton Utilities* Disk Doctor.

If you don't heed this advice, you may turn a problem into a disaster. CHKDSK can completely mess up your file structure far worse than it was, if it should get a confused picture of what is wrong.

How to use it safely: Here are the steps to safely use CHKDSK. Follow them, please, every time you plan to run *SpinRite*. Even better, follow them every time you boot up your computer. (Put CHKDSK on a line by itself in your AUTOEXEC.BAT file.)

1. Run CHKDSK without any parameters.

2. It may stop after reporting problems and ask your permission to fix them. Since you did not give it real permission with the /F command line parameter, it is okay to tell it yes at this stage. It will act as if it were fixing things, then tell you what would have happened if it had. Don't worry, it didn't really do anything to the data on your disk.

3. If it reported no problems other than some lost chains of clusters, do step 4. Otherwise, stop and get a second opinion from another disk utility. (If you are in a batch file at the time, you will have to press Ctrl-Break, possibly several times, till you get a prompt asking if you wish to "Terminate batch file (Y/N)." Answer Y.)

4. Rerun CHKDSK with the /F parameter. When it asks for permission to fix things, say yes. This time it will create a bunch of files in the root directory with names like FILE0000.CHK, FILE0001.CHK, and so forth.

5. Look at the contents of these FILEnnnn.CHK files. The shareware program LIST.COM is an excellent tool to use. (You can get it from almost any BBS or from its author, Vernon D. Buerg, at 139 White Oak Circle, Petaluma, CA 94952. Send him $20 for the latest version.)

6. If any of these files resembles your missing file, rename it and move it to an appropriate subdirectory. If you don't recognize the file or its contents look like garbage, simply delete it.

7. At this point you will have recovered some formerly inaccessible portion of your disk and maybe some valuable files as well. More important, you will have verified that nothing worse is wrong with your disk's file organization.

After completing these steps, you are ready to have *SpinRite* treat your disk. If you stopped at step 3, you will have to do something else to ready it. For specific suggestions of what to do for each possible CHKDSK error message, refer to any good book on DOS or the manual of whatever other disk utility program you choose to use.

When you can't fix the problems

Normally you will not want to run *SpinRite* unless CHKDSK gives your disk a "clean bill of health" from its perspective. Exceptions to this include a situation where your disk is unreadable in some critical areas. CHKDSK may tell you it cannot read the FAT or some subdirectory, or it may say it cannot change directories. If you cannot find a way to fix these problems easily using some other tool, *SpinRite* may do the job. You run some risk using it on a disk CHKDSK says is messed up, but sometimes there is no feasible alternative. With a bit of luck, you may find that all your problems "magically" vanish after *SpinRite*'s ministrations.

The *Norton Utilities* (Version 5.0) Calibrate program incorporates tests that do what CHKDSK does and go a little bit further. Unfortunately, if those tests don't give your disk a complete okay, Calibrate will simply refuse to do anything. If your FAT is unreadable, that could be most unfortunate. *SpinRite*'s willingness to proceed anyway could be your data's only salvation.

Interactive Use of *SpinRite*

Hardly any DOS program is easier to use than *SpinRite*. If you wish, you can make it do its work automatically. Alternatively, you can intervene at various points to customize its operation. Assuming you have booted off a "clean" *SpinRite* disk as suggested above (but without the menu batch files), simply type A:SPINRITE at the DOS prompt. That will start the program. Now watch the bottom line of the screen for prompts for when you have to press a key.

4

> 0110 0110
> **TECHNICAL NOTE**
> To receive *SpinRite* report files, you probably will want to have your DOS default drive and directory be something other than A:\. You could do this (after booting from the clean disk but before starting *SpinRite*) by, for example, typing C: and pressing the Enter key, then perhaps CD SPINRITE and pressing Enter. (This assumes you have a C:\SPINRITE directory in which you want to keep your *SpinRite* report files.) Then type A:SPINRITE to start the program.

In this interactive mode of operation, *SpinRite* prompts you before it proceeds to the next step, giving you the option of modifying how it will execute those steps. You also can choose some options in the non-interactive, or batch, mode by specifying certain command-line parameters. In the interactive mode, you choose most of these options by selecting item 3 from the main menu, "Alter SpinRite's Operation."

Whether to low-level reformat

The first option on this sub-menu allows you to suppress low-level reformatting. In the final section of this chapter, we discuss one reason why you might not want to do a low-level reformatting. If you have trouble giving your PC peace and quiet for the amount of time *SpinRite* requires to run all its tests, you may wish to test your disk extensively without reformatting, then return and do a quick reformat. This option gives you this control.

Let bad clusters become good?

The next option lets you turn off another of *SpinRite*'s features. A capability unique to *SpinRite*, this feature returns to full service sectors and clusters that were formerly marked as bad. It will do so only if you have allowed it to test the disk at the very deepest level, and then only if it finds that the sectors in question are now performing perfectly. In that case, Gibson says, he sees no reason not to let you use the sectors, but you can turn off that feature here if it bothers you.

When to perform the seek test

4

SpinRite needs to be able to place the heads over the tracks of any cylinder it wishes with absolute assurance. To this end, it tests the head positioning mechanism extensively. This is a vital test to perform the first time you run *SpinRite* on any drive.

If you have run *SpinRite* on a given drive many times without detecting any problem, you may wish to skip this test. The third option on this menu allows you to do so.

On a slow drive it can take several minutes to do the seek test. If you run the test in interactive mode, you will have be on hand to interact with the program at later stages of its operation, so you may want to skip this test. Likewise, if you have two DOS partitions on a single physical drive, remember that *SpinRite* tests the head positioning mechanism for the whole drive at once, not just for a particular partition. If you use it on both partitions, one right after the other, you may well want to skip the seek testing for the second partition.

The remaining options on this menu are more often invoked when running *SpinRite* from a batch file. We will discuss them in the section "Batch File Operation" later in this chapter.

Choosing pattern testing depth

Since it is so important, *SpinRite* forces you to choose the pattern-testing depth every time you run the program, automatically bringing up a menu of pattern testing depths. You have four possible choices: none, a little, substantial, or complete pattern testing. In

Chapter 2, you learned that these levels impose 0, 5, 43, or 82 test patterns on each sector in the DOS partition. The more testing you do, the more likely it is that *SpinRite* will detect every problem there may be with your disk and controller. The tradeoff is that more thorough tests take more time.

 Only when the five basic patterns are applied in all their shifted variations will *SpinRite* be able to catch *all* surface defects. This is what Depth 4 (82 pattern) testing does.

The Depth 3 test (43 patterns) will catch most but not all defects. The Depth 2 test (5 patterns) will exercise the read/write circuitry and other aspects of drive and controller, but will have only a poor chance of catching surface defects.

The first time you run *SpinRite* on a new disk or controller, you should choose the deepest level of pattern testing, which applies the test patterns in all their shifted variations. Later on you may not need that same level of assurance and you might, therefore, choose to run *SpinRite* at a lower level of pattern testing to save time.

Any time you are going to change the sector interleave value on your disk, you definitely should choose the deepest level of pattern testing. *SpinRite* will default to Depth 4 testing in that case.

 This is important because when you change the sector interleave value, you are moving data from one location on the track to another. Possibly you will move good data to a bad sector. Running the deepest pattern tests essentially prevents you from making that mistake.

When you are not changing the sector interleave value (and hence not running the risk of relocating data to a bad sector), *SpinRite* will default to Depth 3 pattern testing (43 patterns) to save you some time. Gibson provided Depth 2 (5 patterns) testing as a minimal test for those who aren't willing to spend very much time testing.

You should choose the lowest level pattern testing (none) *only* if you have done some deeper-level testing on this partition recently. An example is the procedure recommended in the last section of this chapter for dealing with an environment in which your PC gets bumped or jiggled from time to time.

Creating a report

Whenever *SpinRite* finishes an operation you have an opportunity to create a report. In fact, you can create a report on an interrupted operation and another one when it is finished.

To create a report you must return to the main *SpinRite* menu and select item 4, "Print Full Operations Summary." Choosing this item brings you to a sub-menu, which presents the following options: Add a Title Block to the Report; Send the Report to a Disk File; and Send the Report to a Printer.

Adding a title block is optional, but it may help you remember why you ran this particular operation at this time. You might want to include the date, since that is not otherwise a part of the report, especially if you are going to print the report (rather than saving it in a disk file, which would at least have a DOS file creation date on it).

If you choose the disk file option, the program will offer a default file name of SPINRITE.RPT. If you accept this name, *SpinRite* will write the file to the current DOS default drive and directory. This is the reason why we suggested previously that you might want to be in a subdirectory where you keep such reports before starting *SpinRite*.

> **TECHNICAL NOTE**
> You are allowed to edit the suggested name, and you can even change the drive or directory to which the report will be sent. The program limits you to a total of 49 characters for the report name, including the path, but that should be adequate for most users.

There are two important differences to note between the *SpinRite* report file and its Detailed Technical Log file. The first has to do with where the file is placed and what it is called. The second is an important caution about overwriting the information.

Although *SpinRite* proffers the name SPINRITE.RPT and suggests placing it in the current DOS default directory, you may choose whatever name and location you wish for the report file. The program always calls the log file SPINRITE.LOG and always creates it in the root directory of the partition being tested.

If you accept the default name for the report file or choose one you had used previously, the new report file will *replace* the earlier one.

On the other hand, *SpinRite* always *appends* to the Detailed Technical Log file. If you want to keep an ongoing record of all operations performed by *SpinRite*, you will have to choose a series of unique names for the report files.

 One suggestion: Accept the default name, SPINRITE.RPT, then exit *SpinRite* before doing another process and re-name the file to conform to some pattern you have chosen. For example, you might name your files to show which partition was being tested, numbering them in serial order: SPINRITE.C01, SPINRITE.C02, SPINRITE.D01, etc.

You may allow the SPINRITE.LOG file to grow in size each time you run *SpinRite* on that partition. Alternatively, after each operation, you may copy that file to the subdirectory that holds your *SpinRite* report files and give it a name that matches the report file name. For example, you might have log files SPINLOG.C01, SPINLOG.C02, SPINLOG.D01, etc.

Remember to delete the original log file \SPINRITE.LOG after creating the copy of it. Otherwise your next log file will include the log of the last session as well.

You also could choose to print the report and not save it in a disk file. This option will create a one- or two-page report with a "form-feed character" at the end of each page. Your printer must be able to print straight ASCII text, and it must be attached to a parallel printer port.

 You can print a report to a printer on a serial port, but you have to do it a special way. Select the option to send the report to a disk file, but when prompted for the name, use the DOS device name for the port (*e.g.*, COM1: or COM2:).

If you have a PostScript printer that only understands PostScript code, your printer will be unable to print the report directly. In that case, use the option to create a disk file and print it later using your word processor.

Something you can't do interactively

Though it might seem that the interactive mode of *SpinRite* would give you the absolute maximum amount of flexibility in controlling the program, there is one thing it can do in batch mode that it cannot do in interactive mode.

When you run it interactively, it offers you a list of partitions to test. They will be described as "C: on First Drive," "D: on Second Drive," and "E: on First Drive." There may be up to 10 partitions listed. It is entirely possible, though not highly likely, that you have more than 10 DOS partitions. In order to get *SpinRite* to test one of them if it is not listed as a choice, you need to log to that partition as the DOS default drive and then run *SpinRite* in batch mode. This brings us to our next topic.

Batch Mode Operation

4

Additional incentives to run *SpinRite* in its batch mode include the fact that you may not want to sit there waiting for each prompt if you plan to accept all of *SpinRite*'s defaults anyway. Or, you may wish to run *SpinRite*, not necessarily with its default actions, as a part of a larger batch file.

Your choices and their default values

The usual way to start *SpinRite* is to type SPINRITE and press Enter. (You may, of course, have to give a drive or path if SPINRITE.COM is not in the current directory or one listed in your current DOS PATH definition.) If you wish, before pressing Enter you can type some "command-line options" after SPINRITE, words that tell the program how you want it to operate this time.

> **0110 0110**
> **TECHNICAL NOTE**
> Remember to separate the program name from the first option, and each option from the next one, with one or more spaces. You may enter the options with any mixture of upper and lower-case letters, in any order, but all on one line.

The command line options fall into three groups. The first are fundamental to batch-mode operation. The next set concerns various aspects of how *SpinRite* does its work. The last simply affects how it appears or sounds.

In all cases *SpinRite* assumes you do not want the effect of any option you do not include. The one exception is the option to choose the depth of pattern testing. We describe its default value as well as that option later in this section.

Fundamental command-line options: The most fundamental command line option is **BATCH**. This tells *SpinRite* you want it to do its work without asking you for any further input.

The other fundamental option is **AUTOEXIT**. This tells *SpinRite* that when it is done it should give control of your PC back to DOS. If you invoke *SpinRite* from within a batch file, this option allows the batch file to proceed with the rest of its actions. If you don't use Autoexit, *SpinRite* will return to its main menu when it finishes its operations.

Functional command-line options: If you want a report file created, you must include the option **AUTOREPORT**. This will force the program to create a file named SPINRITE.RPT, which it will place in the DOS default drive and directory. The file will not include a title block. You cannot direct this report to the printer automatically. You could, of course, copy it to the printer in a subsequent line of a batch file.

The option to choose the depth of pattern testing is the only one that has alternative forms. You can specify **DEPTH1**, **DEPTH2**, **DEPTH3**, or **DEPTH4**, or you can opt not to specify a depth. These depth numbers correspond to using 0, 5, 43, or 82 test patterns on each sector. If you do not specify a depth, *SpinRite* will choose DEPTH4 if the operation it is about to do will include changing the interleave value; otherwise it will choose DEPTH3.

There is no option to choose the interleave value. *SpinRite* will automatically choose whatever it determines to be the optimum value if it is redoing the partition's low-level format.

> **0110 0110**
> **TECHNICAL NOTE** It would not be wise to specify a depth of less than 4 unless you are sure *SpinRite* will not be resetting the sector interleave in your partition. It won't do that if one of the following conditions is true: if the sector interleave value is already set to the optimum; if the hardware does not permit low-level formatting; or if you explicitly command it not to do low-level formatting (with the NOFORMAT option).
>
> By not specifying a depth, or by insisting on DEPTH4, you will be sure not to reset the sector interleave value without the full protection of the deepest level of pattern testing. (One exception to this rule is covered in the last section in this chapter.)

The **LEAVEBAD** command-line parameter tells *SpinRite* that you do not want it to return formerly bad sectors to full use even if they test out perfectly. This option is the default unless you are testing at DEPTH4.

You can force *SpinRite* not to do any low-level reformatting by using the **NOFORMAT** option. You might want to do this if you are specifying DEPTH2 or DEPTH3 pattern testing.

The section "When To Seek Test" earlier in this chapter explains why you might not want to do so. Use the command-line option **NOSEEKTEST** to force *SpinRite* to skip that part of its testing.

One rarely used command-line option is **PERSTOR**. Gibson Research provides this one to make *SpinRite* compatible with some earlier PerStor hard disk controllers. You do not need to use it unless you have a PerStor controller. Even if you do have such a controller and you leave out this option, *SpinRite* reports that it cannot do a low-level format on this drive.

The **QUICKSCAN** option forces *SpinRite* to do its read-only test of the partition, which is the minimum test it can do. QUICKSCAN will not move any data and is always safe to use, but it also prevents *SpinRite* from delivering the full benefits it has to offer.

The last of the functional command line options is **RESUME**. This tells *SpinRite* that if it finds any interrupted processes, it should resume one of them.

> 0110 0110
> **TECHNICAL NOTE**
> If it does so, it will ignore all other current command-line options in favor of the options that were chosen at the time that process was begun.

You could safely add this command-line option in a batch file, knowing it would finish off one interrupted operation each time that batch file is run. The rest of the command-line options in that batch file would take effect only if *SpinRite* had no interrupted operations to finish.

Cosmetic command-line options: Adding the word **BLANK-ING** to the command line will force *SpinRite* to blank the screen as soon as it starts a quick surface scan, pattern test, or low-level format operation. This is never necessary, but it will protect your monitor from possibly "burning in" a pattern from the *SpinRite* screen display. You can force *SpinRite* to unblank the screen at any time by pressing the **B** key. Pressing "B" again will reblank the screen. (The blank screen actually displays a small, moving box announcing that testing is under way.)

The **NOCOLOR**, **NOSHADING**, and **NOSOUND** options do just what you would expect. The first two may be useful if your computer has a gas plasma or liquid crystal display (common on laptop computers) or a monochrome monitor connected to a color display card. The last one suppresses the sound effects. Your co-workers may ask you to choose this one.

Getting Around Some Limitations

Batch mode is useful, and if you have more than 10 DOS partitions, it is the only way you can use *SpinRite* on any of them past the first 10. All you need to do is log to the partition you want to test and then run *SpinRite* with the BATCH command-line option. Remember to add any other options you might want, as you won't get another chance. If you don't include AUTOEXIT, however, you will get a chance to create a report after *SpinRite* finishes the operation and returns to its main menu.

When you create a report in the interactive mode, you have the opportunity to tell *SpinRite* what file name, drive, and directory you want to use. When operating in batch mode, *SpinRite* will create the file for you in the DOS default drive and directory, always naming it SPINRITE.RPT. Also, you cannot have it send the report to your printer.

An easy work-around is to include a couple of lines in your batch file after *SpinRite* is finished that will copy the report file from its default location to wherever you want it and then erase the original copy. You can also rename the report file in this step, or send it to a printer.

The Truth About Hard Disk Head Parking

In the early days of PCs, when hard disks were expensive, users were advised to protect their disks by "parking the heads" every time they shut down their computer. IBM did not want to intimidate users of its first PC (which was introduced as a home computer), and so while they provided a program to park the heads, called SHIPDISK. They only told their customers they needed to run it only before shipping the computer somewhere.

What is head parking?

When you use your PC, each time you read or write any information from or to the hard disk, the heads have to be positioned over the cylinder holding that information. Normally they stay there until you tell them to move elsewhere.

4

Parking the heads moves them away from your valuable data. With some drives this actually means moving the heads completely off the disk surfaces. For most drives the manufacturer will specify a "landing zone," though, which is a cylinder at or near the innermost reach of the head positioning mechanism.

Since parking the heads is nothing more than a "seek" to a specially chosen cylinder, you automatically unpark the disk the next time you ask it to seek to some other cylinder, preparatory to reading or writing data there.

Some horror stories

When *SpinRite* was under development, Gibson asked many people to help test it, keeping careful track of their experiences. One thing he noticed repeatedly was that their SPINRITE.RPT files would show on the track map whole regions of **C**'s. This indicated regions of their disk where correctable errors were happening. Running *SpinRite* corrected those errors, but Gibson wondered what their source was. His testers informed him that the regions in question contained their most-used and most-valued files.

Upon further investigation, he concluded that the magnetic signals for data could get corrupted by having the heads land on them. When you turn off power to your PC, the hard disk stops turning. The heads, which have been surfing on a thin film of rushing air, sit down on the disk platter surface.

Almost all early PC hard disks used stepper-motor head positioners. (See the section on steppers and servos under "Messy Physical Details" in Chapter 5 for more on this.) With those drives, the heads would sit down on whatever cylinder they last had been ordered to find.

When you turn on your PC, the disk starts to turn and the heads start to fly. But first the heads will very likely engage in some quite erratic behavior. They may jerk to one side. They may also have small surges of current go through their windings.

These unscheduled head activities will very possibly flip one or more bits, or perhaps only weaken them. Whatever data damage does occur will happen wherever the heads find themselves. In the case of the early *SpinRite* testers' disks, that was often right on top of their most-used — and usually also most-valuable — files.

Gibson's response was to write a program that would safely park the heads well away from one's valuable data. The user must remember to run this program before shutting off the PC, but that is a significant improvement over not being able to protect your data at all. This program, or a descendent of it, is included with every copy of *SpinRite*.

Self-parking drives

More modern PC hard drives mostly use servo head positioners. These drives are nearly all "self parking," which means that when power is removed from the drive, it will automatically force the heads all the way in toward the spindle or, even better, pull them out all the way off the platters. If you are not sure if yours is a self-parking drive, you should still use a parking program.

An easy way to determine whether your drive is self parking is to listen to your drive. When you power down the PC, if you hear it go "thunk," or maybe even "thunk" followed by "chunk," then it is very likely a self-parking drive. (The thunk is the parking. The chunk is the sound of a locking pin dropping into place to hold the heads safely against the spindle or off the platters.) You can also consult the manufacturer's manual on your hard drive, which you can get from the manufacturer or his distributor.

You may want to park even a drive that will park itself if you plan to leave your PC for awhile while it is turned on. (It stresses a PC much less to keep it running for a few hours than to turn it off and back on again). This strategy guards against the possibility of someone accidentally jarring the computer or knocking it to the floor, which could force the heads to contact the disk surface briefly. If they are already safely parked, they will not damage your most recently accessed file.

In fact, a parked head may not crash when an unparked one would. Consider these facts. Parked heads are near the spindle. The disk platters are much like cymbals, which flex when they are struck. Parked heads rest where the platters cannot flex much, and so a head crash is less likely to occur even when the disk is jarred.

4

Head parking programs

OK, I should park my drives. How? The easy answer for *SpinRite* users is to run the PARK.COM program you will find on your *SpinRite* disk. There are many alternative park programs as well. Many IBM PCs came with a version of SHIPDISK.COM. Some PS/2s come with PARKHEAD.COM, and many bulletin boards boast a plethora of park programs.

Gibson Research operates a bulletin board from which you can download a free copy of the *SpinRite* PARK.COM program. The number is (714) 830-3300. Set your communications program to 8 data bits, 1 stop bit, and no parity. You may call at any speed up to 2400 bits per second.

Not all these programs are equal. In the next section, we describe what distinguishes a good program.

Safe park programs

A safe park program will not ask your disk drive to do anything it would not normally do in the course of every-day operation. In particular, it should ask the drive to seek to a cylinder that exists.

The Hard Disk Parameter Table for any drive contains an entry that ought to point to a safe place to park the heads. PS/2 computers have a special BIOS function to enable one to park the heads (INT 13h, Fn 19h).

For most PCs, using one of these two approaches will succeed. For a few, it is necessary to choose the largest-numbered cylinder on the drive. (To get that, use the BIOS call "Get Drive Parameters," INT 13h, Fn 8.)

Any program that picks some actual cylinder in near the spindle and positions the heads there should be perfectly safe to use.

Destructive park programs

Some park programs are positively dangerous to some drives. Avoid these. They depend on an assumption about hard disk drives that was once usually true, but now is false more often than not.

 A typical hard disk with a stepper motor head positioner often can have its heads moved in a bit further than the highest-numbered cylinder. Eventually the positioner will hit a mechanical stop and go no further. No damage is done by asking it to step in at that point. It simply will not move. (Your machine will make a disconcerting groaning sound, but the program will do no harm.)

When the only drives available for PCs used stepper motors, someone came up with what he thought was a very clever strategy. He would not depend on the BIOS report to determine how many cylinders a drive actually had. Instead, he would ask the drive to go in until it could go no further.

Hard disk controllers have a designed limit. They will not go to a cylinder number higher than what they have been told is the maximum cylinder count. Normally that gets set by the BIOS, based on the numbers in the Hard Disk Parameter Table. But by creating a dummy Hard Disk Parameter Table, pointing to it with INT 41h or 46h, and using INT 13h, Function 9, you can fool the controller. You can tell it the drive has any number of cylinders you want. Then you can tell it to seek to any cylinder number, up to whatever maximum number you just told it.

The controller does not check to see which cylinder it gets to when it seeks. It only checks when you next ask it to read or write some data. Then it will not tell you which cylinder it is on. It will simply give you an error if it cannot find the sector you want. Since it does check all three dimensions of sector addresses (cylinder, head, and physical sector number), that is a way to find out when you are on the wrong cylinder.

This person (and we don't know who it was) apparently used this technique to force the disk controller to move the heads in many cylinders at a time till it gave an error when reading some sector in that cylinder. This indicated it had failed to reach the target cylinder. Next, the program moved the heads in by smaller steps. This continued till the controller was unable to move in even one cylinder without an error. That meant the head was parked at the mechanical stop.

This strategy depends on the controller being able to step the drive's head assembly a given number of cylinders further in, independent of where it is. That is exactly what older, stepper motor drives attached to MFM or RLL controllers do. For them and them only this sort of park program is safe to use.

On a drive with a servo-controlled head positioner, the assumption made by these programs can be fatal. If you run such a program on a vulnerable drive, you will hear it repeatedly slam the head assembly against the stop until eventually something breaks.

4

 A servo-controlled drive can only seek to cylinders for which it has a prerecorded servo track. You cannot ask it to go in several cylinders without it figuring out what cylinder number you are seeking. Asking it to find some cylinder past the range of those prerecorded ones causes great grief.

First the head will move to about where the drive thinks it should go. That is, it will try to go there. In the case of seeking to a cylinder well past the last one, it will slam very hard into the mechanical stop. Now, not finding the servo information to indicate that it is where it should be, the drive controller will order a "recalibration." This is a seek to the outermost cylinder. Once it has done this, it will again attempt to find the requested cylinder.

This process will repeat, moving the head all the way out and then slamming it all the way in (and then some), over and over till the drive breaks.

There is no easy way to be sure how any given park program was written, unless you have access to its source code or its programmer. The safest approach is to use one you trust. The one that the manufacturer provided with your computer should be fine. *SpinRite*'s PARK program is also safe to use on any PC.

Resident park utilities

The one notable weakness of the best parking programs is that you must remember to use them. A resident park program takes care of this automatically when you leave your computer idle for awhile, while a self-parking drive does so when you turn off your PC.

Some computers run for hours without needing to access their hard disks. Then suddenly, they must. Then more hours go by till they do again. One example would be a computer running a bulletin board program that does not get very many calls. It may be on 24 hours a day, but only get used a few times each day. There is no operator present to park the disk, but it would be much safer if it were parked all the times that it is not in use.

For such a computer a timed parking program can be a blessing. This is a park program that can be loaded into RAM as a terminate-and-stay resident (TSR) program. It will monitor the disk activity, parking the heads whenever the hard disk has not been accessed for several minutes.

There are many such programs available on various BBSes. They mostly work as advertised. They are fine if you have that special situation, but most normal PC users don't need them.

Like all TSRs they take up some of the precious first 640K of system RAM. Worse, they may cause conflicts with other TSRs or with other programs you need to use.

Remember that even if you have a resident park utility installed, you still must park the heads manually before turning off power. Either that, or be careful not to use the drive for however long it takes to trigger the automatic parking action of the resident utility and then turn off power (unless yours is a self-parking drive).

Hints and Tips

In this section, we offer a reminder of some essential things to remember to do, along with a brief description of a special situation in which you might want to use *SpinRite* a bit differently than usual.

Some things to remember, always

First, back up your hard disk. Backups are always a good idea, but never so much so as when you are about to let some program work with your data at the low level used by *SpinRite*. You can get away without backing up before rerunning *SpinRite*, though the best advice is always to be fully backed up.

Next, run CHKDSK before you run *SpinRite* — every time. Only proceed to use *SpinRite* if you get a clean bill of health from CHKDSK or if you cannot fix the problems. (See the above section "When You Can't Fix the Problems" for more on this.)

Third, run *SpinRite* in a clean system. That may mean booting the computer off a special Clean *SpinRite* Boot Disk. Or you can simply change your CONFIG.SYS and AUTOEXEC.BAT files appropriately each time. (See the above section "The 'Clean' Boot Disk Approach" for the details.)

Fourth, leave the PC undisturbed while *SpinRite* does its work. Even a gentle bump can make the heads bounce sideways briefly. If that should happen during a low-level format operation, it would create a wavy track.

4

It might not be your disk

If you get a vast number of errors, especially correctable ones, consider the possibility that you may have a loose cable. Another possibility is that the hard disk controller is slightly crooked in its slot. Open the case, remove the cables and replace them. Remove the controller and replace it. (See the section on Simple Things That Sometimes Go Wrong under "Failures" in Chapter 8 both for some **important warnings** and some suggestions on how to fix these and some other problems.)

Part
— II —

How Hard Disks Work
and Why They
Sometimes Die

Chapter 5

Magnetic Storage of Information

The first part of this book told you all about *SpinRite*. Part Two will give you background information so you can understand that information fully. It also can be a wonderful way to learn all about hard disks even aside from any interest you may have in *SpinRite*.

This chapter covers how hard disks work in great detail. Chapters 6 and 7 explain how MS-DOS uses hard disks. You will find some valuable tips for making your disks work more efficiently. The last chapter explains why hard disks die, and what you can do to revive them.

All these chapters cover many topics and their explanations are designed for readers new to those topics and for knowledgeable readers who seek a more thorough understanding. Remember: You need only read what interests you. And as before, especially technical paragraphs are indented so that you can easily go right to them or pass them by as you are inclined.

Fundamentals

A hard disk serves as a depository for data between the times the computer is processing them. Its essential purpose is to store information and, upon request, to deliver it back again. Hard disks function similarly to audio tape recorders: both use patterns of magnetization in a thin film of magnetic material on some support-ing material (called a "substrate") for their information storage.

The two technologies differ in that tape drives use as their record-ing substrate long strips of plastic, wound on spools, while hard disks use rigid metal disks. A more important difference is that audio tape stores information in "analog" form, which means that the magnetic signals mimic in their strength the audio information being stored. Hard disks are "digital" devices: Their magnetic signals are one of two strengths. These magnetic signals encode binary numbers, which represent the data to be stored.

The magnetic recording media used in both cases are only able to support two levels of magnetization: all one way or all the other. We say they are constantly saturated. To record analog informa-tion, one adds the analog signal to a bias oscillator signal and records that composite. The resulting magnetization flips between its two saturated levels with a duty cycle that reflects the analog value being stored. When reading this signal, the read head is commonly designed to average out the bias oscillator signals, thus recovering the original analog signal.

5

Digital data storage is quite different. As you will learn shortly, digital data is a bunch of numbers and they get encoded and stored as transitions in the magnetization at well defined locations on the disk surface. The read head sees each one of these changes and the decoding electronics converts them back into copies of the original numbers.

Finally, we tolerate minor imperfections, such as some extra noise or small gaps of missed information, in analog audio tape record-ings. We expect hard disks to store digital data absolutely perfectly. An error in just a single bit (a binary one or zero) out of many billions of bits could significantly impair your computer's opera-tion. To guard against this, disk makers incorporate a great deal of error correction.

To understand how hard disks work and how they "die" you must first understand how digital data is recorded magnetically. This includes learning the special steps that hard disk manufacturers have taken to make their products appear to have the perfection we insist upon. Once you understand these facts, you are ready to learn how this strategy sometimes breaks down, or "how hard disks die," which is the subject of Chapter 8.

Three Important Physical Facts

Both audio tape recorders and hard disk drives depend on the same physical principles. There are just three facts you need to know to understand how any magnetic recorder works at the most fundamental level:

1. Pass a current through a coil of wire, and you generate a magnetic field.

2. Impose a strong enough magnetic field on a ferromagnetic substance and that field will "stick." That is, part of the ferromagnetic material will become magnetized in the same direction, and that will last until another sufficiently strong magnetic field comes along and magnetizes it in some other direction. This is how magnetic information gets recorded.

3. Change the magnetic field which is passing through a coil of wire and a voltage will appear across the ends of the coil. If, for example, you pass a permanent magnet over a coil, you can detect the magnet's field from the voltage induced in the coil. This is how magnetically recorded information is read.

Now that you know the three basic physical phenomena behind the magnetic storage of information, let us see how they are applied in the design of a hard disk drive.

The basic construction of a hard disk

The principal parts of a hard disk drive are shown in Figure 5-1(a). One or more circular metal platters coated on both sides with a very thin layer of a ferromagnetic material are mounted on a spindle that rotates them at a constant, high speed. For each surface (top and bottom of each platter) there is a "read/write head." These heads are mounted on a "head assembly" that moves them in toward the spindle or out toward the edge of the platters.

> **TECHNICAL NOTE** Recently some drive manufacturers have begun to make hard disk drives using glass platters. Glass platters can be made flatter and smoother more easily, and have higher rigidity. This latter quality is especially important in some new drives that turn faster than the usual 3600 revolutions per minute. So far only a few drives are made using glass platters, but it may become more common in the near future.

When the disk is not turning (when the drive is turned off), weak springs hold the heads in contact with the surface. When the disk is turning, the heads "surf" on the wind created by the turning disk. That air current is strong enough to lift the heads away from the surface, though only by a very small distance, about 0.1 to 0.5 microns (millionths of a meter), which is 0.000004 to 0.00002 inches.

It is important that the head flies above, rather than on, the surface — this prevents it from wearing out the ferromagnetic coating by rubbing. It must not fly too far above the surface, though, or it would be unable either to magnetize the surface strongly enough or read the magnetization that is there.

The "actuator" is what moves the head assembly in and out. There are two common types of actuator: a stepper motor driving a "rack and pinion," as shown in Figure 5-1(b); and a servo-feedback, "voice coil" actuator, as shown in Figure 5-1(c). For an explanation of how these two actuator types function and how they differ, see the section titled "Messy Physical Details" later in this chapter.

Because even minute dust specks can cause disastrous failures of the drive, these parts are sealed in a chamber filled with very clean air. This chamber must never be opened except by qualified technicians in a suitable "clean room." Opening it otherwise will void the manufacturer's warranty and almost certainly lead to destruction of the drive.

> **TECHNICAL NOTE** The chamber is not hermetically sealed. It simply has a fan pulling air into it through a very fine pore filter with holes only a small fraction of a micron (less than a dozen millionths of an inch) in diameter. The air escapes out the inevitable leaks in the housing. This makes the air pressure inside higher than that on the outside, which helps keep dirt from coming in through those same leaks.

The heads are each a small coil of wire wound around a magnetically conductive core. Figure 5-2(a) shows one design. Notice the small gap in the core. That is where all the action is, so far as the magnetic coating on the platter is concerned.

One more important fact is that all magnetic fields are closed loops. Whether they are created by a current passing in a coil of wire or by a permanent magnet, the field lines loop around and connect back on themselves. For a permanent magnet the loop goes through the magnetic material, comes out of its "north pole" and after looping around outside, goes back into its "south pole." In the case of a coil of wire, the loops go through the coil, around the outside, and back in the other side of the coil.

Magnetic field lines also strongly "prefer" to travel through a magnetically conductive material. That is why an electromagnet often has a core of metal or some other ferromagnetic material. The core both guides and strengthens the magnetic field.

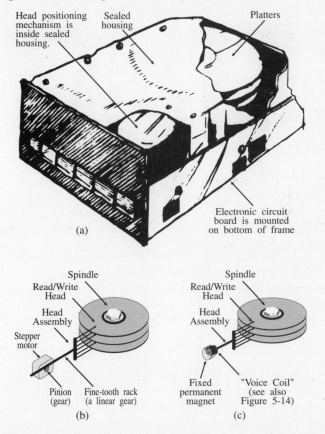

Figure 5-1 (a) A typical hard drive with a portion of housing cut away to reveal the platters.

(b) A stepper motor head positioner.

(c) A servo feedback head positioner.

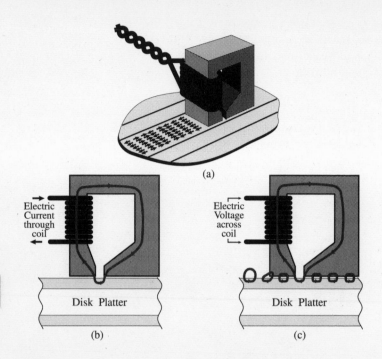

(a)

Electric
Current
through
coil

Disk Platter

(b)

Electric
Voltage
across
coil

Disk Platter

(c)

Figure 5-2 (a) Read/Write head writing regions of magnetization along a track.
(b) Magnetic field lines from current in head coil form permanent magnet in platter surface coating.
(c) Permanent magnets in coating have field lines that close on themselves. Magnet next to gap closes its lines through head core and coil.

When the read/write heads in a hard disk write information to the disk, they act as tiny electromagnets with a ferromagnetic core. But their core does not extend all the way around the loop that the magnetic field lines want to follow. It has a small gap. The field lines cannot have any gaps in themselves, so they have to leave the core material and cross the core gap somehow.

If there is any ferromagnetic material nearby, they will detour through that material instead of going straight across the core gap. In a hard disk the nearby material is the surface coating on the platter. This is illustrated in Figure 5-2(b).

In making that detour, the field lines from the coil's magnetic field force the surface material to become magnetized. Reverse the current in the coil and its magnetic field lines will reverse direction; this will record a reversed magnetic field in the surface of the platter.

As the disk platter turns under the head, the current in the head coil is reversed rapidly, recording an ever-changing magnetic field on the disk surface. This field points forward along the track for a short distance, then backwards, then forward again. These changes provide the means to store information.

When the coil is not carrying any current (and so is not making any magnetic field of its own), it can be used to read the magnetic fields in the platter surface. If a portion of the surface platter next to the core gap is permanently magnetized, the magnetic field lines passing over that portion will close on themselves through the core, and thus through the coil, rather than simply curving back around the permanent magnet over the gap. See Figure 5-2(c).

Once data has been written to it, the part of the platter that passes under the head contains, in effect, a string of permanent magnets, some pointing one way and some the other. As the head passes over each magnet, it closes that magnet's field lines through the head coil in that magnet's direction. Consequently, when the head passes from on top of a magnet pointing in one direction to on top of a neighboring magnet pointing the other way, the magnetic field passing through the head's coil changes. This means that, according to our third "important physical fact," for just a brief moment a pulse of voltage appears across the ends of the coil. These blips of voltage enable the hard disk to sense recorded information.

Besides the platters, spindle, read-write heads, head assembly and actuator, and the sealed chamber that contains and protects all those parts, all hard disk drives must have one more part — an electronic circuit card. This circuitry is connected to the head actuator, the heads, and the drive motor that turns the spindle. In turn it is connected back to the computer or to a disk controller card in the computer, and to the computer's power supply.

Tracks and cylinders

The head assembly actuator moves the head assembly in or out in small, equal-size steps. For any given position of the head assembly, each head traces out a circle on its platter surface as that platter turns under it. Each of these circles is called a "track." Each time the heads are moved to a new position, they sweep out a new set of tracks. Starting from the outside edge of the platter, the tracks form concentric circles and are numbered beginning with zero at the outside edge. (See Figure 5-3.) Tracks with the same number (i.e., all the tracks on all surfaces for a single head assembly position) form what is called a *cylinder*.

5

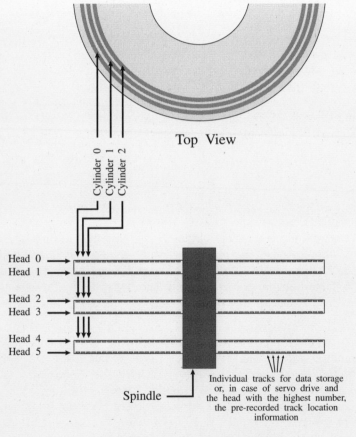

Figure 5-3 Location and numbering of disk heads (surfaces) and cylinders

The significance of a cylinder is simple to explain. A cylinder's tracks pass under their respective heads simultaneously. This means that we can write data to or read data from any of those tracks merely by electronically switching on the appropriate read/write head. Such electronic switching can be done very quickly — much faster than physically moving the head to a neighboring cylinder.

There are as many tracks per cylinder as there are heads, or (since each platter has two heads) twice the number of platters. (In some drives one of those heads is reserved for use by the servo positioning mechanism. This is why you will see an odd number of heads listed for some drives in tables of drive dimensions.) The heads are numbered, starting with zero for the head on the top surface of the uppermost platter. (Computer engineers like to count starting with zero instead of one — the reason is not easy to explain.)

The number of cylinders (or tracks per platter) that any given hard drive has depends both on how narrow each track is (which in turn depends on how small the head is) and on the step size that the head actuator is able to make. Typical hard drives have anywhere from a few hundred to several thousand cylinders.

How big is a bit?

We want our hard disks to store as much information as possible. The number of bits of data a given drive can store depends on how much magnetizable platter surface it has (how many platters and how large each one is) and how much of that surface area must be used to store each bit.

Bits are recorded as patterns of magnetic fields along the tracks, with the fields pointing either forward or backward. As the platter turns under the head, the current through the head is reversed, which in turn reverses the recorded magnetic field in the surface. Think of this as a "flipping and flopping" of the permanent magnets in the surface as you go along the track, as is shown schematically in Figure 5-4. (In an actual disk, there would be many more, much smaller individual magnetized regions than are shown here.)

The size of a bit is its width times its length. The width of a bit equals the width of its track, which is simply the width of the read/write head. That must be somewhat less than the distance from track to track. The length of a bit is a little harder to describe. Three factors affect a bit's length: There is some limit to how closely we can space the flips and flops of the magnetic field along the track. Also, we may need more than one such flip-flop distance to store a bit of information. Multiplying the minimum magnetic field flip-flop distance with the required number of such distances yields the absolute minimum length of a bit for any particular hard drive. Finally, the hard disk's designers may have had some good reasons for making the bit storage regions larger than the absolute minimum.

A circular track of permanent magnets (size greatly exaggerated) which the write head leaves in the platter coating as the platter turns under it.

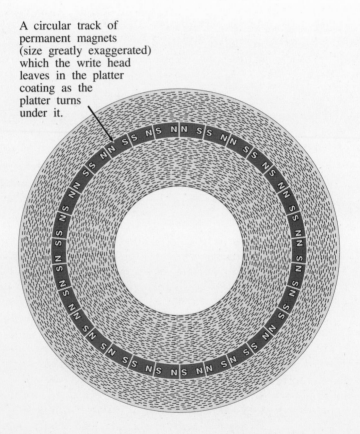

Figure 5-4 A hard disk platter showing (schematically) how the magnetic particles in the surface are aligned circumferentially and the way the read/write head leaves regions magnetized forward and back along the path of its motion (called a track).

The minimum magnetic field flip-flop length turns out to depend on a complex combination of the properties of the platter's magnetic surface, combined with the size of the core gap in the head that does the writing. The number of these flip-flop lengths we need to encode a bit of information depends on how data are encoded into magnetic signals. The last factor, whether we get to *use* the minimum possible space per bit, is the result of a compromise between efficiency and simplicity in the design of both disk drives and disk controllers.

The "Minimum Magnetic Flip-Flop Length": How small can the magnetic flip-flop length be? Again, we can break the answer to this question down into three parts.

First is the nature of the material of which the surface is composed. In drives with *oxide* coatings, the surface consists of small particles of magnetic material suspended in a binder. (This is a special type of paint. Common paint is made of particles of colored stuff suspended in a material that will stick when applied to whatever you wish to paint. This type of paint simply substitutes magnetic stuff for colored stuff.) In *platted media* drives, a deposited film of pure magnetic material comprises the surface. With either surface, there is a minimum size region that can be magnetized, called a grain or domain size. The flip-flop distance cannot be any shorter than this size.

Next is a consequence of the orientation of the recorded regions. (See Figure 5-5 [b].) Notice that adjacent regions of opposite magnetization have a "north pole" next to another "north pole" or a "south pole" next to another "south pole." The bits on the disk repel each other in the way magnets push each other away when you hold them together; the closer you place them, the stronger the magnetic field of one region (or bit) will push onto those of adjacent regions. If the regions are too close together, the field of one region can reverse the field of an adjacent region, causing the two regions to become one. So, the minimum flip-flop distance must be large enough to prevent that from happening.

Usually the flip-flop length is made at least as long as the width of the head's core gap. While you can record regions smaller than this, doing so is not advisable — fields generated by more than one region will simultaneously pass through the head's coil, making it difficult separately to detect the magnetic field of each region. Also, when writing to the disk, the coil current will magnetize an entire core gap length of the track in the same direction, possibly wiping out bits adjacent to the one you wanted to write.

Modern disk manufacturing techniques let the disk designer set all these sizes limits to be about the same. Thus the grain or domain size in the surface, the minimum size regions that will not demagnetize one another, and the head gap width are comparable.

> **0110 0110**
> **TECHNICAL NOTE**
> The minimum-size region of the platter coating that is independently magnetizable is one of the two most important physical parameters describing the recording medium. The other is the threshold magnetic field strength required for magnetizing the surface coating (its *coercivity*). As you might expect, much research has been done over many years to learn how to control these numbers in the manufacturing process. The minimum size of an independently magnetizable region has been made ever smaller, so more bits can be packed into a given length of track. The coercivity has been raised, leading to more firmly locked-in magnetic regions on the disk surface.

The ferromagnetic surface coating can be made in several ways. In the earlier disk designs, magnetic iron oxide particles (so-called gamma Fe_2O_3) are dispersed in an epoxy binder and coated on the platter surfaces. The platters are often spun under a strong magnet as the epoxy cures (gets hard) so that the particles, which are usually made in needle-shapes, will be aligned along the tracks. This ensures that the magnetization is always in the plane of the disk surface and either forward or back along the track direction. (See Figure 5-4.)

Later improvements led to coatings that are more nearly pure magnetic material, sometimes sputtered or plated on the platter surface. The material is oriented so the magnetization will be the same as that for the oxide-in-binder surfaces. The advantages of the plated media are primarily that they can be thinner and still have enough magnetic material in them to make the same strength signals. This thinness in turn makes possible smaller regions in which information can be stored.

The oxide in binder surfaces permit the recording of up to about 20,000 bits per inch along the track. The plated media can support perhaps four times as many. Also, the plated media are mostly used with heads that are narrower and thus with tracks that can be closer together, leading to total capacities per platter for plated media around ten times that of the oxide-in-binder surfaces.

These factors limit the minimum possible size of an independently magnetizable region on the disk surface (the magnetic flip-flop length). The form of data encoding used determines how many of these flip-flop lengths are needed to store one bit. That will be discussed in the next section; for now it is enough to know that you need some fixed number of these regions (up to two) per bit.

Theoretical versus Practical Bit Densities: Let us call the length of track used to store one bit a *bit cell* length. Real hard disk bit cells are not always as small as they could be (that is, one minimum magnetic flip-flop length times the number of flip-flop lengths needed to code a bit), for reasons having more to do with economics than with physics.

The tracks near the spindle are shorter than those closer to the outer edge, which means there is more room for bits on the outer tracks. That's physics. Since the spindle turns at a fixed speed, independent of the head assembly position (which, by the way, is not true in some floppy disk drives), the time it takes for an entire track to move under the head is the same for every track. The longer, outer tracks simply move under the head faster. It is easiest to treat each track as if it were the same length as every other track. The read and write electronics then do not have to consider which track the head is dealing with.

TECHNICAL NOTE We have glossed over a subtle point in this discussion. If you put the same number of bits on every track, those on the inner tracks will be closer together. In order to get as much information as possible on the drive, the bits on the innermost tracks will be jammed together as tightly as feasible. Something interesting happens when they are put this close together. The magnetic transitions actually move even closer together on their own. This is called *bit shifting* or *pulse crowding*.

This makes the signals picked up by the read head come at slightly wrong times, possibly confusing the controller about what information has been recorded at this place on the disk. A common way of preventing this problem is to anticipate the bit shifting and correct for it before it happens.

The signals sent to the write head are forced to have their current reversals spaced just a bit farther apart than would otherwise be the case. Then, after the bits spontaneously shift closer together, the read signals will be spaced correctly. This is called *write precompensation*.

Write precompensation only needs to be done for the cylinders that are close to the spindle. The outer cylinders have their bits spread far enough apart that the bit shifting effect does not occur. The best possible precompensation would be some function of cylinder number, but the more economical approach is simply to do a fixed amount for all cylinders closer than a certain distance to the spindle and not do any for the rest.

Older hard disk controllers will do write precompensation for a range of cylinders if asked. More modern ones do it automatically, whether or not they are asked.

If you are willing to build a substantially more complex drive or controller, you can put more bits on the outer tracks, but the process is more expensive. That's where the economics comes in. So, the designers of most PC disk drives built today settle for putting an equal number of bits on each track, no matter the length of the tracks.

5

TECHNICAL NOTE — Since almost all drives store a constant amount of information on each track (possibly a different constant for different drives), the standard drive controllers do not allow for any other possibility. Thus, you can put more data on outside tracks than on the inner ones only if you forego the use of a standard controller.

As we explain in the section "Popular Products and Standards," SCSI drives contain their own controllers. Some manufacturers, therefore, build SCSI drives that take advantage of this geometrical fact by putting more data on outer tracks. They divide the tracks into *zones*. For example, the tracks in the outer third of the platter will be zone #1; the middle third, zone #2; and the innermost third, zone #3. The amount of data per track within each zone is a constant, but that constant changes from zone to zone. This technique is called *zone bit recording*. Some IDE drives and some of the proprietary format MFM and RLL drive/controller combinations use this technique as well.

So, though we can say the size of a bit on the disk surface depends on the drive, it is likely to fall into the following range: The length along the track is at least .000025 inch (0.6 microns) and at most .0001 inch (2.5 microns). The width of the track is anywhere from about 0.0005 inch (12 microns) up to 0.003 inch (75 microns).

Data Encoding Strategies

The purpose behind a hard disk's complex structure is to store information, specifically a bunch of binary numbers. A binary number is simply a collection of ones and zeros. To read and write the data, these ones and zeros, or *bits*, must somehow be *encoded* as magnetic signals on the disk's surface. You may imagine that we could store the individual bits one right after another along the track, assigning each bit one of two magnetic field directions, depending on whether the bit is a one or a zero. If we could do this, we could get away with just one magnetic flip-flop length per bit.

Figures 5-5(a) and (b) show what this encoding strategy might look like for a particular data pattern. Figure 5-5(c) is a graph of the magnetic field strength versus distance along the track for that same data pattern. When you consider the third "important physical fact" listed at the beginning of the last section, you'll see why this strategy won't work. In order for a voltage to appear across the coil, the magnetic field in the coil must change, which won't happen using this encoding scheme if all the bits you record happen to be identical (i.e., all zeros or all ones). Consequently, there won't be any signal for the head to read.

In addition, if the disk turns at an even slightly different speed when it is reading than it did when writing, the head will traverse the bits at a different rate. If you could "see" each bit as it went by, you could take this different rate into account, but if you are sailing over identical magnetic fields and thus getting no signals at all, you have no way of knowing just how many of those identical bits you have passed over. A more complicated method of recording data is needed.

Think of data encoding as a game in which the goal is to find a way to "hide" the bits of information in the flips and flops of the magnetic field in such a way that one can reliably "find" them again when it is time to read the data back. An obvious solution is to make each bit stand out in some way. Perhaps the simplest way of doing this would be to put a region of no magnetization between each of the bits of data. Unfortunately, that is not easy to do. The grains, or tiny needles, that compose the disk surface are going to be strongly magnetized one way or the other. All you can easily influence is which way each needle is magnetized.

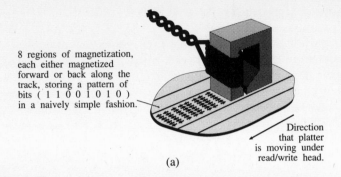

8 regions of magnetization, each either magnetized forward or back along the track, storing a pattern of bits (1 1 0 0 1 0 1 0) in a naively simple fashion.

Direction that platter is moving under read/write head.

(a)

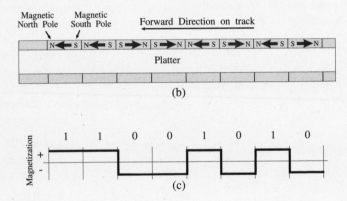

Magnetic North Pole   Magnetic South Pole   Forward Direction on track

Platter

(b)

(c)

Figure 5-5 *Regions of different magnetization store information on disk platter surface.*
(a) Perspective view.
(b) Side view (not to scale).
(c) Graph of magnetization in surface: plus is forward along track, minus is backwards. (Note: This is too simple a data encoding scheme to use for real data storage.)

A simple-minded pulse approach

Here is a simple way that will work: Make each binary one into a bi-directional pulse; and make each binary zero a similarly long absence of pulse. Finally, intersperse between each of the data bits a dummy pulse, or *clock* signal, that is just like the binary one pulses.

(By the way, if you look in other books on this subject and compare their discussion with this one, you may get quite confused. Pulses are signals that go up and down. Many authors, though, speak of recording "pulses" when they really mean the recording of a transition in the magnetic field, either from minus to plus *or* from plus to minus [and *not* back again]. These recorded transitions will result in corresponding pulses of voltage [plus or minus] across the read head later on when the information is read back. Sometimes these authors also use 1s and 0s to stand for both transitions and lacks of transitions and for data bits, without clearly distinguishing between them.)

Figure 5-6(a) shows a graph of magnetic field strength versus position along the track for the same data pattern shown in Figure 5-5, with these extra pulses thrown in. The pulses for the one bits will show up clearly as they pass under the head, while those for the zero bits, since they still have no changing magnetic field, will not. But the clock pulses always show up and will enable the head to detect even long strings of zero bits. This method makes it easy to write and read data, but it is inefficient.

Up to this point we have been looking at data encoding in terms of the distances along the track from one region of magnetization to the next. Another way to look at the same information is in terms of the times between the passage of those regions under the read/write head or, if we simply divide those times into one second, in terms of their frequencies.

Frequency modulation

The graph in Figure 5-6(a) can be viewed as a square wave whose frequency varies. We have one cycle per bit cell when we are recording a zero and two cycles per bit cell when we are recording a one. This is similar to the method used to put information on radio waves at an FM radio broadcasting station, although radio requires a whole range of frequencies to encode the subtleties of music and speech, while we need only two frequencies to encode ones and zeros. This method of representing data is called *frequency modulation* encoding, or FM. Though this approach works, disk system designers soon realized they could create a more efficient strategy.

NRZ coding of FM

The scheme outlined in Figure 5-6(a) gives us exactly two changes for each item we wish to see: a transition as the field goes from backward (negative) to forward (positive) and as it returns. When the head passes over the first transition, a positive voltage pulse appears across the coil, and when it passes over the reverse transition, a negative voltage pulse appears. If we use this data encoding scheme, we will only use the positive voltage pulses, ignoring the negative ones.

We pay a severe penalty for this overkill. Remember that we cannot reverse the field along the track any more often than what we have called the minimum magnetic flip-flop length. In Figure 5-6, a short, double-headed arrow under each graph represents the minimum distance between magnetic field transitions for that encoding scheme. At best we can shrink our bytes of data down until that double-headed arrow distance equals a minimum magnetic flip-flop length. In Figure 5-6(a) you see that this minimum distance is one-quarter of the bit cell size; so, for the bi-directional pulse version of FM encoding, we need four minimum flip-flop lengths just to store one bit of data and its associated clock pulse.

A simple way to halve the track length needed to store a given amount of data is to ignore the direction of each transition when we read the data (the direction shows up as the sign of the voltage pulse on the coil as we pass over that transition); count every transition as significant. We also must change how we write the data.

Figure 5-6(b) shows that change. Compare this with the previous pattern. Every time the signal in (a) goes from minus to plus we see a change in (b), either up or down; when in (a) the signal goes from plus back to minus, we see no change in (b). We see exactly half as many transitions and thus just half as many voltage pulses on playback, yet all the information is there. This is called a *Non Return to Zero* (NRZ) approach to data encoding. We can convert any pattern of pulses by this approach into an identical series of half pulses without any loss of information.

Since we have half as many transitions (and those we have are spaced exactly twice as far apart), we can store this pattern in half as much track length. The increased efficiency is well worth the slight extra bother required to store and retrieve data this way. Since nobody uses the simple-minded version of FM anymore, future references to FM here (and in most works in this subject) really mean NRZ-FM.

MFM

Early makers of magnetic tape and disk drives used FM, but soon clever engineers and mathematicians figured out a way to double the system's efficiency. This simple variation on the FM data encoding, called initially *double density* encoding and now mostly known as modified frequency modulation (MFM), has essentially replaced FM in the world of PC hard drives.

The notion behind MFM is that we need clock transitions only when we don't have nearby data transitions. On the other hand, we must be able to tell reliably which transitions are data and which are clock information.

Figure 5-6(c) shows the MFM pattern of magnetization used to encode the same data as Fig. 5-6(b). Changes from a high to a low level or vice versa indicate field transitions. Figure 5-6(d) shows the voltage pulses that will be seen when the read head moves over this pattern of magnetization.

 Notice that in Figure 5-6 each graph is divided into eight cells, one for each bit of data to be recorded. In that figure, each bit cell is shown at the same size. In Figure 5-6(b), the FM case, there is a transition (clock) at the start of every bit cell, with another one in the middle of every cell storing a binary one.

The rule for MFM encoding is simple. Start with FM and then omit each clock pulse associated with a bit cell, unless that cell and the previous cell hold zeros. All bit cells holding ones and the cells immediately following them are close enough to a transition that we don't need to add any transitions just for clock purposes.

The rule for separating clock and data signals when reading is also simple. You just have to be able to tell if the signal came at the start of a bit cell, indicating a clock pulse (between two zero bits), or in the middle of one, indicating one bit.

The minimum and maximum spacing of the transitions in this method of data encoding are exactly twice that in FM. Since the minimum spacing is doubled, we can put MFM-encoded data into half as much track length — hence the term double density. The doubled maximum spacing means we must have somewhat more stable electronic circuitry and disk motors, requirements that it turns out are not particularly hard to meet.

RLL encoding

Though very popular and effective, MFM is not the most efficient way to encode data. We have reduced the bit cell size down to the minimum magnetic flip-flop length, but we can do even better if we cut back the number of clock signals even more. How far we can go depends on how steadily the disk turns and how sensitively we can time the spacing of the voltage pulses coming out of the head coil.

Disk system designers have tried many different schemes to lower the average number of clock signals per data bit and thus increase the maximum density of bits on the disk surface. The most popular plan, at least for hard disks used in PCs, is called "2,7 RLL" (run length limited). This process uses no clock signals at all! We make up for this by recording on the disk different patterns than the ones in the data we are supposed to store. If we choose just right, we will be able to reverse that process when it is time to read the data back.

The idea behind RLL is that there are two constraints to any pattern of magnetic field transitions we can usefully record on the disk surface: First, the magnetic field transitions must not come any more often than the minimum magnetic flip-flop length (which avoids the risk of erasing the previous field when recording a new field). Second, spaces without transitions must not be so long that we lose track of our position on the disk. Thus there is a maximum and a minimum frequency that we can tolerate for the magnetic field transitions.

> **TECHNICAL NOTE** As in both FM and MFM, in 2,7 RLL we will make transitions only at the beginning or center of any bit cell. Rather than simply translating the incoming data bits into transitions, though, we will take small groups of data bits and store them as specially chosen sequences of transitions and lack of transitions. Let us say that the letter T will stand for a transition and the letter O will stand for an open space. Both a T and an O will take up exactly one-half bit cell of distance along the track.

In 2,7 RLL, we will arrange the sequences of Ts and Os such that no matter what the incoming data stream, we will always have at least two and never more than seven Os between any two Ts. By thinking about these rules, you can see that the minimum spacing of transitions is three half-bit cells, and the maximum spacing is eight half-bit cells.

Figure 5-7 shows a flow chart for generating the sequence of Ts and Os from the incoming stream of data ones and zeros. Look at the sequences at the right side of that figure. Notice that some start with a T and some have some Os before a T. Some have more than one T inside them, but always they have at least two Os between them. Finally, every sequence has at least two Os at the end. Thus no matter which of the sequences is put after the other, we will always have at least two Os between successive Ts.

Similarly, you can see that as no sequence has more than three Os at the end nor more than four Os at the beginning; no matter which sequences are put next to each other, we will never have more than seven Os between successive Ts.

Every sequence of Ts and Os has exactly twice as many symbols as the sequence of ones and zeros it is encoding. Because of the minimum of three symbols from T to T, we can fit three symbols into one minimum magnetic flip-flop length. Since two symbols equal one bit, that means we have reduced the bit cell size to two-thirds of a flip-flop length. This lets us put half again (150%) as many bits into a length of track as was possible with MFM, and three times the number possible with FM.

To summarize, with 2,7 RLL we substitute special patterns of transitions for the actual data patterns we want to record. We choose these patterns so that the maximum to minimum spacing of field transitions will be 8 to 3. Doing this allows us to store 50% more data in the same space. Since most hard disks turn at the same rate, that also means we need only two-thirds as much time to write or read any given information. (Figure 5-6[e] shows how 2,7 RLL encoding of our same data byte looks compared to the other encoding methods.) Though we could possibly improve upon RLL, the process would not be easy nor, at this point, reliable enough for most users. As it is, RLL pushes the limits of practicality.

Since RLL encoding puts down magnetic field transitions no closer than MFM does, people thought at first that they could use any

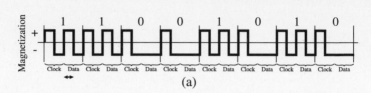

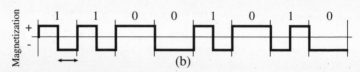

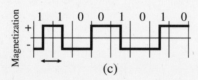

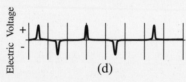

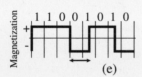

5

Figure 5-6 Data Encoding Strategies
(a) Bi-directional frequency modulation.
(b) NRZ frequency modulation (FM).
(c) Modified frequency modulation (MFM).
(d) Idealized voltage signal across read head when pattern (c)
passes under it.
(e) 2,7 RLL (Run Length Limited).
Note: The pattern in (a) is shown at half the scale of the rest of the figure.

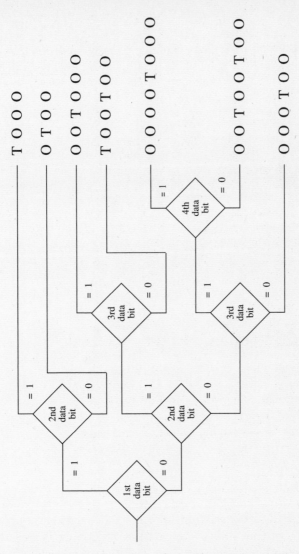

Figure 5-7 Flow chart showing how to convert a data bit stream into magnetic transitions (Ts) and spaces between them (Os) using 2,7 RLL encoding.

MFM drive as an RLL drive by just hooking up to an RLL controller. Unfortunately, when it was first introduced commercially several years ago, RLL data encoding asked more of the disk drives and controller electronics than they could be depended upon to do reliably. The drives and controllers failed over time, often quite soon and quite dramatically.

Manufacturers of RLL controllers have since learned better methods, and the makers of disk drives have devised ways to test their drives for this more demanding application. As a result, there are now many drives available that are "certified for RLL use," though others still are not. Combining an RLL certified drive with an RLL controller makes for a fairly reliable combination.

(Before testing for RLL compatibility was introduced by the drive makers, you might have had as much as a 50% chance of getting an MFM drive to work with an RLL controller at least tolerably well. Almost all the drives that can do this are now marked "RLL-capable"; any that are marked "MFM" are thus very likely not RLL-capable.)

ARLL and other encoding methods

Some people like to live dangerously. Some manufacturers have introduced versions of RLL that go well beyond 2,7 RLL, to what is sometimes called Advanced Run Length Limited (ARLL). The essence of these schemes is that they allow an even larger ratio of maximum to minimum spacing of the magnetic field transitions, letting you pack data on the tracks even more closely — almost twice as densely as MFM.

Drives attached to ESDI and SCSI controllers are sometimes referred to as using ERLL data encoding. Actually they commonly use 2,7 RLL data encoding, but since they record at a higher bit rate they also put more bytes of data on a track than is the case with the standard RLL controllers and drives.

When a drive and controller do use a special form of data encoding it is important that they be closely tuned to each other. This is something that cannot be done unless one manufacturer creates both parts of the combination. Since ESDI, SCSI, hard cards, and IDE drives all include their controllers, this can be done in those cases. Any time a controller is sold separately from the drive, and yet claims to offer much higher data density than RLL, it is most likely an invitation to a data disaster.

A Problem of Imperfection and Some Solutions

You now understand how data can be stored on a hard disk. Since disks cannot work perfectly every time, some additional cleverness has been develped to cope with the inevitable errors. This section describes what is done to make our disks act as if they were perfect, or at the very least, to inform us when they are unable to do so, to keep us from using bad data as if it were good.

A partial solution: error detection

Your computer stores more than just the information it wishes to get back. It also stores extra bits to help it know whether the retrieved information can be trusted.

The simplest form of error detection, used in system RAM, is the use of parity bits. A slightly more complex and more powerful technique, used on disk drives, is the Cyclical Redundancy Checksum.

Parity: In almost every PC's system RAM, every data byte (8 bits) is accompanied by a ninth bit called the parity bit. When writing each byte of information to RAM, the PC computes its parity by counting the number of ones in the byte. If that number is even, the corresponding parity bit is set to a one; otherwise it is set to a zero. Looking at all nine bits you will always find an odd number of bits set to a one, unless an error has occurred. This is called *odd parity.* If any one bit should be read or stored in error, the parity will come out wrong and the PC will know about the error. However, it will not know which bit is in error.

> **TECHNICAL NOTE** If an even number of bits flip, the parity will check out okay, even though the information has been damaged. Fortunately, in RAM memory the most common errors by far are single bit errors, and even these occur rarely. Since the PC cannot fix bit errors, it simply alerts you to the problem and then halts the computer. This is the source of the infamous "PARITY CHECK ONE" and "PARITY CHECK TWO" messages.

Cyclical Redundancy Checksum (CRC): When MS-DOS writes information to a floppy disk, it executes a similar protection scheme. First, it groups the information into *sectors* of exactly 512 bytes of data. It then adds two more bytes to the end of that information. MS-DOS computes this 16-bit binary number by adding up all the other sectors of 512 bytes in a special fashion called a *cyclical redundancy checksum* (CRC).

Like parity, a CRC provides a means to test for corrupted data. CRC can spot any single- and some multi-bit corruptions, but again it cannot detect just which bits got flipped. The message "Error reading drive A" most likely means that the machine read a sector with an invalid CRC value.

A better solution: error correction

5

Hard disks store a great deal more data more rapidly than floppy disks, making errors a lot more likely. Without some means of catching *and correcting* errors, users would experience an intolerable failure rate reading their hard disk, encountering errors as often as several times per day.

Fortunately, some clever engineers and mathematicians have devised *error correcting codes* (ECC). All modern hard disk controllers include special logic to generate and use these ECC numbers. Most of the time we don't even know disk errors occur; they are simply fixed automatically by the controller using ECC.

The Orchard Model for ECC: To understand the magic of ECC takes a bit of patience. Before we discuss how ECC works in a hard disk controller, let us look at a simpler model that is easier to understand. Suppose we have an 16 bits of information that we wish to protect. Arrange those ones and zeros into an "orchard of data," with four rows and four columns. For each row and each column, if there are an even number of ones, add another one bit; add a zero bit if the row or column contains an odd number of ones; and add one more bit where the additional row and column meet (see Figure 5-8), choosing a one or a zero to make an odd number of ones in the bottom row.

This gives each row and column odd parity. If any single bit flips anywhere, we can detect it because the row and column it is in will no longer have odd parity. This now also allows us to correct any single one-bit error with total certainty. Notice that we have protected 16 bits with an overhead of only 9 bits, which takes up less disk space than would keeping a duplicate copy of all the data.

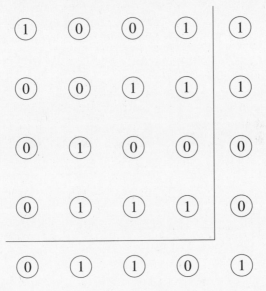

Figure 5-8 The "orchard model" demonstrates the principles behind Error Correction Codes (ECC).

Though not yet a practical ECC, this shows the principle behind any useful ECC. If we wrote a formula for each of the added bits, those formulas would simply be sums of groups of bits, with each group chosen differently. (In calculating these sums, we throw away any carry bits. This is what mathematicians call *modular arithmetic*.) A real ECC is much like this, only it uses more groups of bits, and they are chosen in very arcane ways.

Real ECC: Manufacturers incorporate ECC circuitry in their hard disk controllers, each in slightly different ways. They say their methods are proprietary, so you can't discover what they are in detail or even whether they really are different from one another.

> 0110 0110
> **TECHNICAL NOTE** This is probably one of the reasons why a second controller won't be able to read data on a hard disk formatted with another controller. Because they were written in a different way, the sectors on the drive look strange to the second controller, so it considers the hard disk unformatted.

Typically, any controller's ECC can detect and correct any pattern of errors in an entire sector containing 512 bytes (and, thus, 8 times 512, or 4096 bits) of data, as long as all the errors are contained within 11 consecutive bits in that sector. IBM's standard for MFM drives does this by storing only 32 bits (just 4 bytes) of ECC.

Since RLL stores in the same space 50% more data than an MFM drive, a defect that would damage 11 adjacent bits on an MFM drive would damage about half again that many on an RLL drive. RLL controllers, therefore, often use more bits of ECC. Many RLL controller makers choose to use 56 bits (7 bytes) to protect against any error contained within 17 consecutive bits of data. (This still is only a very tiny fraction of the bytes of data it is protecting.)

Though it's possible that error patterns might span more than 11 consecutive bits (or 17 bits on an RLL drive), such patterns are rare. Most errors on hard disks occur because of some spot defect that makes it impossible to store information reliably over a very small portion of a sector, usually much less than 11 bits long.

The bad news is that if you do have two or more regions of error within one sector, the ECC may *seem* to be adequate for fixing the damage, but the "fix" will be incorrect. Future disk designs may incorporate a much-improved ECC that could detect and correct even this sort of error, but for now we must simply hope such mistakes will rarely crop up on our machines.

What DOS Does When ECC Comes into Play: When the disk controller tries to read a sector of data from a hard disk, three things can happen: The computed ECC matches the ECC on the disk; the controller finds the data to be inconsistent with their ECC, but the ECC suffice to show what the data should have been (known as a *correctable read error*); or the error in the data is so large that the ECC cannot suffice to detect the corrupt bits (called an *uncorrectable read error*).

When errors occur reading data, the disk controller may either use the ECC to correct the data it got and go on to the next sector, or it may attempt to read the questionable sector again and again, perhaps many times, to see if it can get a perfect read. Whether the controller will attempt to reread the data may depend not only on which controller you have, but also on the BIOS on your PC's motherboard, and perhaps on the version of DOS and what application program you are running.

The disk controller then hands the data to the computer with one of three messages. Put colloquially these messages are as follows:

(1) "Here is your data. I read it perfectly."

(2) "Here is your data. I could not read it, but I figured out what it should have been."

(3) "Here is what I got reading your data, but I am pretty sure this is *not* what it is supposed to be."

MS-DOS was designed to take care of disk business without bothering the computer user any more than necessary. For example, we do not have to tell it where on the disk to store information; we let it figure that out for us. When we want our information back again, we just tell DOS the file name and let it figure out where to find it.

This design philosophy makes computers much easier to use in general. But one aspect of this is less wonderful. When DOS gets those three messages from the disk controller, however, it simplifies them into two cases. It lumps together the first two messages, without telling us whether it had to use ECC to fix corrupted data; only if it could not reconstruct the corrupted data with ECC does it report that our data are no longer available.

This is unfortunate, for often disk errors are progressive. What today is a correctable read error may likely develop into an unrecoverable error. If DOS had informed us of the recoverable error when it occurred, we could have moved those data to some safer place on the disk or otherwise dealt with this incipient data loss before it created more trouble.

This is where *SpinRite* shines. These programs can go behind DOS and even the disk controller's own ECC circuitry to decipher what really takes place when data are written to and read from your hard disk. Through such an intimate, down-to-the-platter look at your disk, they can detect problems before they become disasters and either move the data out of harm's way or actually repair the damage.

(A curious side note: Several makers of products like *SpinRite* claim they or their competitors "turn off ECC." Actually none do, because one cannot really force hard disk controllers not to use ECC. The best one can do is notice the use of ECC. Gibson says his claim to "turn off" ECC is phrased that way "partly to confuse our competitors.") We discuss in Chapter 3 *SpinRite*'s particular strategy, including many hitherto unpublished details.

Improving Hard Disk Performance by Sector Interleaving and Head Skewing

One way to speed up your hard disk is to buy a much more expensive, higher performance drive. Such a purchase is not always necessary, however, and if the drive isn't installed with careful attention to its sector interleave and possibly also its head skew, you could be wasting your money.

Anatomy of a Disk Sector

In the last section we introduced the notion that MS-DOS stores information on disk drives in sectors, each of which contains 512 bytes of data. The sectors contain those data bytes and some other things, too. As we will discuss further in Chapter 7, a hard disk straight from the factory must be properly prepared before an MS-DOS computer can store data on it. To create the sectors, we must record a suitable pattern of bits for each sector on every track and surface on the disk drive. A sector has two main parts: its indentifier, and the segment where we store data. (See Figure 5-9.)

The identifier, or *sector header*, contains three numbers that together make up the sector's address: the head or surface on which this sector is located; the track (or cylinder) number; and the position of the sector on the track. The header also contains a field in which a mark shows whether the sector can store data reliably or if some defect has been found that makes its use inadvisable. Some hard disk controllers also record pointers in the sector headers, to direct the disk to an alternative sector or track if the original sector is faulty. Finally, the sector header ends with a CRC value, which the controller uses to make sure it has read the sector head correctly.

We can subdivide the second major part of the sector, where the computer stores data, into the data itself and the error correction codes (ECC) that protect those data. During the initial preparation, the computer fills this area with 512 dummy information bytes — place holders for the real data — and ECC values that correspond to those dummy information bytes.

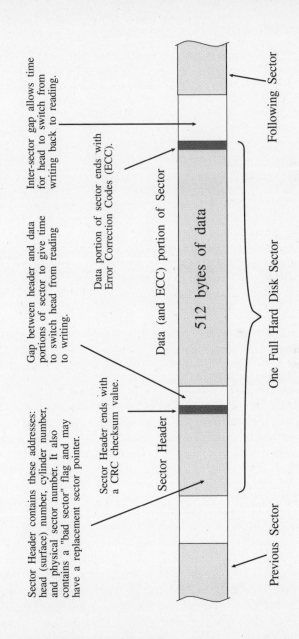

Inter-sector gap allows time for head to switch from writing back to reading.

Gap between header and data portions of sector to give time to switch head from reading to writing.

Data portion of sector ends with Error Correction Codes (ECC).

Sector Header ends with a CRC checksum value.

Sector Header contains these addresses: head (surface) number, cylinder number, and physical sector number. It also contains a "bad sector" flag and may have a replacement sector pointer.

Following Sector

Data (and ECC) portion of Sector

512 bytes of data

One Full Hard Disk Sector

Sector Header

Previous Sector

Figure 5-9 Anatomy of a hard disk sector.

Sector interleave

The sector header contains a sector number that identifies it on the track. We do not have to assign these numbers in any particular order. The design of a sector header allows sector numbers from 1 up to some maximum value, in some cases as high as 256.

The disk controller doesn't care what number in this range we place in any particular sector header. Sectors can share the same number, although that would be most unusual. The disk controller doesn't even care how large the data area is. It just reads whatever it finds or writes whatever it is told to write.

> **0110 0110**
> **TECHNICAL NOTE**
>
> One fairly common use of even the most bizarre of these possibilities is on the floppy disks used to distribute certain "copy protected" programs. They have a few very non-standard sectors on at least one track. The DOS commands COPY and DISKCOPY cannot duplicate such sectors, which is how the copy protection works. Such programs will run only if they see those special, funny sectors on the disk in the A drive.

The disk preparation program, on the other hand, assumes that we will number the sectors in some simple order. We could choose "1, 2, 3, 4, 5 ..." but we don't have to. Let us see why we might wish it to be some different order.

What DOS Does to Store and Retrieve Files: Suppose first that we number the sectors in that simplest order (see track 0 in Figure 5-10). As the disk turns, the sectors present themselves under the head in the order 1, 2, 3, 4, 5.... In this illustration there are 17 sectors per track, which is typical of almost all MFM hard disk drives.

If you ask DOS to store a file on the disk and if all the sectors in that region are available, it will store each set of 512 bytes sequentially in sector number order, switching to the next head in the same cylinder when the first track is full and again filling each sector sequentially. When the cylinder is full, DOS will move to the next cylinder, continuing in this manner till it writes the entire file to the disk. Similarly, it will read the sectors back in the same order. DOS reads a sector by telling the disk controller to read the sector, giving it the cylinder, head, and sector numbers as an address.

Figure 5-10 Examples of Different Sector Interleave Values The outer track (cylinder 0) has its sector interleave set to 1:1, while cylinder 1 has been set to 2:1, and cylinder 2 shows a sector interleave of 3:1. The arrows marked Case A and Case B show two possible places where the head might start reading after it has finished "digesting" the data from reading sector #1. In case A the sector #2 has already partly gone by, but not #3, so an interleave of 2:1 is the best choice. In case B sector #3 has partly gone by, but not #4, so an interleave of 3:1 is optimum.

The disk controller in turn simply steps the head assembly to the appropriate cylinder, turns on the right head, and waits for the right sector to come under the head. The disk controller reads every sector header as it comes along, comparing the address information in those headers with the head and cylinder it is supposed to be looking at (to be sure its head actuator and head switching circuitry work correctly), and looking for the desired sector number. When the controller finds that sector header, it either switches on the write circuitry or it reads the data and trailer, depending on whether it is writing or reading a sector.

Once the disk controller has found the sector, it must "digest" that sector's worth of information before it can go on to the next sector. If it is reading, the controller must compute the ECC for the data as read and then compare that ECC with the recorded ECC; if it is writing data, the controller must compute the ECC to store with those data. The disk turns between reading or writing each sector's worth of data, which takes up an appreciable amount of time.

The simplest (and sometimes the worst) case: Since we are assuming that we have numbered the sectors sequentially around the track, if the disk turns farther than the (small) inter-sector gap, the next sector that the controller wants to read from or write to will already have gone past the head — possibly quite a ways past. (See case A on Figure 5-10.) So, the disk controller will have to wait until the disk has gone almost all the way around again before the desired sector comes into view.

5

How sector interleave solves the problem: An ingenious engineer at IBM many years ago figured out a way around this problem. He did not want to make the inter-sector gaps any larger, for that would waste space on the disk and reduce its storage capacity. Instead, he simply renumbered the sectors in a non-sequential manner. For example, to establish a 2:1 interleave on a track with 17 sectors, the sector numbers go 1, 10, 2, 11, 3, 12, 4, 13, 5, 14, 6, 15, 7, 16, 8, 17, 9 then back to 1 again. (See track 1 in Figure 5-10.) For a 3:1 interleave, the pattern is 1, 7, 13, 2, 8, 14, 3, 9, 15, 4, 10, 16, 5, 11, 17, 6, 12, and back to 1. (See track 2 in Figure 5-10.)

Thus, the *interleave* number is greater by one than the number of sectors you must skip between each sequential sector (for a 2:1 interleave, you skip one sector). It also equals the number of times you would have to go around the track to read all the sectors in order, assuming none of the sectors passed before the controller was ready for it. For example, to read all the sectors on one track with 1:1 interleave will take just one revolution, *if* the disk controller can digest the information fast enough; if not, it will take 17 revolutions.

Increasing the interleave to 2:1 means that you *must* go around the track at least twice to read or write all the sectors sequentially, slowing down their arrival at the head enough so that the disk controller is ready. If a 2:1 interleave is not slow enough, though, the disk will again have to make 17 or even 18 revolutions.

Interleave is a system level problem: In addition to the disk controller, you also need to consider the computer's clock speed in deciding what the ideal interleave value is for a given hard drive. Once most disk controllers have read a sector, they must hand off those data to the computer before they are ready to read the next. Similarly, they will not accept another sector's worth of data to be written until they have finished writing the sectorful they already have. Therefore, the speed at which the computer's *input-output bus* operates can also limit the correct interleave value.

This leads us to conclude that the correct interleave value is decided at the system level — only the person who assembles the disk, controller, and computer can determine this value.

Because of the subtlety of this issue and the effort required to resolve it properly (especially before the introduction of programs like *SpinRite*), until recently, nearly all PCs' hard disks were interleaved incorrectly. Though less common now, it still happens all too often.

If your disk's interleave value is too high, you have to wait only a short while to get your data on or off your disk. If your disk's interleave value is too low, you pay an enormous penalty in reduced disk performance.

Table 5-1 shows just how much an incorrect interleave value will cost you for several common cases. The only way to be sure your interleave is set correctly is to run a program that will evaluate the disk performance in your system for each of several different interleave values. This is a standard feature of *SpinRite* and most other reinterleaving programs.

 Before these programs existed, some other programs, such as HOPTIMUM, could determine your interleave level, but they did so by destructively reformatting one or more tracks, wiping out data if you weren't very careful and knowledgeable. They were not suitable programs for the fainthearted or the uninitiated PC user. *SpinRite* is, in contrast, a perfectly safe program for anyone to use.

Head skewing

Sector interleaving is a subtle concept that many people have difficulty grasping. This next topic, *head skewing*, is similarly

Table 5-1:

The performance penalty from having an incorrect sector interleave setting.

Peak data transfer rate (kilobytes per second)

Minimum interleave your system can handle without missing any sequentially numbered sectors	1:1	2:1	3:1	4:1	5:1
MFM (17 sectors per track)					
If Interleave is set to 1:1	510	30	30	30	30
If Interleave is set to 2:1	255	255	30	30	30
If Interleave is set to 3:1	170	170	170	30	30
If Interleave is set to 4:1	128	128	128	128	30
If Interleave is set to 5:1	102	102	102	102	102
RLL (26 sectors per track)					
If Interleave is set to 1:1	780	30	30	30	30
If Interleave is set to 2:1	390	390	30	30	30
If Interleave is set to 3:1	260	260	260	30	30
If Interleave is set to 4:1	195	195	195	195	30
If Interleave is set to 5:1	156	156	156	156	156
ESDI (54 sectors per track)					
If Interleave is set to 1:1	1620	30	30	30	30
If Interleave is set to 2:1	810	810	30	30	30
If Interleave is set to 3:1	540	540	540	30	30
If Interleave is set to 4:1	405	405	405	405	30
If Interleave is set to 5:1	324	324	324	324	324

NOTE:

The above figures were derived using the following data:

Data on different encoding schemes

	MFM	RLL	ESDI
Revolutions per second	60	60	60
Kilobytes per sector	0.5	0.5	0.5
Sectors per track	17	26	54
Maximum possible data transfer rate	510	780	1620
Data transfer rate for one sector per revolution	30	30	30

(Some RLL drives have as few as 23 or as many as 27 sectors per track. ESDI drives range from 34 up to 56 sectors per track.)

subtle, but your knowledge of sector interleaving should help you comprehend it.

Remember the steps that DOS goes through to write a file to the disk? First it fills one track, then goes to the next head in the same cylinder, and then when the cylinder is full goes on to the next track. Each transition from one track to another and from one cylinder to another takes time, during which the disk inexorably keeps on turning. Considering this, you can see that you can incur a similar penalty in disk performance every time you read or write a file that goes across a track or cylinder boundary. This is where head skewing comes in.

The idea is simple enough. Suppose you have just finished writing to the last sector on one track. Since you have presumably already set the interleave to its optimum value, you are now ready to write to the first sector of the next track. But you must wait till you get the head switched, or the head assembly repositioned, over the correct, next track. If that takes more than just a very little time, you will arrive there just too late, despite the interleaving. The solution is to move all the sector numbers for the tracks on the new track or cylinder around by one (or more) positions, relative to where they were on the previous track.

Figure 5-11 shows this for a case in which a single sector displacement is appropriate when going from one head to another, but a displacement of three sector times is called for when going from one track to an adjacent one. Figure 5-11 assumes there are two platters, and thus four heads. Proceeding from the first surface, each succeeding surface moves one sector further than the previous one; so the tracks start at 1 on Head 0 and at 15 on Head 3. The sectors on the next cylinder are shifted by six sectors — three sectors accumulated from the surface to surface shifts, plus three sectors to compensate for the time delay needed to shift the heads over one cylinder.

Most disk controllers do not permit the head skew to be set, though high-performance ones do. Head skew is not yet a commonly understood idea in the marketplace, though it will probably become more prevalent as we move to ever-faster disk drives.

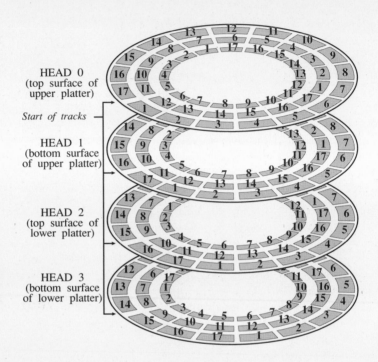

HEAD 0
(top surface of
upper platter)

Start of tracks —

HEAD 1
(bottom surface
of upper platter)

HEAD 2
(top surface of
lower platter)

HEAD 3
(bottom surface
of lower platter)

Figure 5-11 Head Skewing. This figure shows a 1:1 sector interleave, with a head-to-head skew of +1, and a cylinder skew of +3.

Where sector interleave and head skew information is stored

The sector numbers are stored in the sector headers. Thus the interleave and skew values are set by whatever writes those sector headers. Initially that was the disk preparation program (the low-level formatter), which simply invokes a special function of the disk controller to do the work. Since this process destroys all the data on the tracks that are low-level-formatted, it used to be done as infrequently as possible. If you wanted to reinterleave your disk in the old days, you had to first back up all the data, redo the low-level format, recreate the partition table, redo the high level format, and then restore all your data. This would very likely take you at least a full working day. (We discuss the above terms and process in detail in Chapter 7.)

How can I alter interleave and skew?

The advent of *SpinRite* and the other non-destructive reinterleaving programs made it possible to alter your sector interleave value at any time, to test out different values.

> ▐ ▌ While it is always a good idea to do a full backup of your
> system before the first time you use any utility program that
> messes with your hard disk at such a deep level, it is most
> unlikely that you will need that backup. After you have proven the
> compatibility of your system and your reinterleaving program once,
> you may reuse it any time you wish without doing a full backup first.

The head skew is harder to reset. Fortunately, since it comes into play only when you are reading or writing a file that extends across the end of a track, you pay a much lower time penalty than you would with an incorrectly set sector interleave. If you are technically sophisticated and daring, you can experiment with different skew settings by use of the HTHF program, available from Kolad Research, 1898 Techny Court, Northbrook, IL 60062-5474; (708) 291-1586.

When and how to set the interleave wrong

If you are going to set your interleave to anything other than the optimum value, you certainly should set it too high. Remember that when 3:1 is optimum, setting it to 4:1 means you will have to wait only 4 revolutions to read a full track of data, whereas setting it to 2:1 will mean you will have to wait 17 or maybe even 18 revolutions.

But why might you wish to set the interleave to a non-optimum value? Remember another fact: The optimum value depends on several factors, including how fast your computer bus operates. If the bus operates at different speeds at different times (e.g., a Turbo XT which might run at 4.77 MHz or 10 MHz), the optimum interleave value most likely won't be the same for both. Thus, you should set it to the optimum value for the lowest bus speed, unless you know you will not be using your computer at that speed much.

Does every track have to have the same interleave value?

Since the sector interleave is set by numbers written into the sector headers, each track can and does have its own sector interleave. On most drives, all tracks have the same interleave value, but this need not be so.

If you interrupt the operation of a reinterleaving program, then some of the tracks will have been changed and others will not. This will not adversely affect your computer's operation. But the tracks that are optimally interleaved will work faster than the others.

One special case where the interleave will not be the same on all tracks

5

The detailed discussion of *SpinRite*'s operation in Chapter 3 included mention of some curious facts. While it normally redoes the low-level format and resets the sector interleave value for almost every track in a DOS partition, *SpinRite* is very careful not to do this in the very first track. It also may skip the track whose location is cylinder 100, head 0. Finally, it uses a track in the diagnostic cylinder to experiment with different sector interleave values. When it is finished, it restores the sector interleave for that track to its original value. Thus there will be at least one and maybe several tracks on your disk for which *SpinRite* does not permanently alter the sector interleave.

This becomes more than a bit of trivia when you learn that several of the popular disk performance testing program, such as the CORETEST program from Core International and SYSINFO from.Peter Norton Computing, use the very same tracks for much of their testing. If you run them on a disk that has had its interleave changed by *SpinRite* to the optimum value, these programs will not correctly report the improvement in disk speed.

Popular Products and "Standards"

When IBM introduced the PC in 1981, it did not offer a hard disk as a standard option, though not because there weren't any available for personal computers; some already had been used with a few Apple II and S-100 bus systems. They were simply considered too expensive for an individual's home computer.

By 1983, IBM realized that they could successfully sell PCs to small businesses, and that people wanted and would pay for the added storage capacity and convenience of hard disks. So the IBM-PC/XT, introduced that year, came standard with a 10-megabyte hard drive.

 The fact that IBM specified the XT as having a "5-year design life (8,000 hours Mean Time to Failure)" reveals that they thought these machines would not be used even as much as 40 hours per week, let alone around the clock as so many PCs now are.

IBM implemented the hard drive through an "option card" that you could plug into one of the bus slots on the PC/XT motherboard. This card, christened the "Fixed Disk Adapter," in turn was connected to the drive by two ribbon cables.

The XT also contained a four-wire cable from the power supply to the drive, similar to that powering a floppy disk drive. All later versions of disk drives for PCs receive their operating power in a similar fashion, though many modern designs have only two wires in their power cable.

You could put that same hard disk controller and hard disk into a PC, but first you would have to be sure your power supply was able to provide enough power to operate the disk; the original PC power supply was not.

Also, you would have to be sure you did not have one of the very earliest ROM BIOS chips in your PC. It is likely your ROM BIOS is too early if your PC can accept only up to 64K (kilobytes) of RAM on the motherboard. If yours is one of the older ROM BIOS chips, you can upgrade to one dated October 1982. This and all later versions of the ROM BIOS for the PC support what is called the *option ROM scan*, without which the hard disk controller (and several other plug-in cards) will not work. All PC clones are actually XT clones and already have a sufficiently up-to-date ROM BIOS.

As with many of the parts in the PC, IBM bought off-the-shelf technology for its hard drives. It made its own controllers, which were very similar to some existing controllers, and had the drives made to its specifications by experienced drive manufacturers.

Because the IBM-PC, XT, AT and PS/2 models have sold so well, their basic design has become a standard. They define what is meant by a personal computer today. (Well, yes, there are other important designs, but the lion's share of the personal computer market is for "IBM compatibles.")

Thus the way IBM chose to implement their first hard disk controllers and disk drives defined by example an important standard for these products. IBM never gave a name to that design standard. Since the design for the first IBM-PC/XT hard drives bears a very close resemblance to a couple of earlier designs by the Seagate Technology Company, blending features of both of them, it is now known by the numbers of those models as the ST412/ST506 interface.

ST412/ST506

This designation describes a particular variety of hard disk interface. That is, it says in detail how the disk drive and its controller "talk" to one another. How the controller talks to the computer is described in the definition of the PC input-output (I/O) bus that connects to all the motherboard slots, since the hard disk controller plugs into that bus.

The specification of this (or any) interface has several aspects. The first concerns the physical description of the cables through which the controller and drive conduct their conversation, and the connectors at the ends of those cables. Another is the electrical aspect, giving the voltage levels and signal timings on each wire. Yet another is the logical aspect in which the function of the signal on each wire is described. When you mention a standard, like ST412/ST506, you are implying all these aspects.

> **TECHNICAL NOTE** The disk controller is connected to the drive by two ribbon cables. One has 34 wires in it (with a 34-pin connector, so the wires are sometimes referred to as "pins") and is used to command the head actuator to move one track in or out, set the level of write current for the heads, and for the drive to report back to the controller on its success or failure in carrying out a controller command and on its readiness for further work. Digital in nature, these signals change slowly for the most part. If you have two hard drives attached to the same controller, this cable will be routed from the controller to first one and then the other drive.
>
> The second cable contains 20 wires, most of which are connected to "ground" and serve as shields for the other wires. All the data the controller writes to the drive travel on just one of these 20 wires,

with the complementary signal traveling on another specific wire. Yet another pair of wires carries the read signal and its complement from the heads to the controller. These are high-frequency signals, up to 5 million bits per second. These signals are much more susceptible to noise contamination than those on the 34-wire cable. To keep these signals clean, if you have two drives attached to one controller, each drive gets its own 20-wire cable, which you should keep as short as possible.

Significantly, only one bit of data can travel in the data cable at a time, even though it has 20 wires in it. Thus when one says that the data bits travel at 5 million per second, that means that since one byte requires eight such bits, the bytes of information can only go in or come out at most one-eighth that fast (625 kilobytes per second). This is in contrast to, for example, SCSI drives, in which the data cable carries the information at least 8 bits, and up to 32 bits, at a time. There the byte data-transfer rate can be as much as four times the maximum bit-frequency on the cable (on a 32-bit-wide date path).

The name ST412/ST506 does not imply any particular data encoding strategy, though manufacturers at first used it to describe an MFM drive with 17 sectors per track. Since encoding data using 2,7 RLL leads to the same maximum frequency of magnetic field transitions (but with a lower minimum frequency), the signals on the wires in the cable between an RLL controller and its drive look very much like those for an MFM controller/drive combination. Thus, an RLL drive can also be said to have an ST412/ST506 interface.

> **TECHNICAL NOTE**
>
> Because RLL packs more data into less distance along the track, an RLL drive has 25 or 26 sectors per track instead of the 17 typical of an MFM drive. Also, since in an RLL drive there are more bits encoded into a given number of field transition times, even with no higher frequency signals than on an MFM drive, the RLL drive can convey 50% more bits per second across the cable (up to 937 kilobytes per second).

The "more daring" ARLL controllers are sometimes also described as using this interface. But since they use signals to and from the head that exceed the standard's frequency specification, their interface ought to be given some other name.

The ST412/ST506 interface design was simple to build in 1983 using available hardware. It also adequately met the needs of PC owners when the largest hard drives available were 10 MB (megabyte) models, and the maximum PC bus speed was 4.77 MHz (megahertz). It did not take long for that happy situation to change, however. Prices of hard drives began to plummet, available disk sizes grew, and new PCs ran at ever-higher clock speeds. The interface limits soon became at the very least annoying. Hard disk manufacturers proposed two different solutions to this problem.

ESDI

One hard disk maker, Maxtor, began to push for an *Enhanced Small Device Interface* (ESDI) standard in the early 1980s that evolved from the ST412/ST506 interface. Only a few, subtle, yet very important changes were made. This solution still works with a disk controller card plugged into the PC bus and connected to the drive with the same two ribbon cables, one with 34 wires (going to both drives if you have two) and one with 20 wires (or two 20-wire cables if you have two drives).

 Most important, circuitry called the *clock-data separator* is put on the drive itself instead of on the controller. This has at least a couple of very important advantages.

The companies that make drives generally do not also make controllers. This meant that with the ST412/ST506 interface, MFM or RLL controllers had to incorporate clock-data separators that had a somewhat "vanilla" design — they were able to work with anybody's ST412/ST506 hard drive. Now, with an ESDI interface, the drive makers can incorporate a data separator that has been very finely tuned to their own disk's design.

The other important advantage is that since the data is recovered from the head signals before entering the cable, their bit rate can be raised without undue degradation. The maximum frequency of bit information transfer for the ESDI design is to 24 MHz. Drives now on the market go up to at least 15 MHz. Proposed extensions to the ESDI standard would raise the maximum frequency to around 50 MHz.

Don't forget, though, that this is still a standard that sends data along the cable one bit at a time. So the maximum byte information rates are one-eighth of these values. Thus the ESDI drives on the market today offer at most about a 2-million-byte-per-second data transfer rate.

In this standard, some more minor changes from its predecessor include provisions for the controller to tell the drive to go to a certain track by giving it the track number (instead of having to tell it to step in or out some number of steps), allowing it to ask the drive to report on some additional status items, and to tell it to do some drive diagnostics.

SCSI

The *Small Computer System Interface* (SCSI, pronounced "scuzzy") is a very different kind of disk interface. Properly speaking, it is not a disk interface at all.

The SCSI standard was first developed in the late 1970s under the name SASI (Shugart Associates System Interface). Over the past dozen years, disk makers have upgraded it several times; its latest name is SCSI-2 (SCSI, second version), though its basic design philosophy remains the same. SCSI differs in many important ways from the other interfaces we have discussed.

The most important idea is that this interface presupposes that only rather intelligent devices are attached to its interconnecting cable. There may be up to 7 SCSI slave devices and one SCSI master sharing a single cable. The nature of these devices may be quite diverse. You can attach large, fast hard disk drives, tape drives, optical disks, laser printers, and even such slow devices as a mouse, so long as each one has the appropriate SCSI interface electronics between it and the SCSI cable. In many ways, SCSI is more of a small *local area network* (LAN) than a normal PC-to-hard-disk interface.

The SCSI host sends a command to one of the slaves, which in turn possesses enough intelligence to execute the sequence of operations using the SCSI cable (i.e., it becomes a temporary master). When the slave completes its task, it relinquishes the cable and the original SCSI host may permit some other slave device to control the cable for awhile.

Apple Macintosh computers popularized the SCSI interface, but it is rapidly gaining favor in the PC world as well. ESDI drive/controller combinations and SCSI host adapter/SCSI slave disk drive combinations now offer competitive performance at competitive prices.

Users most often prefer the ESDI solution when they need only a drive and desire the maximum compatibility with the earlier standards. SCSI wins out when users need to support multiple SCSI devices, although there may be some cost in compatibility.

> ▐ SCSI devices communicate via a ribbon cable with 50 pins (or in the SCSI-2 standard, a 50-pin cable plus an auxiliary 68-pin cable). All the signals are digital. The data is carried 8 (or 16 or 32) bits at a time in parallel. There are relatively few control signals in the cable.
>
> It is possible for each of seven SCSI slave devices to have up to 8 *logical units* within them. So in principle, you could have one SCSI host adapter in a PC communicating with up to 56 logically separate subdevices.
>
> The data transfer rate in the original SASI interface was only 12 megabits per second, or 1.5 megabytes per second over 8 parallel wires. In the latest version of the SCSI standard, the bit rate may be as high as 10Mhz, with a corresponding data rate as high as 40 megabytes per second (using 32 parallel wires).

Most drive makers now offer both ESDI and SCSI versions of their newest drive designs. The only difference is the electronics board attached to the drive and the cable connector it presents.

A SCSI hard disk contains in effect its own disk controller electronics. The SCSI host adapter merely manages the SCSI bus, which in effect is a mini-LAN.

One important implication of this layered approach to controlling the drive is that many of the physical details of the drive may, and indeed must, be hidden from the computer.

No longer does the computer, or a disk controller plugged into the computer bus, command the drive to step one track in or out. The computer does not know how many tracks a SCSI drive has. Instead, a SCSI drive appears to the computer as an idealized, logical disk drive.

> ▐ The actual drive may have, for example, 5 platters with 10 heads, of which one is used for servo-positioning of the head assembly. It might have a couple of thousand tracks. The inner tracks might have 30-some sectors and the outer tracks as many as twice this number, with some of the intermediate tracks having some intermediate numbers of sectors. The SCSI interface reduces this complexity to a logical drive that appears to have 64 heads, 32 sectors per track, and just a few hundred tracks.

Since the SCSI interface electronics "makes up" this logical drive, it can and usually does make it appear to have utterly no defects. The SCSI interface uses spare sectors to store data, in lieu of using any partially damaged sectors.

> **0110 0110**
> **TECHNICAL**
> **NOTE**
> This is an extreme example of *head translation* and *sector translation*, which is discussed in more detail in the next chapter, in the section "Evading the Limits." Because of this unreality, SCSI drives significantly limit the function of a program like *SpinRite* (though *SpinRite* can still do some wonderful things).

IDE

The latest wrinkle in hard disk interfaces for the PC is the so-called *integrated drive electronics* (IDE) drive. The drive maker Conner Peripherals has popularized this approach, which includes an entire RLL or MFM controller on the drive itself, eliminating the need for a controller card. To connect to the computer, IDE drives do not take up a bus slot, which is one of their most attractive features. Instead, they use a special connector on the motherboard, which is, in effect, a mini-slot carrying only those bus slot signal lines that the IDE interface needs.

Since the IDE drives, like SCSI drives, incorporate the entire drive controller on the drive, they can and many times will do some nonstandard things, such as sector translation. If an IDE drive appears to the computer exactly as an MFM or RLL drive, then *SpinRite* may be able to treat it like one.

Often it will mask some of its real personality, preventing *SpinRite* and any other low-level reformatting programs from performing all their functions. These programs may still provide useful services, just not everthing they can do for MFM, RLL and most ESDI drives. Again, see the details in the section of the next chapter "Evading the Limits."

Hard disks on an option card

Several years earlier, the Plus Development Corporation made a departure like IDE, but in the opposite direction. They moved the hard disk onto the controller card. Since Plus' first *Hard Card* was introduced in 1985, many other drive makers have introduced similar products. Plus Developments' models have evolved from an initial 10-megabyte capacity to around ten times that capacity, yet they still fit into a single slot in a PC.

> **0110 0110**
> **TECHNICAL NOTE**   *Hard Card* is a trade mark of the Plus Development Corporation, but some people use it as a generic term for similar products from any manufacturer. In this book we shall use "hard-disk card" (all lower case letters) as such a generic term.

The makers of hard-disk cards have often opted to take advantage of the same tight integration of controller and drive as the makers of SCSI and IDE drives, using zone bit recording, sector translation, and other non-standard approaches in order to get the maximum capacity into the minimum space. Hard-disk cards appear to the computer as more or less standard MFM drives, but they deny the computer the lowest levels of control that it could expect for such drives. Again, *SpinRite* and similar programs can do only some of their usual work on a hard-disk card.

5

Drive Geometries

We've given you a lot of information about fundamentals and about the variety of products and standards. After reviewing a bit, we introduce a new way of looking at how hard drives store information.

Heads, cylinders, and sectors

You have learned that a hard drive is built with platters and heads. The heads (one per surface of a platter) are attached to a head assembly and are moved in toward the spindle or out toward the edge of the platters by an actuator. For each position of the actuator and head assembly, the heads each read or write a track on their respective platter surfaces. The collection of tracks for a single head assembly position is called a cylinder (see Figure 5-3).

The cylinders are numbered starting at zero at the outer edge of the platters. The heads are numbered also starting at zero on the top surface. Some drives use one of the heads for a servo-feedback head positioning system, and thus they appear to have an odd number of heads as far as data storage is concerned.

The tracks are divided into sectors, each storing 512 bytes of data (plus sector header and ECC information). The sectors are numbered starting at 1.

Thus, if we wish to send some information to a particular spot on the drive, we would expect to have to tell the drive controller to put it on some particular head (surface), in a certain cylinder, and into some numbered sector.

Physical versus logical structures of information

We've just described a *physical* way of addressing data on the disk, a method the hardware must ultimately follow. We seldom wish to be bothered with this point of view, however, because it is much easier to think of the disk in a simplified, *logical* sense instead.

After all, MS-DOS is designed to relieve us (and our programs) of the need to know in any great detail about the disk drive. DOS attempts, instead, to manage that resource so that we and our programs need give DOS only the simplest of instructions to save and retrieve our information.

 The operating system of your PC is divided into several parts: The BIOS (basic input output system) ROMs (read-only memory chips) on the motherboard and on various option cards that contain very low-level hardware control programs; the BIOS program, which is contained in one of the two hidden system files; and the highest level DOS program, which is contained in the other hidden system files on bootable disks. The BIOS programs, both those that live in ROM and that which comes off the disk, deal with the hardware in a way that is close to the physical reality. The DOS program tends to abstract the hardware into some simpler, logical form.

Chapter 7 includes a discussion of the various parts into which a disk drive's space gets divided when it is prepared for use with DOS. At this point, suffice it to say that there is a region before the DOS information storage area and there may be another region after it. For now we will ignore those non-DOS regions.

DOS, in its highest level form, regards the portion of the disk into which it may store data as simply a large number of logical sectors. It numbers these sectors in a simple list, starting at logical sector number zero.

This numbering scheme for logical sectors is not to be confused with the numbering scheme for physical sectors, which starts over with sector number 1 on each track.

Almost every program that runs under DOS is thereby relieved of much complexity in its dealings with the disk. Even many disk utility programs deal only with this abstract, logical disk drive, instead of with the actual, physical drive. It is precisely these properties of DOS that allow our programs to work with so many different kinds of hard disk drives. DOS has hidden their diversity from our and our programs' view.

For some of its purposes, *SpinRite* can work with a disk in this abstract way too, but to deliver all its potential benefits it must get behind DOS and see the physical reality by talking directly to the controller. Unfortunately, if the controller, rather than DOS, is hiding reality, even *SpinRite* may not be able to penetrate this veil, which may limit its capability to fix certain problems.

5

Messy Physical Details

In this section, we briefly describe what is special about the spindle drive and discuss the differences between stepper and servo head actuators and what the electronics do on the drive and on the controller. We also define *recalibration* (and tell why your hard drive makes those weird and sometimes scary sounds).

What the physical parts of the drive do

The disk platters turn, the head assembly moves in and out, and the heads read and write data to the surfaces. That much we have covered already.

The main drive motor turns the platters at a constant speed, usually 3,600 revolutions per minute (60 revolutions per second). It does this by driving the spindle with a specially designed multipole DC motor, driven by a crystal-controlled oscillator. The torque the motor delivers is very nearly constant, making the speed at which the platters turn nearly the same at every part of a revolution, as well as from minute to minute.

How the heads move in and out gets a bit more complex. We should also say a bit more about how the read/write heads work.

Steppers and servos: Many actuator designs exist for moving the head assembly in and out, but we can simplify them to two common types of actuator: steppers and servos, both of which are specialized motors. Steppers tend to be cheaper, slower, and less accurate at positioning the heads than servos, and thus they are used in the less expensive, smaller-capacity drives.

Any electric motor works by having two magnets pushing or pulling on one another. One of them is bolted to the frame of the motor (the part that stays put) and the other one is mounted on the portion that moves. (See Figure 5-12.) Depending on the motor's design, one or the other magnet may be permanent, but at least one must be an electromagnet so it can be turned on and off at just the right times. This is a little like a swing, which you push only at a certain point in its swing.

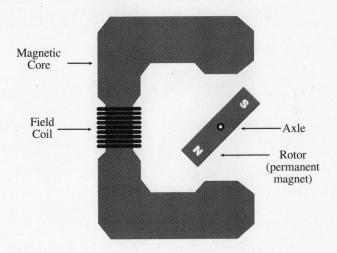

Figure 5-12 A simple electric motor

TECHNICAL NOTE   To make a motor work more smoothly, some incorporate several magnets attached to the frame; these take turns pushing on the magnet mounted on the shaft. In making a good motor, one must try to make the pushes merge into one another as smoothly as possible. This is especially true for the spindle motor of a hard disk, where the constancy of rotation speed is critical to the drive's performance.

5

You can use just two or four magnets on the frame in a way that makes them act as if there are many more than that. This is done by making each such *field coil* supply its magnetic field through a *multipole core*. The several field coils have their cores interleaved. Then if the shaft magnet is drawn near to one of these poles by having its field coil turned on, it will next "feel" the pull of the adjacent pole when that magnet is turned on. After receiving one pull from each magnet in turn, it is pulled by the first one again. (See Figure 5-13.)

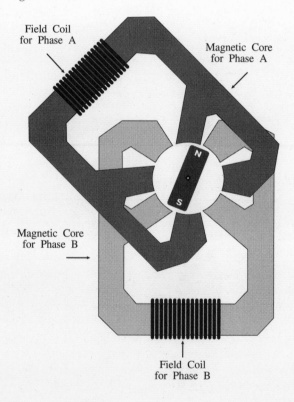

Figure 5-13 A multipole motor

If one turns on current through just one of the field coil magnets and leaves it on, the motor will turn a part of a turn and then stop, with its rotor "locked" to one of the poles of the energized field coil. If then a different field coil has current put through it, the shaft will turn to a different position and stop.

Motors that are not carefully designed will tend to "cog," which means they will tend to jump from one of these positions to the next and, as they reach each one, try to pause there. Though considered a defect in a normal motor, it is the whole point behind a stepper motor.

A stepper motor is simply one which can be operated by DC signals to turn its shaft to a succession of positions "a step at a time."

If the motor in Figure 5-13 has many poles for each of the magnets, and if one drives one of the electromagnets in the frame at a time with a steady (DC) current, it is possible to move the motor shaft in small, well-defined steps simply by switching on a different field coil. Since this strategy involves turning the magnets all the way on or off, it is inherently a digital technique. Since the distance the motor turns is fixed by the construction of the motor, its step size does not depend on the electric signals at all; they govern only *when* it will take a step.

If a small gear with a few fine teeth (called a pinion) is mounted on the shaft, and if it engages what amounts to a large gear with many fine teeth that has been sort-of unwrapped (this is called a rack), then as the motor steps, the rack will be moved back and forth in a straight line, also in steps. This is the essence of a *rack-and-pinion, stepper-motor head-positioning actuator*. Such an actuator was included in the first IBM-PC/XT hard disk drives and it has been common in most of the lower cost drives built since then.

When a stepper motor is used with a rack-and-pinion gear arrangement, it can move something (in our case a head assembly) in a straight line in small, well-defined steps. There are variations on this technique, including mounting a shaft on the stepper motor that has a spiral groove cut in it and then having a carriage ride along in this groove, or replacing the rack with a portion of a large round gear and transferring its rotation to the head assembly through a taut metal band. All these different mechanical arrangements share the stepper motor's ability to move in small, clearly defined steps.

We commonly encounter, in something you may not recognize as a motor, a completely different way to make an electric motor move something in a straight line. A speaker in a radio or hi-fi is simply a cone of paper attached to a linear electric motor of a special kind. Once again there are two magnets, one permanent and the other an electromagnet, that push against each other. One of these magnets (the permanent one) is fixed, while the other one is able to move (see Figure 5-14).

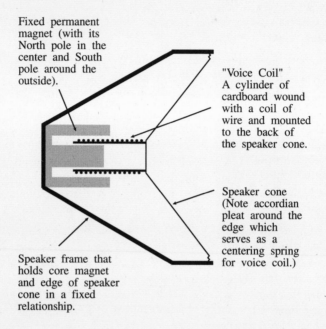

Fixed permanent magnet (with its North pole in the center and South pole around the outside).

"Voice Coil" A cylinder of cardboard wound with a coil of wire and mounted to the back of the speaker cone.

Speaker cone (Note accordian pleat around the edge which serves as a centering spring for voice coil.)

Speaker frame that holds core magnet and edge of speaker cone in a fixed relationship.

Figure 5-14 Cross-section view of an audio speaker showing voice coil

Unlike the usual electric motor that rotates a shaft, this kind of motor can move only a short distance, instead of turning for as many revolutions as one might want.

> **TECHNICAL NOTE** A physical stop is built into this sort of motor at each end of its range of motion. A positive current in its coil will push the moving part in one direction and a negative current will push it in the other direction. The stronger the current, the larger the force, and the more rapidly the moving part will accelerate in one direction or the other. There may also be a weak spring tending to hold the moving part near the center of its range of motion, but the forces from the current will be much stronger than those of the spring during normal operation of the motor.

Since this sort of "motor" was first used in radio speakers, the moving part (which is the electromagnet) is commonly called a *voice coil*. It pushes the speaker cone in and out to make sounds you can hear.

Notice that in a stepper motor, current is applied steadily and the motor moves to a new position and stops. In a voice coil motor, the moving part accelerates as long as the current is applied. Once it is moving, the only way to get it to stop short of the end of its range of motion is to reverse the current in the coil briefly.

There is an important difference between the rack-and-pinion, stepper motor way of moving things and the voice coil way. In the first case, the motion is in steps whose size is a built-in feature of the stepper motor and its gear arrangement. All one can influence with the electric signals is when a step will be taken and in what direction. This is an inherently digital system. With the voice coil, in contrast, the technique for moving something in a straight line by a distance depends directly on how much electric current we pass through a coil and for how long we apply that current. Thus the voice coil positioner is inherently an analog system.

If we attach such a voice coil "motor" to a head assembly for a disk drive, we can position the heads to any cylinder just by passing the current through the coil in a carefully controlled pattern of plus and minus signals. But if we get that pattern wrong by the least amount, the heads will move somewhere else. To make sure our current pattern is exactly right, we use *negative feedback*: Servo disk drivers function analogously to car drivers in that they watch the current pattern much as a driver watches the road, making adjustments as necessary to stay in the proper highway lane.

5

The manufacturer prerecords a special magnetic pattern on one surface of one of the platters. Though not data in the usual sense, this information is critical to the operation of the drive. It consists of a signal for each cylinder, recorded all the way around the track. The magnetic pattern operates like a highway lane. By watching the strength and nature of the signal picked up by the head as it moves over the recorded information, the electronics on the drive can tell if the head is precisely centered over the track and if not, in which direction it is off. Each of these tracks also contains the actual cylinder number for that track.

This system tells the electronics on the drive which cylinder number to find; the system then varies the voice coil current up and down, plus and minus, until that track number is found. It then must constantly fine-tune the current to keep the heads centered over that track.

Some servo disk drives do not have a reserved head and platter surface for prerecorded servo information. Instead, they put that information on every track in between the sectors. These are called "embedded servo" drives. They have a couple of advantages over the other servo drives. The obvious advantage is they have one more platter surface on which to record data. A less apparent advantage is that since the head is following a servo track on the same surface as the data, it will follow the recorded data accurately even if the head assembly tilts. (This is called "tower drift.") The one significant disadvantage with these drives is that they have less prerecorded servo signal to use, and thus may be less accurate in their ability to follow the tracks.

A servo system has several advantages over a stepper motor positioner. First, as the head actuator parts age and wear, the servo system uses a built-in tendency to compensate for that wear. It does this because the system constantly "looks" to compare the heads' position with the prerecorded track position information. This also helps compensate for any tendency of the head assembly to sag under gravity in different positions, such as if you turn your PC on its end and place it on the floor to free up your desktop.

5

The servo system also has the advantage of being quicker than a stepper positioner. This is in part because you can simply pour an excess current into the voice coil briefly, in order to push the heads more forcefully. With the stepper, the size of the currents in the coils are fixed.

Finally, the servo system has a certain degree of built-in disk-surface protection. These designs come standard with circuitry that will force the heads in toward the spindle whenever you turn off the power. In contrast, a stepper positioner does nothing special when you power it down. As a result, the heads in stepper drives stay in whatever position you last put them.

This difference is described by saying that servo drives are "auto-parking" or "self-parking." Stepper drives must be parked by the deliberate use of a special "head parking" program before the computer is powered down.

A stepper motor takes a step and stops. When a stepper motor loses power, it does not move. A voice coil motor is likely to be moving in or out a little bit all the time. When a voice coil loses power, it will tend to continue moving in whatever direction it was moving just before that. To ensure that when power is turned off the voice coil motor used in a hard drive will do something predictable, the machine stores up energy in a capacitor. Then, whenever power to the drive is turned off, special shutdown circuits dump that energy through the coil, causing the motor to slam the head assembly all the way in toward the spindle until it hits the mechanical stop, or out all the way off the platters. Sometimes a pin is then dropped into the actuator to lock it in that position. We call this behavior *auto parking*.

Chapter 4 includes a section that discusses in some detail just why parking the heads on a disk drive is *vital* to your data's safety and describes some *dangerous* park programs you should never use.

Read/write heads: You have already learned that the read/write heads are small electromagnets, one for the top and one for the bottom of each platter, that write information to and read it back from the disk. You know that as the disk turns, the heads skim along just a fraction of a micron above the platter's surface. When the disk stops turning, the heads sit down on the platter.

You don't need to know much more about the read/write heads. We described the heads as having coils of wire wound on a ferromagnetic core; that core has a small gap, which is where the magnetic field lines leak out and go through the platter's magnetic coating. (See Figure 5-2.)

An interesting, though not essential, fact is that the head core gap is not simply a space. It is filled with some hard non-magnetic material that not only assures that the gap will remain the same size; it also makes sure that there will be no sharp edges on the heads to scrape the surface when they park.

Manufacturers make the heads (and the assembly that holds them and which connects them to the actuator) as lightweight as possible and yet as rigid as possible. This is so that the assembly can be moved quickly and easily and yet will put each head in a predictable place for any given position of the actuator.

Perhaps the most important thing to know about the read/write heads is that they almost certainly will acquire some permanent magnetization. This magnetization can be useful, for if it is properly engineered into the head design, it can increase the sensitivity with which the head can pick up the magnetic fields from the platter surface. Unfortunately, such magnetization can also play a negative role.

The problem is that since the heads are always magnets — not just when the computer is using them to record signals on the platter surface — sweeping them over the platter tends to weaken the recorded signals on the platter surface.

One of the causes of premature hard disk death, this is also one reason why we should always park the heads over a safe cylinder before we turn off the disk drive motor.

What the drive electronics does

Near the start of this chapter, we discussed the general function of the electronic circuit board that is attached to every hard disk drive. What the circuit board does in detail depends on the kind of drive we are talking about.

5

Spindle motor drive circuit: In all PC drives, this board contains circuitry to drive the spindle motor (thus turning the platters at a constant speed). The board can use one of two strategies to keep the spindle turning at the desired rate.

> **0110 0110**
> **TECHNICAL**
> **NOTE**
> Some spindle motors are *synchronous motors* — they turn synchronously with an oscillating electric signal, much like a kitchen clock that uses the frequency of the AC power line to keep accurate time. The circuit card has an oscillator whose frequency is crystal controlled (like a "quartz" wrist watch) and an amplifier to make that signal strong enough to drive the spindle motor.
>
> The other kind of spindle motor is more tightly integrated into the driving circuitry. It forms a part of the oscillator, called in this case a *phase locked loop*. Again, the frequency is controlled by a quartz crystal. The only essential difference is that in this case the oscillator will not oscillate unless the motor is turning.

Head positioner drive circuit: The drive circuitry also controls the head positioning actuator. Just what circuitry is needed to control the actuator depends on two things. One is the kind of positioning mechanism the drive has (stepper motor or servo-feedback). The other is the kind of interface used with that drive (ST412/ST506, ESDI, SCSI, IDE, or a hard-disk card).

MFM and RLL controllers simply tell the drive to step in or to step out some number of cylinders. Unlike ESDI and SCSI controllers, they do not specify the destination cylinder by number.

Stepper motor drives are naturals for the MFM or RLL approach. After all, these motors take a step whenever they get a suitable pulse of electric current, and they have no means of knowing what cylinder number the heads are over. There is a buffer on the drive circuit card that can store up several step commands, but nothing to keep track of absolute cylinder number.

If you command a stepper motor drive, for example, to go in 4,000 cylinders, it will cheerfully go in as far as it can, then simply push the heads against some physical stop several thousand times, not noticing that it isn't moving them at all.

In a servo-motor drive things are a bit different. Again, if you are talking about an MFM or RLL drive, the controller will command it to step in or to step out by a single cylinder at a time. Again, the drive electronics will store up a number of those commands in a buffer until it has time to carry them out.

Unlike the stepper drives, though, servo drives *must* keep track of where (over which numbered cylinder) they are supposed to have put the heads. This is because the only way they properly position the heads is to read the signals coming off the special servo head on the last surface, see which cylinder number it finds its heads sailing over, and then compare that with the desired cylinder number.

If you tell this sort of drive to step in 4,000 cylinders, it will compute some huge cylinder number that it is supposed to find and then start ramping up the voice coil current in the appropriate direction, looking at the servo head signals all the while to see if it is yet where you commanded it to go.

Since no PC drive today has that many cylinders, it will inevitably fail to find what it is looking for. What happens then?

The circuitry is clever enough to notice that it didn't get where it was going even by using a large, long pulse of voice coil current. Noticing that, it tries again. First, it will reverse the current and hold it there until it sees cylinder number zero, out at the very edge of the platter. Then it reverses the current again and goes back to looking for the cylinder you have requested. Again, of course, it will fail.

The drive will simply continue this forever, or until it completely destroys itself. (You will hear it going bang, bang, bang, bang until your turn off power to your computer.)

Unfortunately, the previously mentioned dangerous head parking programs are dumb enough to ask a servo drive to do this.

Since MFM and RLL controllers only command the drive to step in or to step out by one cylinder at a time for some number of times, they are well matched to the stepper design of head positioner. The higher performance MFM and RLL drives, though, will add the extra circuitry needed to operate a servo-feedback head positioner.

All ESDI and SCSI drives must have that circuitry because those kinds of controller will typically send to the drive a command to go to a particular cylinder by its number. As it happens, these drives are high-performance models that use servo-feedback head positioners, which means they have the absolute cylinder-number positioning capability built-in anyway.

IDE drives and hard cards are essentially combinations of a drive (usually an RLL or ERLL drive) and a controller card. They too include the absolute cylinder positioning circuitry.

Switches and amplifiers: Finally, the circuit card on the drive has to have some circuits connected to the read/write heads. There are three parts to these circuits: A set of switches that let you choose which head to turn on and whether to set that head to reading or writing; a write amplifier that takes the signals from the controller and makes them strong enough to record information on the platter surface; and the read amplifier circuitry, whose job it is to strengthen and clean up the signals coming off the heads when data are being read. (See Figure 5-15.) In addition, some drives, such as ESDI, SCSI, IDE and hard cards, have a clock-data separator circuit on the electronics card.

This circuit takes the analog signals from the heads (after they have been amplified and somewhat cleaned up) and converts these pulses into binary digital data. If the drive is using MFM data encoding, that means it figures out which pulses are clock signals and which are data signals and then separates them. Hence the name clock-data separator. If RLL data encoding is used, the job is a bit more complicated, but the circuitry that accomplishes it is still called a clock-data separator.

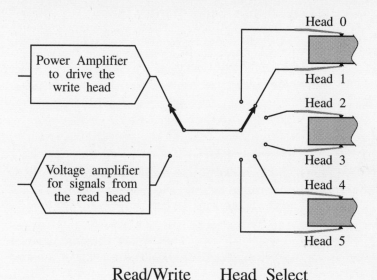

Head 0

Head 1

Head 2

Head 3

Head 4

Head 5

Read/Write
Switch

Head Select
Switch

Figure 5-15 Block diagram of the read/write head switching circuits of a typical hard disk controller.

For ESDI, that is the end of the story. For SCSI, IDE, and hard cards, there is one more part.

Interface electronics: IDE and hard cards are each essentially a complete controller plus hard disk all in one. The basic drive design is most likely similar to RLL drives. In any case, these drives must have circuitry that is able to talk to the PC input-output bus, in addition to performing the tasks described above.

SCSI drives have the full circuitry of a controller plus drive as well as the SCSI interface circuitry, which gives them the "intelligence" to conduct a proper conversation with the SCSI host adapter and to control the SCSI bus when permitted.

What the controller electronics does

MFM, RLL, and ESDI drives connect to controller cards plugged into the PC's input-output bus. Those controller cards take commands from the PC and translate them into the language understood by the drives, then do the reverse from the drives back to the PC.

 The controller cards' job includes packaging the data as it comes from the computer by adding the ECC bytes. In the case of ST412/ST506 interface controllers (for MFM and RLL drives), this also includes encoding the bytes of data plus ECC according to the chosen data encoding strategy (MFM or RLL). For ESDI drives, that job is done on the drive.

Going the other way, an MFM or RLL controller must separate clock and data signals or otherwise infer the actual binary data from the string of pulses coming off the drive's heads. ESDI systems do this separation on the drive. Any of these controllers (MFM, RLL, or ESDI) will then have to compute the ECC and compare that with what was read, attempt to reread the data if there is a discrepancy, and finally deliver those data back to the PC (with the ECC removed and perhaps with the data corrected by use of the ECC). Finally, it must message the PC to describe what level of confidence it has in the data just delivered.

The most important thing to know about the workings of disk controller cards is that each one does its job in a unique manner. This means first that you must always use the right sort of controller for the drive. MFM drives do not generally work correctly when attached to RLL controllers, and certainly neither controller can be used with an ESDI drive, or vice versa.

Also, as we mentioned earlier, you cannot format and fill a drive with data with one controller and then expect another controller, even the same kind of controller, to be able to read the data. Only if the two controllers of the same model and revision number were made simultaneously by the same company would such a swap work.

SCSI controllers (which are more properly called SCSI host adapters) are completely different. The disk controller, per se, is located on the SCSI drive along with the SCSI slave interface circuitry.

Recalibration and other strange sounds in the night

Sometimes horrible grinding noises may emanate from your computer. Clearly the disk drive is doing it, but what, exactly, is it doing and why? Should you be worried?

Some unusually noisy disk drives *always* make strange sounds. If they work once, you may assume that they will continue to work more or less as long as any other, similar drive. For such drives, you can safely ignore the strange noises.

You should, however, worry about drives that make inconsistent noises — such as when a drive that was working quietly suddenly starts grinding away. This scares people, as it probably should.

There are two main reasons for these strange noises. In both cases, the drive is doing a *recalibration*.

5

0110 0110
TECHNICAL NOTE
In the first case, the drive has lost its sense of where it is— in particular which cylinder its heads are traveling over. Perhaps it is a servo-feedback drive, and the servo head signals tell the drive electronics that it is no longer over the track it meant to be over. Perhaps it is a stepper drive, and the signals read from the sector headers on a data track tell it the same thing. This can happen even when the drive is neither reading nor writing any information. (That is, you could be sitting at the DOS prompt or in some application program that was waiting for your input.)

The usual ploy the drive electronics will use to get (literally) back on track is to go first to the outermost track (cylinder zero) and then come in from there. This makes most sense in a stepper drive, in which the most obvious way to find cylinder number 12, for example, is to go to cylinder number zero and take 12 steps in toward the spindle. It also is used in servo drives to confirm which way it should be looking.

In the second case, the drive is trying to read a bad sector. Either it could not find a sector header with the right address numbers in it, or the CRC value for that sector header did not agree with the header's contents. Here the drive may be quite sure which cylinder it is over, yet it again tries to reread the sector by going first back to the start of the disk (cylinder zero) and then returning to the desired track to look for the desired sector. This is to insure that it is not failing to read the sector simply because it was looking in the wrong place.

These noises mean the disk is having some trouble carrying out its orders; you are right to be concerned. If some of the sectors lie in places on the disk where it cannot reliably store information, perhaps it is enough to mark those sectors as bad and then avoid trying to write or read data there. Of course, if you have already written some data there, that may not suffice.

> **TECHNICAL NOTE** You may also hear these noises when you first prepare a hard disk. Both in the low-level and the high-level formatting, the machine tests every sector on the disk to be sure it can be used reliably to store and retrieve information. When it finds a bad spot, the program will tell the controller to try again and again and again. Only after a very large number of failures will it give up and mark that place as bad, so that DOS will never try to store information there.
>
> You will very likely hear these noises when you run *SpinRite*, too. This is because it tests even places that have previously been declared "bad," just in case they are no longer defective.
>
> The worst time to hear these noises is when some ordinary DOS program is trying to read or write information on the disk. That is when you might lose some data if you are not careful (and a bit lucky).

If you hear these noises while you are running an ordinary DOS program, you should immediately back up to a floppy disk or tape cassette any active files. If DOS doesn't allow you to back up, telling you "sector cannot be found" or that there is an "error reading the drive," then you may be able to recover your data by running *SpinRite*. See Chapter 8 for additional details.

Disk Caching

This is the last section of this rather long chapter. You are near the end of our story of how disk drives work to store and retrieve information.

Disk caching facilitates access to the information on our disks. A primitive version of it is essential to the operation of all PCs. More sophisticated versions are becoming increasingly popular. In this section, we will examine the workings of disk caching and describe most of the varieties you may encounter. Finally, we will answer a question you may have wondered about and never found carefully discussed: What is the "correct" value to put in the BUFFERS statement in the CONFIG.SYS file?

Purpose of a disk cache

A disk cache, at its most fundamental level, provides a place to store information on its way to or from a disk drive. Its purpose is to speed up disk reading and/or writing. (See Figure 5-16.)

In this way, a disk cache resembles cache memory, which is a special place to store information on its way to or from the computer's main RAM. Conceptually similar, the two differ in detail. In this book, we will cover only the details of disk caching.

To state that difference in a bit more detail, a disk cache is a temporary storage location (some RAM) for data moving in between the PC's main RAM and its disk drive. A memory cache is a temporary storage location (some very fast RAM) in between its central processing unit (CPU) (the 8088, 8086, 80286, 80386, or 08486 chip), and its main RAM. Your PC might have both (the fastest PCs do), or one, or neither.

Any computer is an "information processor." For your PC to process any information both the data and the program to process it must reside in the PC's RAM. When you turn off your PC, it loses all the information in RAM. Consequently, we must store the programs and information on a hard disk or some other less-volatile medium, which in turn means we must have a method to load everything from the disk into RAM and back again.

DOS routes such information through the *DOS disk buffers*, which are special regions of RAM set aside for this purpose. We will discuss them in detail after covering *hardware disk caching* and *software disk caching*. An important point to remember is that the PC will ask for information from or send information to the disk drive just one sector at a time.

There is an exception in versions 3.3 and above of MS-DOS and PC-DOS. These versions of DOS can request the hard disk controller to read or write multiple sectors at one time. Most programs, however, do not take advantage of that possibility. Also, some controllers are not able to handle those requests correctly if there is any error, even a fully correctable one, in the data that is being read or written more than one sector at a time.

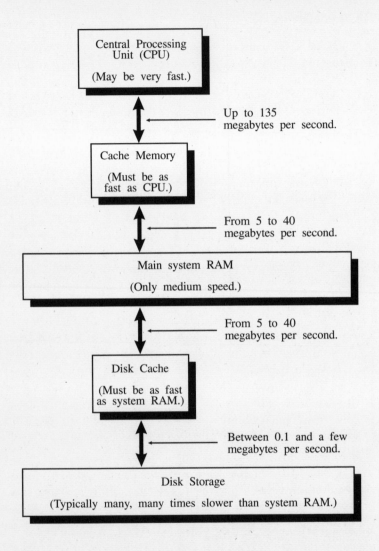

Figure 5-16 Cache memory versus disk cache with the typical speeds of each component and of data transfer between them.

An even more important point to remember is that the disk drive has moving parts. This means that a disk drive handles data *far* slower than the CPU can shuffle data around in RAM.

The varieties of caches

A hardware disk cache consists of a chunk of RAM on the disk controller in which we can temporarily park information while waiting to send it either to the disk drive or to the computer. It also is the program built into the controller to manage that RAM. Not all disk controllers offer this feature, and those that do offer it in many different forms. Here are the most popular ones.

Track buffer: In this version, the controller has a chunk of RAM whose data capacity matches that of one full track on the disk. When DOS asks for a sector of information from the disk drive, the controller reads not only that sector but also the rest of that track, anticipating that DOS will ask next for another sector out of the same track, which it generally does. The controller can supply the data right away, without waiting for the disk to turn and bring that next sector into view.

> **TECHNICAL NOTE** The presence of a track buffer on the disk controller can greatly mitigate the effect of an improper interleave on the disk drive. For optimum performance, though, you want to have the appropriate interleave *and* a cache buffer of some sort on the disk controller.
>
> Since the typical MFM drive has 17 sectors, each holding 512 bytes, a track buffer requires only 8.5K of RAM. For an RLL drive, that number may be about 13K, and for an ESDI or SCSI drive, it could be as high as 25.5K. These days this much RAM is not very expensive, so more and more disk controllers are including at least a track buffer.

This kind of disk buffering can speed up disk reading enormously, especially if you are reading a file that is stored in successive sectors on the disk. It does nothing to speed up disk writes.

Read ahead cache: A slightly fancier sort of disk cache, the *read ahead cache*, has more RAM that it uses a bit more cleverly. This version may provide enough RAM to store several tracks worth of data. Typical amounts of RAM cache range from 32K to 16 megabytes.

As the controller reads information from the disk, each time a sector is requested, the controller will again read the remaining portion of that track. With a cache, if it gets a request for a sector that is not on that track, it need not throw away the information it has just read; instead it will read the new track into another part of its cache memory. It will keep this up until it has filled the cache with information from some number of different tracks (which could be located anywhere on the disk, not necessarily next to each other).

Once the read ahead cache starts to fill up, chances increase that DOS will ask for sectors that are already in the cache, causing the effective speed of your disk drive to soar.

 The technical term for finding what you are seeking in the cache is a *cache hit*. The percentage of hits is a measure of how effective the cache is. In favorable circumstances, a large cache can achieve hit rates over 90%. That means the drive will appear to operate more than ten times as fast as usual.

Most of the time, such "favorable circumstance" won't prevail; then the cache will not do nearly that well. Still, even if it only *doubles* the speed of your disk drive and just occasionally makes it appear to run ten times as fast, the cache is a boon.

5

Like the track buffer, the read ahead cache does nothing for disk *writing* speed; it speeds up disk *reading* only.

Write through cache: Some disk cache techniques also speed up disk writing, by setting aside some of the cache memory to remember recently written information. Then when DOS asks the controller to write something to the disk, it first checks to see if that data already resides in the cache. If so, it tells DOS it has finished writing the information, even though it didn't have to do any writing at all.

 There are many different ways to manage the cache memory resource. Once the cache is full, almost all such strategies call for discarding the least recently used information in favor of retaining the most recently written or read information. (Some caching controllers discard the oldest information, even if the controller used it more frequently than more recently acquired information, but that is not common.)

These controllers differ in the number and size of pieces into which they break the cache memory, or how much cache they allocate to information being read and how much to information being written.

Every manufacturer of a caching disk controller will assure you that his design is "best." It probably is — for the test situation he has analyzed. The diversity that abounds in the marketplace suggests that the "best" solution depends on your particular needs and system.

Advanced write through cache: Mostly marketing hype, an *advanced write-through cache* is a caching disk controller like the previously described ones, but with either more cache RAM or a "better" cache control method.

Deferred write cache: A *deferred write cache*, on the other hand, is really a different sort of caching disk controller. Such a cache differs from a write through cache in one very significant way: it doesn't write information to the disk when it gets it; it does so later on, when it is good and ready.

 When DOS asks for information from the disk, this kind of controller acts just like the other disk caching controllers with a lot of RAM. It looks to see if it already has the sector DOS wants. If it does, it gives that sector to DOS immediately. If not, it goes out and reads the whole track containing that sector, keeping that information in the cache in case DOS requests it shortly.

The difference comes when DOS asks it to write information to the disk drive. The deferred write cache, as its name suggests, simply takes the information and puts it in the cache—for the moment. It writes it to the disk drive later on.

This provides the fastest performance of any of the caching disk controllers. It speeds up even the first write, whereas any other caching controller doesn't improve performance until DOS asks it to rewrite something it recently wrote (and remembered).

These controllers are fast! But they have a dark side: possible data loss if power fails before the deferred write cache has written the data from RAM to disk. If that was your accounts receivable, you could be in big trouble.

 We can force the controller to "flush its buffers" (write the information in the cache to the drive) in various ways. In some cases the buffer flushing will happen automatically, whenever you leave an application and go back to DOS. In others you may have to press some special "hot-key" combination to force it. Otherwise the controller may wait till the buffer is full or perhaps until the disk drive is free for some preset time period. Whatever the case, just remember that until the controller flushes its cache buffers, you remain vulnerable to data loss.

An *elevator cache* is an especially elegant version of the deferred write cache. This variation not only speeds things up as much as possible, it even makes the actual disk drive work less hard.

The elevator caching controller will organize in cylinder order accumulated data in the cache that it has not yet written to disk. Then when it goes to write the information to disk, it needs to move the head assembly from outside to inside only once, writing all the sectors of data in the order they go on the disk drive, instead of in the order they were delivered to the controller by DOS.

This method is the fastest, but remember the vulnerability of your data. If you use this sort of disk cache, you may well want to invest in an uninterruptible power supply (UPS) for your computer to prevent inopportune power failures.

Buffers versus cache

Some manufacturers tout that their disk controller has a cache when all it has more or less is a large buffer. A mass of RAM that the controller can fill at one end and empty at the other, a buffer may also be accessible in the middle, but it is all one block of data. If it doesn't hold what you ask for, then the controller will fill the whole block with new data.

Functioning like a track buffer (or like the DOS disk buffers), a buffer might be much larger, yet not offer much, if any, improvement in speed. Its main drawback is that it lacks the flexibility to cope well with DOS' tendency to dart around the disk drive.

Caching software in the computer

Hardware disk caching controllers may soup up performance, but they will lighten your wallet, too. A software disk cache offers a much cheaper solution that often works just as well. Such a program takes advantage of some otherwise unused RAM in your PC, in much the same way that the caching controllers use their RAM.

A disk cache program might store the information in extended memory (on an AT or higher model PC) or in expanded memory. It would be a very bad idea to ask it to store the information in the system RAM (the bottom 640KB of RAM in a DOS machine); you should reserve that memory for other purposes.

With a software cache program, such as *Super PC-Kwik* from the Multisoft Corporation (15100 SW Koll Parkway, Beaverton, OR 97006. Telephone: 800-274-5945, 503-644-5644) — to name just one good one — you get most of the benefits of all but the deferred-write hardware disk caches. These programs cost only a fraction of what a hardware disk cache costs, even when you include the cost of the extra RAM you may have to add to your computer.

This might not seem true, for the hardware caching disk controllers have a separate processor on them devoted to managing the cache, whereas the software cache programs use the PC's main CPU for that job. The reason that the software cache programs can compete effectively with the hardware ones is that the speed of the input-output bus limits both of them. So, unless you have a PC with a fast, 32-bit (or wider) input-output bus (which is to say, an MCA or EISA computer or one with a special slot and a matching proprietary disk controller), you may as well stick to a software disk cache program.

DOS disk buffers

Now let us turn our attention back to the buffers that everyone has in their PC: the DOS disk buffers. If you do not have a line in your CONFIG.SYS file that says BUFFERS = nn, where nn is some number, then DOS will assign a default number of disk buffers. That default number is only 2 for PCs and XTs and it is just 3 for ATs, 386, and 486 computers. Though reasonable back when a minimum PC might have only 16K of RAM total, or at most 64K of RAM, these levels are now definitely *un*reasonable.

Such a small number of DOS disk buffers makes sense only if you also have a large, fast buffer or cache on the disk controller or in a disk caching program running in your PC's RAM. In those cases, follow the cache manufacturer's suggestion. Otherwise, you will have to assign your own value to the BUFFERS statement.

The "correct" value for the BUFFERS statement

At last, we can reveal the correct number to put in the BUFFERS statement in your CONFIG.SYS file. If you use a disk cache, either software or hardware, consult the manual for the recommendations to follow. On a PC without disk caching, the DOS disk buffers perform the equivalent job.

TECHNICAL NOTE Whenever DOS asks for a sector of information from the disk, it asks for as many sectors as you have DOS disk buffers. Then when you ask for the next sector, it checks to see if the one you need is in the buffers. If it is, you get it right away, without waiting for the disk drive.

The legal number of DOS disk buffers is anything from 2 to 99; more, however, is not always better.

For one thing, before reading anything from the disk, DOS must spend some time checking all the buffers to see if what it wants might be there. If you have too many buffers, you'll slow things down. Also remember that if it decides it must read from the disk, DOS will order up enough sectors from the disk to fill the buffers. That may take a lot of time.

Another problem with too many buffers is that they will use up too much of your precious first 640K of system RAM. Each buffer requires a few bytes more than can fit in one sector. (With the usual DOS 512-byte sectors, a buffer is 528 bytes long.) Ninety-nine buffers would use up over 50K of system RAM, which your programs most likely could use much more profitably.

You can decide the best number of DOS disk buffers in a particular situation only by conducting a careful (and time-consuming) test. If you constantly read large files that are located in consecutive sectors on the disk, you will want more buffers than if you tend to jump from one part of the disk to another, each time reading or writing only a small amount of data.

The best, general rule to follow is to specify a number in your BUFFERS statement that equals the number of sectors in a track on your hard disk. This will give you the benefit of a track buffer, without incurring any unnecessary penalties.

This concludes our chapter on the structure and function of hard disks. Next, we turn our attention to the way that these disk design details interact with the design of MS-DOS.

5

5

Chapter 6

Hard Disks Under MS-DOS

All IBM PC or compatible computers (what we term PCs) can run MS-DOS (the Microsoft Disk Operating System). If we lump together all the varieties of MS-DOS, including PC-DOS (IBM's brand name for MS-DOS), then most PCs run MS-DOS every day.

To run MS-DOS, a computer must be designed around an Intel 80x86 microprocessor chip (the notation 80x86 is how Intel refers to their 8088, 8086, 80186, 80286, 80386, and 80486 family of microprocessor chips as well as future members), and it must follow the Microsoft additions to the Intel design. (One consequence of this is that one cannot build an MS-DOS machine using the Intel 80186 microprocessor.) Further, to be an IBM PC compatible, a computer also must follow some apects of the IBM PC and PS family design. So, the label "PC" implies a bit more than merely that a computer uses an 80x86 microprocessor.

An operating system like MS-DOS manages the physical resources of the computer, particularly the disk drives, for the benefit of any programs that wish to use its help. This means that computers running DOS look at disks in a particular way. This chapter explains how hard disks operate under MS-DOS.

 For convenience, from now on we will use DOS as a synonym for both PC-DOS and MS-DOS, unless we are discussing a point that applies to only one of them.

165

Some people use a different operating system on their PCs. Scientific computing and design work is often done on PCs running Unix. Larger business systems sometimes run OS/2. The most popular PC network, Novell, uses a custom operating system on their file servers. (In Chapter 7, we offer a short discussion on how Unix, OS/2, and Novell differ from DOS in their use of hard disks.) Still, since most of us use MS-DOS, this book focuses on how that affects hard disk operation. Also, *SpinRite* and the other reinterleaving programs work only on PCs running MS-DOS.

Block versus Character Devices

We call the source of information going to, or the destination of information coming from, a PC's RAM a *device*. DOS lumps all devices into two classes: character devices and block devices.

A character device is any device that can accept or deliver only one character of information at a time. A block device only handles information in blocks of some fixed size containing many characters.

The screen and the keyboard are both character devices. You press one key and the computer gets one keystroke. That same keystroke is then sent to the screen for display, which informs you that the computer noticed your action. A mouse or a modem is also a character device.

All disk drives are block devices, as are tape drives. Any block device must have a buffer in RAM where the computer can assemble information to be sent to it or into which the device can dump the current block of information it is delivering. You must have at least one such buffer. DOS disk buffers, discussed in the preceding chapter, serve as buffers for disk drives.

 Under DOS, a disk buffer normally holds 512 bytes of data—just enough to fill one disk sector. Its actual size is 528 bytes; DOS uses the extra 16 bytes to help manage the buffer.

Some manufacturers have created special programs to allow users of early versions of DOS (before version 3.3) to access large hard disks (those with more than 32 megabytes of total storage capacity). These programs modify DOS as it is loaded into the PC's RAM to achieve their purpose, sometimes enlarging the apparent size of the hard disk's sectors. Whenever one of these programs is active, the DOS disk buffers also will be enlarged so that they each will still hold one sector's worth of data.

DOS allows you to create as many or as few of these disk buffers as you wish, from 2 to 99. The default number is only 2 for an IBM PC or XT (or a clone of one of these) and only 3 for all other PCs.

Increasing that number with a BUFFERS statement in your CONFIG.SYS file can make access to your disk much more efficient. Before you go hog wild, setting BUFFERS = 99, notice how much memory that will use. Your 640K of system RAM is a very precious resource. Even without enlarged sectors, setting BUFFERS = 50 takes up more than 25K. This is one good reason not to define any more of these buffers than you need. The last section in the previous chapter discusses this point more fully.

When your program wants to read a few bytes from the disk, it must ask DOS to get the entire sector containing those bytes into a disk buffer. Then your program can extract the information it wants from that buffer.

Similarly, if your program wishes to write a few bytes to the disk, it actually will merely write that information to a disk buffer. Only when that buffer is full will its contents be written to a sector on the disk. When your program finishes writing all its information, then the last, partially filled sector must be filled with something and written to the disk.

6

 Often that last buffer is written out as it is. This means the beginning of the buffer holds the end of your file. The end of the buffer holds whatever it held the last time you used it, whether reading or writing some previous sector.

This means that any file that does not exactly fill the last sector it has been allocated will have some unrelated information tacked onto its end. Ordinarily this does not cause any problems, since DOS records how long each file is right down to the byte. It is not supposed to read a file past that length.

Various disk utility programs do let you look at what really is stored on the disk, showing you that "garbage" after the end of the file. Also, you may see this sort of garbage tacked onto the ends of files sent from one computer to another over a phone line, because the exact file length is not always transmitted with the file.

To summarize, character devices accept or deliver information "retail," while block devices only deal in information "wholesale." See Figure 6-1.

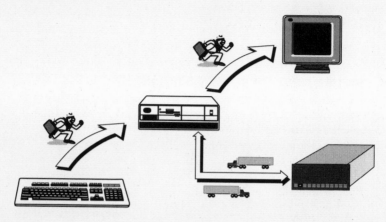

Figure 6-1: Block versus character devices

6 How DOS Makes Things Happen

There are many layers of programs in our PCs. You may only be aware of the very highest couple of layers, but those layers could not function without help from other programs operating at the lower levels.

The layers of programs in a PC

For example, when you load a document into your word processor, you just press some keys and specify the file name. Neither you nor your word processor needs to know how the document is loaded; the program just asks another, lower-level program to do it.

Your word processor turns your request over to DOS. DOS "understands" requests in terms of file names. It translates that request into a series of more detailed requests to the BIOS (the basic input output system), which is one of those lower-level programs. DOS must phrase each of those requests to the BIOS in terms of the actual disk location where the file's data is stored (the particular cylinder, head, and physical sector values).

Before making those requests, DOS must first find out where on the disk the file is stored. To do this, it must ask the BIOS to get copies of the disk's FAT (file allocation table) and one or more of the disk's directories. By inspecting these tables, DOS can pinpoint your file on the disk.

The BIOS translates these low-level requests further into a series of yet lower-level and more detailed requests to the hard disk controller. For example, to read any one sector, the BIOS tells the controller to position the read/write head assembly to the right cylinder, then turn on the correct head, and finally notice when the desired sector comes into view and read it. Figure 6-2 shows just a few of the very many steps in this process.

These layers allow a person or team of people writing a particular layer to focus on just that specialized level of the PC's inner workings, a big advantage. If you later want to modify how the PC does things at one level, you need only replace the program that works at that level, such as if you decide to switch word processor applications.

Interrupts

6

To function, this multilayer programming needs a standardized method of passing messages between the different layers. PCs do that by using *interrupts*.

Interrupts are events that cause whatever program is running to be suspended while some other program takes over to handle that event. When the event-handling program ends, it returns control of the PC to the first program, which resumes operation.

Hardware events cause some interrupts. For example, the hard disk controller may need to signal the PC's BIOS program that it has finished reading a sector and has the data ready for use. Or it may need to say why it could not get the sector.

Software causes other interrupts. For example, DOS will cause an interrupt each time it wants the BIOS to do something for it.

The Intel microprocessors in our PCs were designed to make the interruption procedure work easily and well. When a hardware or software interrupt occurs, the microprocessor finds a subprogram created for handling that event and lets it "do its thing." This

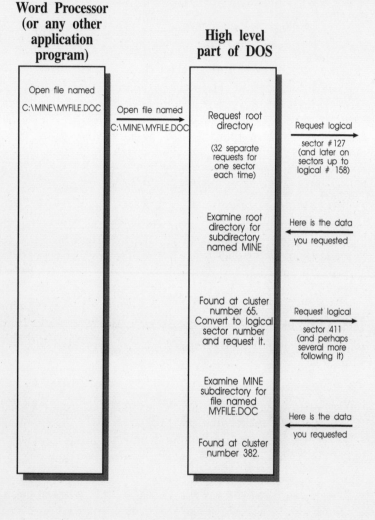

Figure 6-2(a): Layers of programs handling a file request

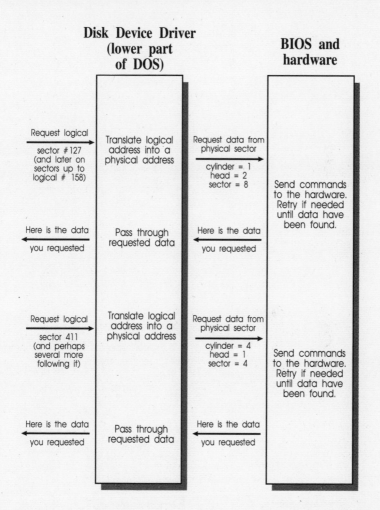

Figure 6-2(a): Layers of programs handling a file request — continued

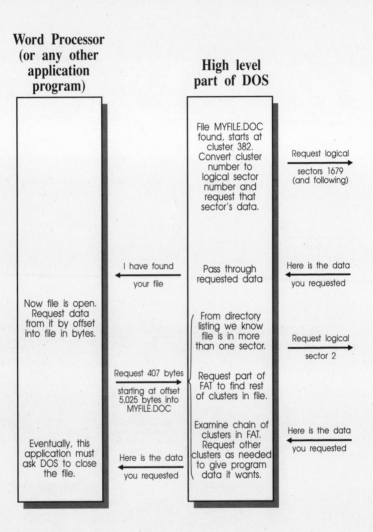

Figure 6-2(b): Layers of programs handling a file request — continued

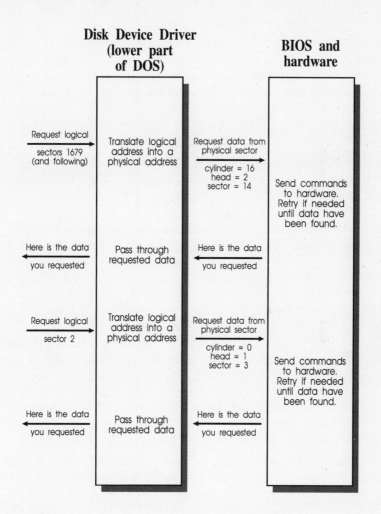

Figure 6-2(b): Layers of programs handling a file request — continued

method may seem roundabout, but it has proven to be extraordinarily flexible and powerful.

TECHNICAL NOTE The Intel 80x86 chips reserve the first 1,024 bytes of RAM for a table, called the *Interrupt Vector Table*. This table holds 256 addresses, four bytes per address. The first two bytes store a segment value and the next two bytes store an offset into that segment. The addresses stored there are those of the mini-programs called *Interrupt Service Routines* (ISRs) that will be called upon to handle events of types 0 to 255.

The primary purpose of DOS is to provide various services to programs. The programs request these services by calling one or another interrupt. So, from this point of view, DOS is simply one huge collection of ISRs.

When an event of a certain type occurs, the microprocessor "interrupts" whatever else it is doing and looks in the interrupt vector table for the address that goes with that particular type of interruption. It then runs the program stored at that address, which it assumes is the proper way to deal with that event. After that program finishes its work, it tells the microprocessor to return to its original task.

6

Figure 6-3 shows this process schematically. This diagram shows memory addresses only up to 1,024 kilobytes. That is the maximum amount of memory an 80x86 processor can access when it is operating in "real mode." The 8088 and 8086 processors have only that one mode of operation. The 80286, 80386, and 80486 processors have some other modes of operation in which they can access more memory, but DOS does not know how to use those modes.

Many recently introduced programs such as Windows, Version 3.0, and Lotus 1-2-3, Version 3.0, do know how to use the memory beyond a megabyte. Still, DOS or the BIOS handle all the interrupts and they are restricted to working in the first 1,024K of memory address space. The OS/2 and Unix operating systems use the same hardware but in ways that DOS cannot. They do not have this memory-range limitation.

Having pointers that specify where the processor can find programs to handle various events means that one can easily alter the way in which any particular kind of event is handled. One merely has to run a program that will establish itself in memory and then run every time a particular event occurs. We call this a *terminate-and-stay-resident* (TSR) program.

THE PLAYERS

All programs that are running in the computer must be in the computer's "system memory." That is memory whose addresses are between 0 and 1024k.

The first 640k addresses are used only for random access memory (RAM) and hold programs and data that change. The last 128k addresses are reserved for read only memory (ROM) which contain unchanging programs. These ROM programs are the most fundamental parts of the Basic Input-Output System (BIOS) program. This includes the default Interrupt Service Routines.

From 640k to 896k is a mixture of ROM and RAM used for a variety of purposes. Video display adapters live here. So do option ROMs.

The lowest addresses are used by DOS and the BIOS for interrupt vectors and tables of data about the system.

THE ACTION

(1) Normally the computer executes a program one instruction at at time from successive memory locations.

(2) When an "interrupting event" occurs, the computer is forced to stop what it is doing. It saves "its place" and looks for a special Interrupt Service Routine (ISR) program to handle the event.

(3) It finds the address of the ISR from the Interrupt Vector Table.

An event of type 5 is handled by ISR whose address is in location 5 in the Interrupt Vector Table.

(4) When the ISR is done, the computer goes back to the saved place and resumes executing the original program.

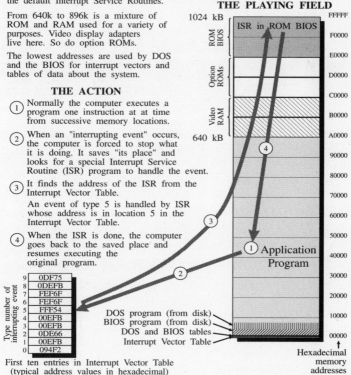

THE PLAYING FIELD

First ten entries in Interrupt Vector Table
(typical address values in hexadecimal)

Type number of interrupting event	
9	0DF75
8	0DEFB
7	FEF6F
6	FEF6F
5	FFF54
4	00EFB
3	0DE66
2	00EFB
1	00EFB
0	094F2

DOS program (from disk)
BIOS program (from disk)
DOS and BIOS tables
Interrupt Vector Table

Hexadecimal memory addresses

Figure 6-3: How interrupt vectors and interrupt service routines are used to handle events.

TECHNICAL NOTE Before the TSR program is first run, the interrupt vector table will contain entries pointing to various interrupt service routines (ISRs). When you first run a TSR program, it will examine certain entries in the interrupt vector table. It will then copy some of those numbers into a safe place inside itself. Next, it puts into those places in the interrupt vector table some other addresses. These are pointers to still other places within itself. At those places it has a mini-program.

Finally, the TSR tells DOS that it is through running, but it asks DOS to please leave it in memory and protect it from being overwritten by any other program. The name of that last step is "terminating, but staying resident." This is where these programs get the name TSR.

Now, if one of the events that this TSR has "hooked" occurs, the PC will stop whatever program it was running. It calls on the program pointed to by the entries in the interrupt vector table for that kind of event, expecting that to be the appropriate program to handle this kind of event. It will not invoke the original ISR, but will instead run the mini-program inside the TSR.

Like any other ISR, that mini-program can do whatever it wishes. When it is through, it does something a bit different. A normal ISR will end by telling the microprocessor to go back to running whatever program it was in when the interrupting event occurred. A TSR will instead turn around and call the ISR whose interrupt vector table address it stored and replaced.

6

At that point, the original ISR can do whatever it normally does. When it finishes it will tell the TSR to go back to what it was doing, and then the TSR will tell the main program to resume.

That is what happens when one TSR hooks itself between the normal ISR and the main programs. It is even possible for several TSRs to hook themselves together in that way. Called "chaining off an interrupt," this has proven to be a very powerful way to make our PCs do many useful things.

That may sound more complicated than it is. Figure 6-4 diagrams a single TSR hooked into one interrupt. Actual TSRs often hook many interrupts, and you may have several TSRs loaded in memory at once. That situation is much too complex to show easily in a diagram. Your PC manages amazingly well to keep track of what to do even in such complicated cases.

Intel allowed for up to 256 different kinds of interrupt. Since we don't need that many, some space in the interrupt vector table goes unused. DOS puts some of that "waste space" to use by storing address pointers that point to tables of information, instead of to interrupt-handling programs.

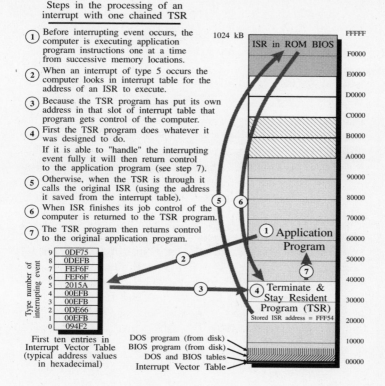

Steps in the processing of an interrupt with one chained TSR

① Before interrupting event occurs, the computer is executing application program instructions one at a time from successive memory locations.

② When an interrupt of type 5 occurs the computer looks in interrupt table for the address of an ISR to execute.

③ Because the TSR program has put its own address in that slot of interrupt table that program gets control of the computer.

④ First the TSR program does whatever it was designed to do.
If it is able to "handle" the interrupting event fully it will then return control to the application program (see step 7).

⑤ Otherwise, when the TSR is through it calls the original ISR (using the address it saved from the interrupt table).

⑥ When ISR finishes its job control of the computer is returned to the TSR program.

⑦ The TSR program then returns control to the original application program.

Type number of interrupting event	
9	0DF75
8	0DEFB
7	FEF6F
6	FEF6F
5	2015A
4	00EFB
3	00EFB
2	0DE66
1	00EFB
0	094F2

First ten entries in Interrupt Vector Table (typical address values in hexadecimal)

DOS program (from disk)
BIOS program (from disk)
DOS and BIOS tables
Interrupt Vector Table

Figure 6-4: Chained TSRs and the associated ISRs

Hard Disk Parameter Tables

DOS can talk to a vast variety of disk drives by using some stored parameters which describe key aspects of particular drives. The name of the main parameter table is, not surprisingly, the *Hard Disk Parameter Table*. Since most PC hard disk controllers can control either one or two hard disk drives, DOS' design provides for two hard disk parameter tables.

 You may think your PC has more than two hard disk drives. You may call them C:, D:, and E:, for example. These are what we call *volumes*. They act logically as if they were

separate disk drives, but in fact they are only different partitions of one, or at most two, physical hard disk drive(s). Down deep DOS knows which of these volumes belongs to each physical drive.

Partitioning a hard disk into volumes is one step in preparing it for use. We describe the details of how to do that in the next chapter. Later in this chapter, in the section "Evading the Logical Limits," we discuss one reason you may wish to create such volumes.

For interrupts number 41H and 46H, DOS uses the locations in the interrupt vector table that would normally point to ISRs to point instead to the first and second hard disk parameter tables. If both drives have the same dimensions, DOS can get away with only one hard disk parameter table simply by putting the same sets of numbers in both these locations in the interrupt vector table (see Figure 6-5).

(A number followed by the letter H means a number expressed in base sixteen, or hexadecimal notation. Translating to decimal, 41H becomes 4 times 16 plus 1, or the decimal number 65. Similarly 46H becomes 4 times 16 plus 6, or decimal 70. Since it takes four bytes to specify an address for an ISR program, the actual locations at which these particular interrupt vectors get stored are just four times these numbers, or 00104H [260 decimal] and 00118H [280 decimal].)

6

In the hard disk parameter tables, DOS stores the number of cylinders and heads (or surfaces) for each drive, as well as the numbers telling it how large an error the ECC (the error correcting codes stored with the data in each hard disk sector) can correct and how many times to retry reading a sector that it cannot read right the first time. DOS also stores some timeout values (to govern when the controller should give up trying certain operations that aren't succeeding) and a couple of very arcane numbers: the cylinder at which to start *reduced write-current* and that at which to start *write precompensation*.

 Each hard disk parameter table is 16 bytes long. Figure 6-6 shows its structure. Not all hard disk controllers will use every number in this structure, but since DOS can't tell which type of controller it's working with, it will fill in every number.

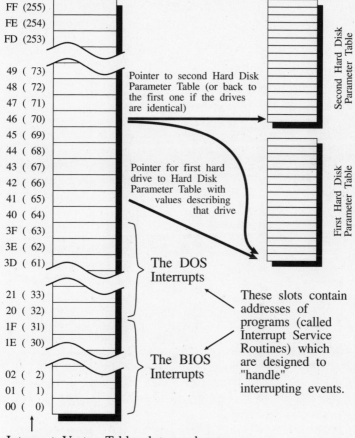

Interrupt Vector Table slot numbers, given in both of the common ways of specifying numbers: hexadecimal (decimal)

Figure 6-5: Pointers in the Interrupt Vector Table to the Hard Disk Parameter Tables

You can put the hard disk parameter tables almost anywhere in the first megabyte of the PC's memory-address space. The first 640K of that space is what we call *system RAM*, while the remaining portion (anywhere from 32K to 128K) holds the main BIOS ROM chips. Where the hard disk parameter tables lie depends upon the type of PC and disk controller you have.

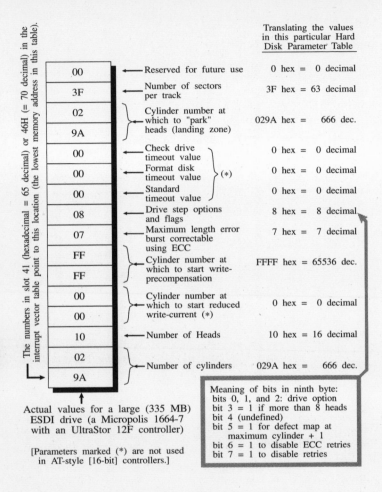

The numbers in slot 41 (hexadecimal = 65 decimal) or 46H (= 70 decimal) in the interrupt vector table point to this location (the lowest memory address in this table).

Translating the values in this particular Hard Disk Parameter Table

00	Reserved for future use	0 hex = 0 decimal
3F	Number of sectors per track	3F hex = 63 decimal
02 9A	Cylinder number at which to "park" heads (landing zone)	029A hex = 666 dec.
00	Check drive timeout value	0 hex = 0 decimal
00	Format disk timeout value (*)	0 hex = 0 decimal
00	Standard timeout value	0 hex = 0 decimal
08	Drive step options and flags	8 hex = 8 decimal
07	Maximum length error burst correctable using ECC	7 hex = 7 decimal
FF FF	Cylinder number at which to start write-precompensation	FFFF hex = 65536 dec.
00 00	Cylinder number at which to start reduced write-current (*)	0 hex = 0 decimal
10	Number of Heads	10 hex = 16 decimal
02 9A	Number of cylinders	029A hex = 666 dec.

Actual values for a large (335 MB) ESDI drive (a Micropolis 1664-7 with an UltraStor 12F controller)

[Parameters marked (*) are not used in AT-style [16-bit] controllers.]

Meaning of bits in ninth byte:
bits 0, 1, and 2: drive option
bit 3 = 1 if more than 8 heads
bit 4 (undefined)
bit 5 = 1 for defect map at maximum cylinder + 1
bit 6 = 1 to disable ECC retries
bit 7 = 1 to disable retries

Figure 6-6: Hard disk parameter table structure

The BIOS ROMs are the read-only memory chips that contain the most fundamental portions of the BIOS. These include the startup program the PC runs when it first is powered up and whenever it is reset.

Determining the Drive Types

DOS employs several methods to make sure its hard disk parameter tables get filled with the right numbers.

Original XT and similar older controller cards

The original XT hard disk controller had a couple of jumpers that you set to specify the kinds of first and second drives you were attaching. There were just four places for the jumper to go for the first drive and four for the second. Thus, this approach could accommodate only a very small set of choices.

When you boot your XT or XT clone, the initial program that gets control does many things, including reading the position of these jumpers. That tells it what numbers to put into the interrupt vector table to point to the right hard disk parameter tables.

The newer autoconfiguring XT controller cards

More modern XT hard disk controllers will work with a wide variety of drive types. When you low-level format the drive (see Chapter 7), you tell the controller what the drive's "dimensions" are (the number of heads, cylinders, and sectors per track), as well as the numbers for the cylinders at which to start write precompensation and reduced-write current. As a part of the low-level format, these controllers record all this information somewhere on the drive itself.

When you boot your PC, these types of controller eventually get charge of the computer. The controller then reads the dimensions of the first drive off the drive itself, builds the first hard disk parameter table, and puts its address into the interrupt vector table, repeating the process for a second drive if you have one.

AT and higher PCs

If you have an AT or higher-level PC, then as a standard part of the design your PC will have *CMOS memory*, which stores several facts about your PC, including the number and type of disk drives (both floppy and hard) that you have attached to your PC.

CMOS stands for "Complementary Metal Oxide Semiconductor" and refers to a process for making integrated circuits that require very little electric power to operate. The

CMOS chip in your AT is a small RAM chip made by use of that process. Like all other RAM, it would ordinarily lose any resident data when you turn off your PC, were it not for the small attached battery providing its power.

The CMOS stores the date and time of day, the amount of memory (RAM), the type of video display, and some other information about your computer's configuration. A crystal-controlled oscillator, powered by the same battery, constantly updates the CMOS record as to the date and time. This is why ATs, but not XTs (which do not have CMOS), usually "wake up" knowing the correct date and time.

When you turn on your AT, it may complain that the CMOS values are invalid, for one of two reasons: the date or time is invalid, or the configuration information (which includes the record of what drives you have) is invalid.

In either case, you need to run your computer's *setup* or *reference* program to correct those values. If the data in the CMOS are chronically wrong, you may need to replace its battery. The setup program may be on a disk (as it is for IBM PCs and PS/2s) or it may be located in the BIOS ROM chips on the motherboard (common for clones). In the latter case, you can run the setup program by pressing some special key combination.

6

To save space in the CMOS, it holds just a single number called a *drive type* for each drive. The computer stores the actual dimensions of that type of drive in the *AT Drive Type Table* in the BIOS ROM chips on the PC's motherboard.

The AT drive type table is a collection of possible hard disk parameter tables, one for each type of drive that the AT "knows about." This lets the startup program merely inspect the CMOS to see which types of drives are installed (by type number) and then put into the interrupt vector table the addresses of the appropriate places in the AT drive type table. The hard disk parameter tables are then ready to go.

> **TECHNICAL NOTE** The numbers in the interrupt table location for interrupt number 41H point to the first hard disk parameter table. Interrupt 46H points to the second table (if you have a second drive) or back to the first table (if your second drive is identical with the first).

AT drive type table

Since the AT drive type table is in ROM, you cannot ever change it (except by replacing that ROM chip, which is something most people never do). When IBM first introduced the AT, they had a modest table, listing only 14 different types of hard drive. Later IBM models and AT clones have extended the BIOS ROM AT drive type table substantially, some listing nearly a hundred different types of hard drive. This is still not enough.

Some newer hard disk controllers, especially those for RLL and ESDI drives, use perhaps the cleverest way to get around the limited number of drive types in the AT drive table. Their approach is essentially the same as that of the XT "autoconfiguring hard disk controllers" described above. These controllers expect you to tell your AT setup program that you have a type 1 drive installed (the smallest possible size).

This means that the BIOS startup program will initially put in the interrupt vector table's pointers to the hard disk parameter table in the BIOS ROM for a type 1 drive. Later in the boot process, during what is commonly called the *option ROM scan*, the hard disk controller's BIOS extension program will get control of the PC. At that time it reads the actual drive dimensions off the drive itself, creates in RAM a new hard disk parameter table(s), and repoints the interrupt vectors to the new table(s).

6

When you first start your PC, the startup program first finds
TECHNICAL out how much RAM the PC has, what disk drives, what
NOTE video display, and possibly some other information. Next it tests all those parts, at least briefly, a process called the *power on self test* (POST).

After the POST is complete, the startup program will look at some special places in memory address space to see if it can find any additional ROM BIOS chips containing extensions to the main ROM BIOS. (The possible places are at C0000H and every 2K after that, up to E0000H.)

If it finds any such ROM BIOS extensions, it will execute a program that must be in a standard place within such a BIOS. That program may do anything it likes. When it is through, it must give control of the computer back to the startup program, so the startup program can go on looking for other option ROMs and eventually try to load an operating system from a disk drive.

The BIOS extension ROM chips are most often located physically on plug-in cards (also called *option* or *add-in* cards). For example, if you have a VGA display card, it will have a ROM BIOS on it containing information on how to make its special hardware work. That information is in the form of mini-programs that your applications will use when they want to display data on the screen. The mini-program will usually announce its presence with a message on the screen, then do whatever it needs to do to make all future video messages display correctly.

Another common kind of ROM BIOS extension is that found on some disk controller cards. If it is an AT-style disk controller, it may simply have an extension to the main AT drive type table. The more flexible solution is the "autoconfiguring" controller, which can accommodate a disk drive with almost any dimensions by recording those dimensions on the drive itself. The initialization programs of some hard disk controller option ROMs put a message on the screen during the boot process; others do not.

SCSI hard drives

SCSI drives connect to a PC through one of three sorts of SCSI host adapters, each of which looks very different to DOS.

> **TECHNICAL NOTE** The distinction between these three types of adapter applies not only to SCSI host adapters but generally to any option cards you may have that control a DOS block device. Examples include optical disk drive controllers and some tape drive controllers.

Fundamentally, SCSI treats a hard disk as simply a large number of sectors, just like the high-level DOS "logical" view of a disk drive. This method requires only one number to point to a location on the drive — a logical sector number.

DOS and the BIOS talk to a hard disk on a much more physical level, using the cylinder, head, and physical sector numbers to specify a place on the drive. The three types of SCSI host adapters differ mainly in how they convert information on the hard drive from the BIOS's way of addressing to that used by the SCSI standard.

The simplest type of SCSI host adaptor to install and use is a *register-compatible* controller. It looks to the computer exactly like a standard AT hard disk controller for an MFM drive. This sort of host adapter may have an option ROM, but when that program gets control of the PC, it does not hook any of the interrupts.

 Since this sort of SCSI host adapter presents the full appearance of a standard AT hard disk controller, the PC can and does give commands to it exactly as if it were talking to an MFM controller. However, the adaptor differs from the standard AT controllers in that it doesn't have to make the drives it controls look like any of the drives in the AT drive type table. To accomplish this, it must be an autoconfiguring controller and build its own Hard Disk Parameter Table during the option ROM scan portion of the boot process, instead of using the AT drive type table entries.

The most common SCSI host adapters are not register compatible, but they are "INT 13 compatible." These controllers have an option ROM that repoints the INT 13 entry in the interrupt vector table to a program within itself. Thus it does not use the BIOS program in the motherboard ROM of an AT.

 This sort of SCSI host adapter presents the computer with a fictitious drive having some convenient number of cylinders, heads, and physical sectors per track. It then translates all INT 13 requests into a logical sector number and sends those translated requests on to the SCSI slave adapter. The slave adapter will, in turn, translate the logical sector numbers back into real cylinder, head, and physical sector numbers using the actual dimensions of the drive. (Figure 6-8 shows an example of sector translation.)

The third variety of SCSI host adapter is neither register nor INT 13 compatible with the standard AT hard disk controller design. To use an adapter of this sort for hard disk access requires an *installable device driver*. This driver is a program that may be in the option ROM on the host adapter, or it may get loaded into RAM off the boot disk.

The purpose of any installable device driver is to replace a low-level part of DOS. In this it resembles many TSR programs, but it hooks itself into DOS in a different way.

 DOS includes two interrupts for accessing the disk at the "logical" level. They are INT 25H (for reading a sector) and INT 26H (for writing). Strangely enough, DOS does not use them. Any other program may use them, in which case it will get the same result DOS gets by its different strategy.

The higher-level part of DOS (or an external program) does this in order to be able to get at a spot on the disk by specifying only the logical sector number. The DOS resident block device driver normally converts such requests into ones using the actual physical addresses (cylinder, head, and physical sector numbers). Finally that driver calls on the BIOS through INT 13 to do the actual disk access.

DOS gets to the device driver by an absolute call to an address known to itself. Changing any of the entries in the interrupt table (*e.g.*, those for INT 25H or INT 26H) will *not* allow one to interfere with this action.

The lower-level part of DOS maintains a linked list of device drivers. That means that DOS holds the address of the first one, then each driver points to the next one in the chain. There is a standard way of inserting character devices at the head of the chain and block devices at the end. There is no standard way to insert a block device except at the end.

Since DOS searches the chain in order looking for a device driver that can perform whatever task it has to do, an installed character device can easily supersede a resident one. An installed block device normally cannot. Anyone wishing to replace the DOS resident block device must learn how to do some very non-standard things.

Makers of the third kind of SCSI host adapter created installable device drivers that insert themselves in front of the normal DOS resident block device driver (see Figure 6-7). They usually also hook INT 13H so that they can respond to requests for disk service at that level too.

Since a SCSI controller looks at a disk as a one-dimensional string of sectors, its special block device driver has a very easy task at the INT 25H or INT 26H level. It merely must add some offset to the DOS logical sector number to get its sector number. When it intercepts an INT 13H BIOS call it must do the inverse of the job normally done by the DOS resident block device, this time converting from a 3-dimensional disk address back into a one-dimensional one.

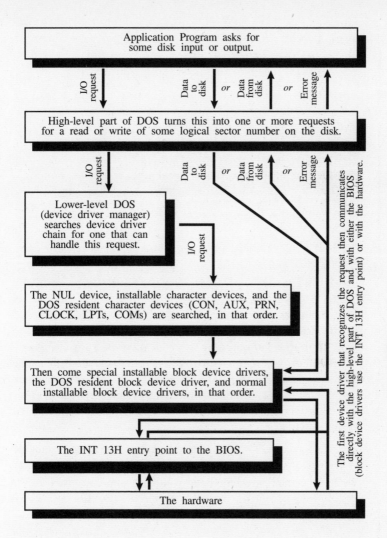

Figure 6-7: An installable device driver replacing a low-level part of DOS

Physical Size Limits Under DOS

Whenever a program wishes to have some information read from or written to the disk, that request must eventually get translated down to the physical level. It may start as a request for a file, which DOS may translate to accessing some particular cluster or logical sector on the drive. Eventually, before the hardware can be commanded to do the needed read or write, the address must be resolved to a particular cylinder and head (thus specifying one track) and then to the particular sector on that track.

> ▌ `0110 0110`
> ▌ **TECHNICAL** The highest level part of DOS does this translation by
> ▌ **NOTE** calling a device driver (either the resident block device or
> ▌ an installed replacement). In either case, the called
> program translates the request to a physical address and then calls
> the BIOS through INT 13, subfunction 5 or 6. (See Figure 6-7.)
>
> The numbers that this device driver uses to do this translation are
> the dimensions of the drive. The device driver learns those di-
> mensions at boot time by another call to INT 13, this time to
> subfunction 8.

The interrupt call that DOS uses to give the translated information to the BIOS (INT 13) has some severe limits on the size of the numbers it can accept for the physical address components. It only allows the use of a 10-bit binary number to specify the cylinder number. It limits head numbers to 4 bits and sector numbers to 6 bits. This means you can have cylinder numbers from 0 to 1,023 $(1,023 = 2^{10} - 1)$, heads from 0 to 15 $(15 = 2^4 - 1)$, and sectors from 1 to 63 $(63 = 2^6 - 1)$. Anything beyond that could perfectly well exist, but you couldn't get information about it to the hard disk controller through the BIOS.

> ▌ `0110 0110`
> ▌ **TECHNICAL** Actually the head number is only *supposed* to be kept in the
> ▌ **NOTE** range 0 to 15. The places in DOS and the BIOS that hold
> ▌ the actual maximum head number can take numbers up to
> 255. Nothing in DOS or the BIOS checks to see if the number of
> heads is less than 16; the documentation just says it is *supposed* to
> be. This is an important "loophole" in what would otherwise be a
> painfully tight set of size restrictions even with the best of modern
> "DOS limit evasion" techniques. You will hear more about this
> loophole shortly.

When PCs were new, these limits did not seem a particularly severe restraint. With the latest, largest hard drives, they are posi- tively unacceptable. Though we can evade these limits using clever techniques, doing so has some serious consequences. These are discussed in the section "Evading the Physical Limits" a bit further on in this chapter. First, we would like to describe another famous limit, as well as how to evade it.

Logical Size Limits

Prior to DOS 4, DOS could not handle a hard disk larger than 32 megabytes.

DOS at its higher levels looks at the disk drive as simply a long string of sectors. It numbers those sectors, starting at 1. This is the "logical" view of the disk drive. Later, when DOS gets ready to command the hardware to read or write something, it must translate each logical sector number into a real, physical address (head, cylinder, and physical sector).

The higher levels of DOS have a designed-in limit on the number representing the *logical* sectors. There is no reason that this limit on the disk's size is either smaller or larger than the limit imposed by the allowable sizes for the physical address numbers.

In all versions of DOS before 4.0, the logical sector number had to fit into a 16-bit number. This meant there could be no more than $65,536$ (2^{16}) sectors in a DOS-addressable portion of a disk drive.

The standard size for sectors under DOS is 512 bytes. This size times the maximum number of sectors is 32 MB, which was the maximum storage capacity that DOS could address before version 4.0.

DOS 4.0 raised the size limit on the sector number. Instead of only a 16-bit number, the sector size can now be a 32-bit number (up to $4,294,967,296$). This implies a maximum disk size, with the standard 512 byte sectors, of 2 TB (2 terrabytes, which is 2 mega-megabytes, or approximately 2.2 million, million bytes). That seems like a large enough limit — for now!

| 0110 0110 |
| TECHNICAL |
| NOTE |

Versions of DOS before 4.0 used a 16-bit register to hold the logical sector number. The new method, under DOS 4, is to use a pointer to a table holding a 32-bit logical sector number.

This is the maximum *logical* size to a disk under DOS. The *physical* limits are more binding, even with DOS 4. The limit to the size of

6

a disk, based on the official BIOS limits on the physical addressing, is just over 500 MB. Even when one realizes that there is a loophole in the official size description and takes full advantage of it, the maximum physical size of a DOS disk is just a bit over 8 GB. Either way, it is a far smaller limit than the new DOS 4.0 logical size limit.

Years ago, long before DOS 4.0, people began to want to exceed the 32-MB storage capacity. Various people found a variety of ways around this limit. Using one of these non-standard methods may bring on some unpalatable consequences.

Evading the Logical Limits

If you want to use a disk larger than 32 MB, you could simply upgrade to DOS 4.0. Even before we had that option, there were two other techniques in common use: larger sectors and disk partitioning.

Large sectors

Before DOS 4.0, you couldn't have more than 65,536 sectors in a DOS-addressable disk. One way to handle a disk with a storage capacity greater than 32 MB without violating that limit is simply to make each sector larger than 512 bytes. DOS allows you to do this but requires some help. The sector size can vary, but it is customary to use an integer multiple of 512 bytes. So people have used sector sizes of 1,024 bytes, 1,536 bytes, 2,048 bytes, and all the way up to 8,192 bytes.

One serious consequence of this strategy is a potential loss in efficiency in the use of your disk space. Any file takes up at least one sector, and perhaps several sectors (if the cluster size is several sectors). This is true no matter how small the file. If you store many tiny files on a disk with very large sectors, you may waste much of the disk drive's space. Each of those tiny files has a cluster all to itself. The space in each cluster after the end of the file it holds is called *slack space*. Large sectors (and thus large clusters) make for lots of slack space.

The other important consequence is that you must use some non-DOS program to set the sector size to your chosen non-standard value. That makes your computer operate just a bit less compatibly. That does not *often* cause any problems, but it can.

Wyse Technology introduced a way for DOS to deal with disk drives larger than 32 MB. They did this first in their Version 3.21 of MS-DOS. Their technique was simply to allow the FORMAT program to write larger sectors. They used the same technique with Version 3.3. At Version 4.0, they changed to the IBM- and Microsoft-blessed method for dealing with large disk partitions, using only standard 512 byte sectors.

The sector size is stored in the boot record on any disks formatted by recent versions of DOS. Thus, any version of Wyse's MS-DOS after 3.21 can recognize their large sector size way of dealing with large disks and access them successfully. Other manufacturer's MS-DOS versions may not.

The actual physical sectors created by the hard disk controller continue to have exactly 512 data bytes in them. These larger apparent sector sizes are simply logical sections created out of smaller physical sectors.

Compaq introduced its special technique for dealing with large disk partitions starting with its version 3.31 of MS-DOS. They did not say so at the time, but later it came out that they had developed their method in close consultation with Microsoft. The technique they used was the same one used later by IBM and Microsoft starting with PC-DOS and MS-DOS, Version 4.0.

If you use some special driver program to modify DOS by setting up a larger than normal sector size, you run a risk. If you lose that driver program, you will be unable to access the data on your hard drives. Also, any such non-DOS solution carries with it the potential for a nasty interaction with some DOS application program that expects your operating system to be pure DOS.

Disk partitions

The other common way to evade the 32 MB limit is to break up a larger hard drive into several virtual, or logical, drives, each less than 32 MB in total capacity. DOS version 3.3 enabled you to do this in a Microsoft- and IBM-blessed manner. Before that, you could evade the limit only by using some additional software to augment the basic DOS procedures.

What are the consequences of logical drives? Since your disk drive is initially all one volume, when you add files to it they go into whatever space is available. Once you divide it into partitions, those boundaries are not flexible. Thus, if you fill one partition, you cannot automatically "borrow" space from another partition. This means you must do a bit more thoughtful management of what goes into each partition.

This is not necessarily all bad. First, it may force you to organize your files better. Second, it can make your disk work faster, because you have the files and the FAT tables and directories that refer to them in a partition that spans only a few cylinders, letting DOS access them more quickly.

This approach is inappropriate if, for example, you bought a large hard drive to have some place to put data files larger than 32 MB. In this case, the large sector approach makes sense, as does the use of a single huge partition under DOS 4.0. Either way, you can address the whole disk as a single partition.

If you partition your disk using a third party add-on software solution, you can access the first partition of any physical drive using only DOS. You can access the rest only when you have that special driver installed on top of DOS. If you use DOS 3.3 or later to partition your disk, you will not have this problem.

6

 Some popular DOS add-on programs that can do this partitioning are *Disk Manager* from On Track Software, *SpeedStor* from Storage Dimensions, the Priam EVDR.SYS driver, and *Vfeature Deluxe* from Golden Bow Software. You can also use the latter program to alter the sector size or even to make two physical drives appear as if they were one even larger drive.

DOS 3.3 has been available a long time, and most of its bugs have been expunged or techniques for dealing with them are well known. Thus it is no longer appropriate to use third-party DOS add-on programs to partition new hard disks. Still, many people continue to do so, out of habit more than anything else. They make the systems they build needlessly dependent upon those device drivers. If you have DOS 3.3 and your system uses one of those device drivers, you may wish to make some changes.

Regardless of what method you use to partition a disk, you must do so at the time the disk is formatted. We provide the details on how to do this in the next chapter, which also describes what is involved if you decide to change from a third-party solution to one of the pure DOS solutions.

Evading the Physical Limits

The physical limits on disk size are harder to get around. You can choose from several methods.

The pure software evasion technique

On Track Software, maker of the *Disk Manager* disk partitioning software, has a companion product called *SWBIOS*. It can only be used on AT compatibles (PCs using the 80286 processor chip) with a hard disk controller that is "register compatible" with the Western Digital controller that IBM used with their original PC-AT. (This is the highest possible level of compatibility, meaning essentially the hardware looks so much like Western Digital's that the computer really cannot tell the difference.)

SWBIOS is a program that adds itself to DOS. *Disk Manager* knows how to find and use it instead of the BIOS Interrupt 13H program for reading or writing to the hard disk. The Western Digital controller design allows up to 12 bits for the cylinder number, instead of the 10 bits allowed for by INT 13H. Thus this program in effect modifies the BIOS limit from only permitting cylinders numbered 0 to 1023 to permitting them in the range 0 to 4095. It does nothing to evade the BIOS (INT 13H) limits on head and sector numbers.

This solution works only if you are using *Disk Manager* to partition your hard disk. It also is a bit peculiar in that you must read the program from your disk. But once it is read and linked into DOS and Disk Manager, it changes how DOS reads the disk. The engineers at On Track had to be very clever to make it possible to read the disk in one way to find *SWBIOS* and then in another way to use it.

As often happens when someone is that clever, some other software turns out to be incompatible with it. Shortly after Microsoft's *Windows*, version 3.0 started shipping, people reported that they were losing all the data on their hard disks. The problem turned out to be an unfortunate interaction between On Track's clever software and the version of *SMARTDRV.SYS* that shipped with *Windows* 3.0.

In time, vendors can work out all such incompatibilities with patches to one or the other program. The more dependable method of evading these limits is to use a specially built hard disk controller.

Sector mapping

Remember that DOS at its highest levels views a disk as simply a long string of sectors into which it can store information. Only as it gets ready to ask the BIOS to command the drive to do the actual disk access does it convert the logical sector number into a physical cylinder, head, and sector set of numbers.

The hard disk controller can do something similar in reverse. It can take all the disk space on the actual physical disk drive and convert it to a single long list of sectors. Then it can convert a location in that list back into a fictitious cylinder, head, and sector address that it presents to DOS. We call this *head and sector translation* or *sector mapping*.

> **TECHNICAL NOTE**
>
> For example, suppose you have a drive that in its physical reality has 7 heads, 1,781 cylinders, and 54 sectors per track. (These are the dimensions of the Micropolis 1664-7 ESDI drive.) Multiplying this out, we see that there are a total of 673,218 sectors. (With each sector holding 512 bytes, and remembering that a megabyte is 1,024K or 1,048,576 bytes, this becomes a 328.7 MB disk drive, formatted capacity.)
>
> Suppose the hard disk controller pretended to DOS that the drive it was controlling had the maximum DOS legal values of 16 heads and 63 sectors per track. This would make it appear to have 16 times 63 or 1,008 sectors per cylinder. That, in turn, would imply that the fictitious disk drive would have only 667 and a fraction cylinders, which is well within the DOS limit of 1,024 cylinders.
>
> The mapping would actually be done as follows: The first 54 sectors would be put on the first track (cylinder 0, head 0). The next 9 sectors, which DOS thinks are still on that same track, would instead be put on the next track (cylinder 0, head 1). What DOS thinks of as the second track (its cylinder 0, head 1) would be started on cylinder 0, head 1 (the first 45 sectors), and would finish 18 sectors into cylinder 0, head 2. And so on. See Figure 6-8.

6

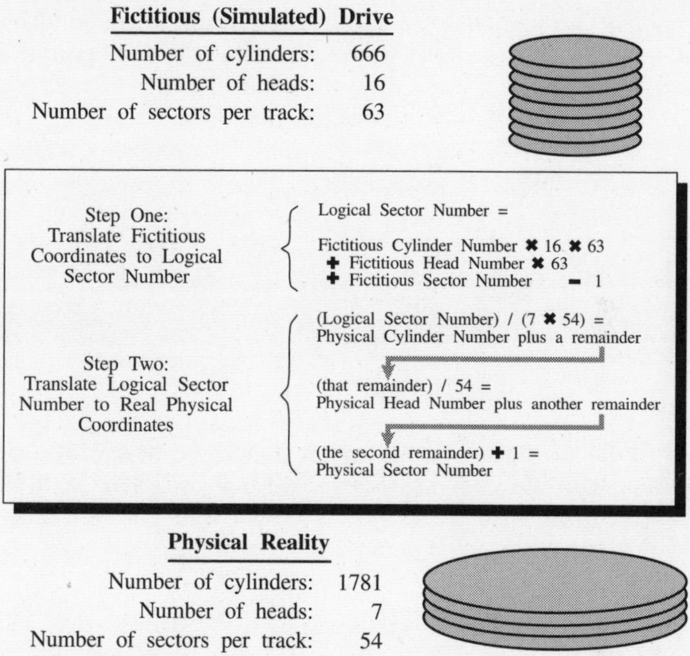

Fictitious (Simulated) Drive

Number of cylinders:	666
Number of heads:	16
Number of sectors per track:	63

Step One:
Translate Fictitious
Coordinates to Logical
Sector Number

Logical Sector Number =

Fictitious Cylinder Number **✖** 16 **✖** 63
✚ Fictitious Head Number **✖** 63
✚ Fictitious Sector Number **━** 1

Step Two:
Translate Logical Sector
Number to Real Physical
Coordinates

(Logical Sector Number) / (7 **✖** 54) =
Physical Cylinder Number plus a remainder

(that remainder) / 54 =
Physical Head Number plus another remainder

(the second remainder) **✚** 1 =
Physical Sector Number

Physical Reality

Number of cylinders:	1781
Number of heads:	7
Number of sectors per track:	54

6

Figure 6-8: Head and sector translation example

Sector translation mapping appeared in hard disk controllers in another context, before evading the physical limits was an issue. Some early software written for the PC "knew" that all disk drives had 17 sectors per track (as MFM drives do). These programs would not operate correctly with RLL drives, which have about 26 sectors per track. One solution was for the hard disk controller manufacturers to put in sector mapping.

TECHNICAL NOTE For this purpose they make the controller fool DOS in a direction opposite to that in the previous example. Specifically, these controllers present to DOS a fictitious MFM drive with 17 sectors per track, and therefore about half again as many tracks as the real drive has. That might be by pretending the drive had half again as many heads as it really had, or half again as many cylinders. As long as both those numbers stayed below the DOS limits, it would not matter which way the controller designer chose to make her controller "lie."

The advantage of having your hard disk controller lie in this manner is that your hard disk will appear to be a more standard, DOS-addressable disk. The drawback is that neither DOS nor any other program knows what the real disk dimensions are. For most of what DOS and DOS applications do, that does not matter. One case where it does matter is with programs like *SpinRite*. Without real numbers for the drive dimensions, they simply cannot deliver all the benefits for which they were designed.

Other controller mapping strategies

Controllers are sometimes designed to do other kinds of mappings for a variety of reasons, one of which is to make the drive appear to have fewer defects than it really does. Another reason is to cram more data into less space.

The UltraStor 12F is a typical modern ESDI controller (and a good choice to use with the Micropolis drive mentioned above). When you use it to do a low-level format, it will present you with many options.

One choice you have is whether to request Head Skewing. That adjusts the sector numbers from one track or cylinder to the adjacent ones, to allow for the time involved in head switching or in moving the heads from cylinder to cylinder. (See Figure 5-11.)

Spare Sector, another option, means that the controller will format the tracks of the drive with 55 sectors, but if all the sectors are good it will only use the first 54. If any one sector on a track is bad, that one will be marked as such and ignored. The remaining sectors on that track will then have their physical sector numbers decreased by one (assuming 1:1 sector interleave).

That same controller also offers four choices for Sector Mapping: to make it present 17, 32, or 63 sectors per track, or the real number, which for the Micropolis 1664-7 drive is 54 sectors per track.

The reason for offering 17 sectors is clear: to make the drive appear to be a normal MFM drive. The reason for offering 63 sectors per track is also clear: That is the maximum number of sectors per track allowed according to the INT 13 design. Offering no translation allows programs access to the real, physical drive. The one strange option is 32 sectors per track. It turns out that some versions of DOS have an FDISK program that cannot deal with more than 32 sectors per track and so this option allows the maximum number of sectors that those versions of DOS can handle.

For drives with a capacity of over 500 MB, you must use Track Mapping, the next option, with DOS. To see where 500 MB comes from, multiply the official BIOS maximum number of heads (16) by the maximum number of tracks (1,024) and sectors per track (63). This ought to be the absolute maximum size drive DOS could handle, which works out to be just over 500 MB (or more like about 528 million bytes). Since DOS and the BIOS really can handle head numbers from zero all the way up to 255, this limit is artificially low. The real limit is just over 8 GB (gigabytes or kilo-megabytes). Track Mapping takes advantage of this loophole in the BIOS limits on disk size by artificially increasing the maximum head number enough to keep both sector and cylinder numbers in bounds even for very large drives.

Finally, the UltraStor 12F offers the option of 1,024 Cylinder Truncation, which merely means asking the controller to ignore any cylinders the drive may have past number 1,023. Using this option will make the controller present an acceptable drive to the BIOS, but at the cost of not using a part of the drive capacity.

SCSI drives do something even a bit more complex. They have a special extra pointer in each sector. If a given sector is good, that pointer will not be used. If it has some defect, this pointer will show where to find an alternate sector. SCSI drives have several spare tracks and may have some spare sectors on each track. This approach permits SCSI drives to appear to DOS as if they are perfect. CHKDSK, for example, will report no bad sectors at all for such a drive.

Finally, there is zone bit recording. This technique was mentioned in the last chapter as one used in some SCSI and IDE drives and sometimes on hard cards to cram as many bytes on the drive as possible. Here the number of sectors per track is not constant from cylinder to cylinder. This *mandates* having the controller lie to DOS, since everything in DOS assumes that whatever the number of sectors per track, at least it will be a constant for any one drive. Thus, for these drives the controller must always do head and sector translation.

Error Messages

We discussed earlier the several layers of programs in our PCs. Requests for action filter down from the top level and finally, at the bottom, get turned into commands to hardware. The results of those actions often mean that information will be passed back up the same chain in reverse order (see Figure 6-9). This is how the system returns an error message, among other things. Any layer can generate an error messages if it fails to understand the request it got from above. An error message also results if the hardware fails to operate correctly.

Each level of program can react to an error message in several ways: It can ignore the message; it can decide to pose its request again in hopes that this time it might succeed; or it can decide to try something different.

The actions we care most about in this book are requests to the hard disk drive (or to its controller) to read or write data on the disk. There are many ways that these processes can fail. For each failure mode, there is an error message that the controller will send to the BIOS, which in turn will send it on to DOS, which may or may not send it on to you or your application program.

6

> `0110 0110`
> **TECHNICAL NOTE**
> For example, the drive may be asked to position the heads over a particular cylinder ("seek" to that cylinder). The controller may attempt this and then find that it was unsuccessful. The usual recovery procedure from this error is to "recalibrate" the drive (seek to cylinder 0) and then try again to seek to the desired cylinder.

The controller may be asked to read a particular sector. Two kinds of error can occur in this process. One is that the sector header cannot be found or, if found, its CRC (cyclical redundancy checksum) may be invalid. That means it is not possible to be sure that you are where you thought you were on the drive. Again, a recalibration followed by a retry is an appropriate response.

The other kind of error in reading is that the controller may find the sector header, but the data it read may turn out to be inconsistent with the ECC (error correction codes) that were also read. This case further subdivides, depending upon whether the ECC seem adequate to correct the data or not. Either way, a retry may be the simplest way to deal with this problem. At some point, if the ECC are adequate, it may be easier (and quicker) to use them to correct the data. If the controller uses the ECC, it must pass along those corrected data with a message saying that it had to use ECC.

If the program receiving an error message chooses simply to repeat its request, when does it stop retrying? Most often the BIOS will ask the hard disk controller to retry several times to read a sector that it could not find. Then, if it must, the BIOS will accept defeat and tell DOS that it didn't find the sector. At this point DOS may ask the BIOS to ask the controller to try again. Then another round of retries starts. Since DOS may make that request of the BIOS several times, and each time the BIOS may force the controller to try again several times, the total number of retries quickly escalates to a large number. Hundreds of retries are not unusual.

Finally, DOS may decide to accept defeat. Two things may happen next. Most of the time DOS will announce this fact with a brief message and then give its infamous choice, "Abort, Retry, or Ignore." Or, if the request for that sector's data came from a modern, sophisticated application program, it may intercept DOS's message of defeat and do whatever that program's designers thought appropriate. They could even ask DOS to try again, thus forcing several hundred more retries.

There is one case where DOS is neither so diligent nor so informative. That is when the ECC seem adequate for reconstructing data initially read incorrectly. Then no retries are called for. DOS simply accepts the reconstructed data as gospel truth, without informing the application to which it delivers the data about the original error.

This is most unfortunate. It hides from us the impending doom, only revealing it when a disaster is already upon us. Fortunately even a DOS application can "go behind DOS" and intercept the error messages from the disk controller before they get masked.

| | This is done, simply enough, by putting some code into the DOS application that loads an address inside itself into the interrupt vector table in the location for Interrupt 13H (INT 13H). Then whenever DOS tries to ask the BIOS to access the disk drive, it will ask the special bit of code in your application to do the job. |

TECHNICAL NOTE

Rather than performing the task, all the program has to do is call on the BIOS at whatever address the BIOS had originally inserted into the interrupt vector table at those locations.

Why get in the way if you aren't going to do anything but pass along the request? Because that puts your program in the path along which the system returns the "announcement" of the results of that request to the higher-level programs. Your program will get those results before DOS has a chance to receive and perhaps ignore them. See Figure 6-9.

SpinRite is one such program. In this way it can see any place on the disk where there is a struggle to get data back. It can then move these reconstructed data to some safer place before the problems become insurmountable.

This completes our discussion of the essential facts about how MS-DOS treats hard disks. In the next chapter, we focus on how to prepare a hard disk for use under DOS, and to a lesser extent, under the Unix, OS/2, and Novell operating systems.

6

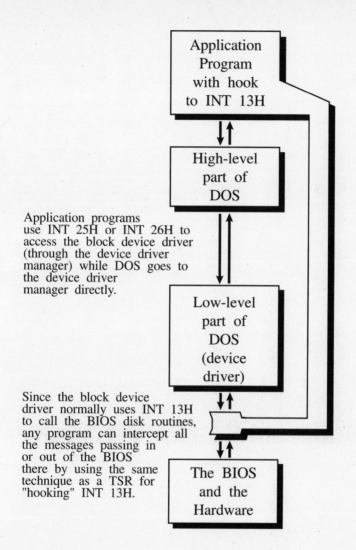

Application programs use INT 25H or INT 26H to access the block device driver (through the device driver manager) while DOS goes to the device driver manager directly.

Since the block device driver normally uses INT 13H to call the BIOS disk routines, any program can intercept all the messages passing in or out of the BIOS there by using the same technique as a TSR for "hooking" INT 13H.

Figure 6-9: Passing disk service requests, data, and error messages through the program layers with an application hooked into INT 13

6

Chapter 7

Preparing a Disk to Store Information

You now know how hard disks work and how MS-DOS works with them. Before any hard disk can work with DOS, though, you need to prepare it. As it comes from the factory, a hard disk is incapable of storing any information, since it lacks any organizing magnetic marks on the platter surfaces. In this chapter, you will learn what those essential marks are and the process of putting them on the disk.

Remember that the controller looks for sectors of information. It expects each sector to be complete with sector headers containing address information and a valid CRC (cyclical redundancy checksum), plus a data area and the corresponding ECC (error correction codes). It anticipates that this information will be encoded according to its particular data-encoding method *e.g.*, MFM, RLL, or ARLL. But before the drive is "properly introduced" to the controller, no such information exists on the disk.

The first job in preparing a hard disk is to get the controller to record the skeleton of the data patterns for which it will look. We call this a *physical format* (or a *low-level format*). After the drive has the necessary structure into which to store information, you must take it through *partitioning* and *logical* (or *high-level*) *formatting* to make it usable with DOS.

To understand the three-level process of preparing a hard disk, consider this analogy: A new hard drive is much like a brand new parking lot — each has a vast expanse of potential storage space. In a parking lot, you first put down marks to show people where to park their cars, analogous to providing a physical format on the disk. Then, you may divide the lot with fences to separate different groups of drivers, such as customers and employees, just as you partition a hard disk. Next, you might provide a valet parking service (just as DOS "parks" our files on disk), which requires a place to keep keys, along with a "directory" of their owners' names and the stall number where each car is parked, much like the directory created by a high-level format. In this way you can know both which stalls are empty and where to find each person's car.

While most cars are about the same size, files on your disk may be large or small. If we stretch the analogy a bit to fit our discussion, we can assume that sometimes a group of cars will come together, and the leader of the group will specify when the whole group will leave. The valet parking directory will show the location of only the group leader's car. Some other table showing which spaces are available and which are occupied will indicate which cars are in which groups. Figure 7-1 shows a whimsical representation of this analogy.

Low-Level Formatting

7

There are at least three ways to impose a low-level format on a hard disk, but whichever of these options you choose, in the end they amount to the same thing. Some controllers come with a disk that has a low-level formatting program on it. (IBM included this program for its PCs on an Advanced Diagnostic disk shipped with the Technical Reference Manual for each model.) Some controllers use a program that is permanently on the card in its BIOS extension ROM (read-only memory) chip. You also might use some third-party disk setup software like *Disk Manager* or *SpeedStor*. Each of these three methods simply asks the controller to place a physical format pattern on the disk.

To do so, the controller moves the head assembly from the innermost cylinder to the outermost, one cylinder at a time. At each cylinder position, it switches on one head at a time, stepping through all the heads before going on to the next cylinder position.

For each cylinder and head, it records a full track of information in the format it will need to find whenever it reads or writes additional data.

Figure 7-1: An analogy to how data is stored on a hard disk

> **TECHNICAL NOTE** By starting the low-level formatting at the inside cylinder, the controller provides the maximum amount of time before it gets to the outer cylinders, where the most critical data on your drive lies. Thus, if you discover part way through that you really did not want to format your drive, you can stop the process in time to save some of your data. (Redoing a low-level format wipes out all your data.)
>
> The original hard disk controllers for PCs did their low-level formatting in precisely the opposite manner, wiping out the most critical data immediately. The controller makers changed this after too many users came to too much grief and suffered too many near heart attacks. Be glad if you have a modern hard disk controller. Consider getting one if you don't.

This low-level format is done one track at a time. Usually you can command the controller to do this for a single track, and sometimes for the whole drive. Some third-party software (*e.g.*, *Disk Manager*) will allow you to do it for a range of cylinders as well. This just means they repeat the command for the controller to format a track until all the heads over the specified range of cylinders are formatted.

A very important point to remember is that *only* at the time of this low-level format does the controller write the sector headers. It also writes the data sections of the sectors (filling them with some dummy data and the corresponding ECC). The sector headers are, of course, read to find where to read or write data, but those headers are never again rewritten.

Only the controller can do it

Only the controller can actually format the disk at this level, which means that the controller's design dictates the way the format is carried out. Each controller design accomplishes low-level formatting differently. (If a controller lacks the ability to perform low-level formatting, then no program can make it do it.)

> **TECHNICAL NOTE** All floppy disk controllers, on the other hand, perform low-level formatting in the same way (for disks of that size and capacity). In part this is because there is only one standard set of integrated circuit chips used in the design of floppy disk controllers. More important, though, it reflects our need to be able

to take a disk formatted on one PC and use it on any other. Since hard disks stay put, they do not share this requirement.

Some hard disks are removable. They work with only those PCs that have the same special hardware in them. One cannot take, for example, a Tandon AdPac removable disk pack and insert it into a MegaDrive system and expect it to work.

Different controllers sometimes put the head, cylinder, and physical sector numbers into the sector headers in varying order. They may further differ on their choice of the formula by which they compute ECC, on where they put the bad sector flag, and on any other information they may put in the sector header. Finally, even for controllers of the same nominal sort (*e.g.*, RLL), they also may differ on precisely how they encode data. The result of all this individuality is that you must redo the low-level format on a drive each time you attach it to a new controller.

TECHNICAL NOTE At least you must do so each time you attach it to a new *kind* of hard disk controller. Naturally all the Tandon AdPac controllers, for example, must be sufficiently alike so that you can switch AdPac disk packs between them successfully. Being able to move data that way is the main selling point for any removable hard drive. Thus this is a crucial limitation on the design of their controllers. Other makers, without those restraints, seem to change their low-level format patterns nearly every time they introduce a new model, and sometimes more often.

An exception to this generalization, PerStor hard disk controllers are unusual in that they store information with twice the density of normal MFM drives (even more densely than RLL drives). They number their physical sectors starting with zero (instead of one, as the BIOS normally expects), then hide this fact from the BIOS.

These tricks enable a PerStor controller to recognize the low-level format of a drive formatted by any other PerStor controller. You even can move a drive formatted on a PerStor XT controller to a PerStor AT controller.

Because they are so unusual, you may have to inform *SpinRite* if you are using it on a PerStor controller. You do this with a special command-line parameter. Then *SpinRite* will recognize the controller's quirks and deal with it accordingly. (You may be able to run *SpinRite* without this special command-line parameter, but if it complains in any way, try it again with the special parameter.)

Please understand: Redoing the low-level format on a hard drive utterly destroys previously recorded data. (The most insidious computer viruses order the hard disk controller to redo the low-level format on one or all of your hard drives.)

> **0110 0110**
> **TECHNICAL NOTE** Some data recovery specialists claim to be able to detect the residual magnetism in the disk surface. They say they can (at least sometimes) recover data even after they have been written over, whether by a low-level format or by a simple copying of one file on top of another. This possibility worries the government enough that when national security is at stake, they specify that files should be erased by writing over them many times with many different (prescribed) data patterns. Still, for all normal purposes, once a file or a disk full of data gets written over, that information is gone for good.

Generally, DOS does *not* destroy data with its high-level, or logical, format (though some versions of DOS do.) This makes it possible to create utility programs that let you "unformat" (undo the high-level format) a drive. (More on this in the next chapter.)

SpinRite introduced the capability to re*do* the low-level format on a drive without destroying the data stored there. *This is not the same as* **un***doing the low-level format. SpinRite* refreshes the sector header information, without requiring you first to back up the data on the disk and afterward redo the disk partitioning and high-level format, as well as restore the backed-up data.

In essence, *SpinRite* does this by making a copy of the data on one track at time. Then it asks the controller to reformat just that one track. It tests the newly formatted track to be sure it can safely hold the data, and then puts the original data back. This is not really an exception to the rule that the low-level format wipes out the data. *SpinRite* simply keeps a copy long enough to replace it after the reformatting is complete. The data it replaces includes the DOS high-level format information, which lets you avoid both the reformatting and the backup/restore cycle.

Some weird alternate formats

While almost every hard disk controller has its own idiosyncratic approach to performing a low-level format, some take a weirder tack than others, preventing programs like *SpinRite* from redoing the low-level format.

Certain disk/controller combinations: Some manufacturers who ship controllers and drives already matched together put the low-level format on their drives at the factory, and do everything in their power to prevent anyone from redoing that low-level format. For these drive and controller combinations, it does not matter if a program like *SpeedStor* asks it to do a low-level format in preparation for the initial storage of data, or if *SpinRite* asks it to do so as a means of increasing data transfer rate or improving the integrity of data already stored; the controller simply will refuse to do the job. And if the controller won't do it for you, no one can.

> **TECHNICAL NOTE** One example of this is the *Hard Card* series of products from the Plus Development Corporation. Plus does two things that lead them to refuse to allow other programs to redo their low-level formats. One is zone recording, in which they put more sectors per track on the outer tracks than on the inner ones. The other is spare-sector mapping, in which they replace defective sectors with some otherwise unused sectors to make the drive appear to have no defects, at least when they ship it from the factory. They think these special strategies justify denying anyone but them the right to do a low-level format on their drives.

Most IDE and SCSI drives use similar strategies. They often also prevent any programs from redoing their low-level formats.

Another interesting and strange example is what Toshiba does on the hard drives in their laptop computers. They call it *head multiplexing*, a strategy they employ in order to fit the maximum data possible on some small hard drives and yet make them look to the computer as if they are standard MFM drives. They found they could put 34 sectors per track. That doubles the data on each track, but if they admitted to the BIOS what they had done, it would not see the drive as standard.

They solve that problem by making the controller do something special. When the BIOS tells it to read a particular sector number for a particular head number, the controller translates that requested location into a real location, by using the following translation rule: First, double the requested sector number and add one if the head number is odd to get the real sector number. Divide the requested head number by two and discard any remainder to get the real head number. For example, if you tell it to read sector 5 for head 0, it will actually read sector 10 for head 0. If you tell it to read sector 15 for head 1, it will actually read sector 31 for head 0.

The most unusual aspect of this is that it means that heads 0 and 1 share the top surface, instead of each head having a surface to itself. Head 0 gets every other sector on the track and head 1 gets the rest. This means that the disk appears to have only 17 sectors per track, as any normal MFM drive does.

So the low-level format for that track can only be done once for both heads 0 and 1. Toshiba thinks this unusual treatment means they should deny all programs the right to do a low-level format on their laptop computer's hard drives. Unfortunately, they don't *prevent* a program from doing the low-level format, nor do they force it to come out right for you. Programs that might want to do the low-level format on Toshiba laptop computer hard disks need to recognize this problem and avoid doing anything dangerous. Fortunately, *SpinRite* does.

Some autoconfiguring hard disk controllers: Some autoconfiguring hard disk controllers take a slightly less weird formatting approach. They put the drive dimensions in a special place on the drive, somewhere within the normal data area, but "out of sight." For example, they may put those dimensions in a special, tiny sector located on one of the data tracks, in addition to the usual sectors for that track.

These controllers may allow you to request a low-level format of any track you wish. If you are imprudent enough to do so on the track containing their special disk dimension table, you will most likely wipe it out, possibly rendering the whole drive inaccessible.

Gibson carefully designed *SpinRite* to watch out for these controllers. Thus you can use it safely with any controller.

One situation in which it is unsafe to use *SpinRite* is if you have partitioned your disk with a version of Priam's EVDR.SYS program earlier than Version 5.0. In that one case, you must be sure *not* to use *SpinRite* on your system — as the *SpinRite* documentation well notes.

Almost all other autoconfiguring controllers put the drive dimension information on some cylinder that is safely out of harm's way, where only the controller can access it, and then only for that one purpose. These controllers won't let you destroy their drive dimension table no matter what you request.

Perhaps the weirdest solution is what Western Digital uses on some of their controllers. They noticed that a part of the Master Boot Record is always left empty. This sector, which is also called the Partition Table, is the very first sector on the disk. (The nature and use of this sector is discussed in detail a few sections further on in this chapter.) Western Digital decided to use that unused space.

The controllers they make that use this strategy put the drive dimensions into the middle of this blank space in the master boot record. Then they make the controller hide it from view. If you read or write that sector, the controller will make you think that area contains zeros. Only it can read or change the actual numbers stored there. As long as no program tries to store information there, you will never know the controller is doing this.

Partitioning

Once you finish the low-level format, the disk is ready to store information. All one has to do is tell the controller to write some data, and in which physical head, cylinder, and sector to put it. But before you store files on an MS-DOS computer, you must still partition the disk and perform the high-level format. To refer back to our parking lot analogy, we have defined the parking stalls, but we still need to erect some fences and establish a valet-parking kiosk.

Floppy disks don't have partitions. DOS' designers didn't need to require partitions for hard disks either, but they did so mostly due to the high price of hard disk drives when PCs (and DOS) were very young, about a decade ago. Back then, the designers of DOS felt they had to accommodate users who might want to install more than one of the several competing operating systems, including DOS, Softech's P-system, and CP/M-86. They did so by allowing each operating system to use a portion, or partition, of the very costly hard disk.

Hard disks today cost between 10 and 50 times less per megabyte than they did during DOS' infancy. So, committing a disk to only one operating system is a whole lot less extravagant now than it was then, but DOS still requires partitioning.

Carving up the disk

Partitioning means dividing into parts. Most of your disk gets divided into some partitions in which you can store files of information. Your computer will not know about nor can it use these parts, however, unless there is a special, "introductory" section on the disk. This section, which comes at the very beginning of the disk (starting at cylinder number 0, head number 0, physical sector 1), holds something called the *Master Boot Record*, also known as the *Partition Table*.

At the very end of the disk, there are one or two other special-purpose parts. These are the *Diagnostic Cylinder* and, on some controllers, a "secret" cylinder to store the drive dimensions.

Figure 7-2 shows the three major parts into which partitioning divides a disk. It also shows some ways you can further subdivide the middle partition.

The Master Boot Record (aka the Partition Table): The very first sector on a hard drive (cylinder 0, head 0, physical sector 1) is the Master Boot Record, or the Partition Table. We call this sector the Partition Table because its data table specifies regions, called partitions, into which we divide the bulk of the hard disk. The sector is also called the Master Boot Record because it contains the program that reads this table, goes to the correct partition, and loads from the very beginning of that partition another boot sector.

7

If the bootable partition is a DOS partition, that boot sector will be identical to the boot program and data table on any DOS disk. If that partition is, for example, a Unix partition, the boot sector will contain the Unix standard boot program.

 The Master Boot Record takes up only a single sector (cylinder 0, head 0, sector 1). DOS, Version 2, allocates only that one sector for it; the disk's first partition under that version of DOS starts in the very next sector (cylinder 0, head 0, sector 2). Beginning with Version 3.0, in recognition of the generally larger size of hard disks and to keep things simpler for itself, DOS "wastes" the rest of the first track. Thus, the first partition on disks using modern DOS versions starts at cylinder 0, head 1, sector 1.

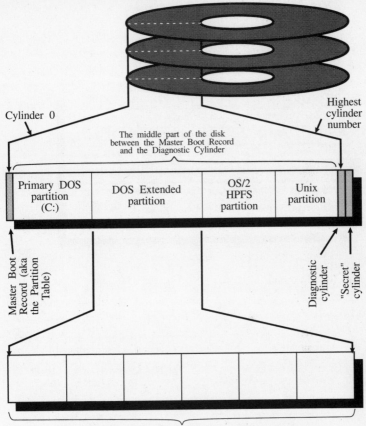

Figure 7-2: *The regions into which a hard disk is divided*

The bulk of the disk lies between the Master Boot Record and the diagnostic cylinder. You can use this space as a single partition, or you may subdivide it into two, three, or four partitions. The Partition Table lists the starting and ending address (cylinder, head, and physical sector) for each of these partitions. It also shows for each the operating system that gave it a high-level format. Finally, it shows which one of these partitions is "active" (bootable). Figure 7-3 gives the details on what is stored where in the partition table.

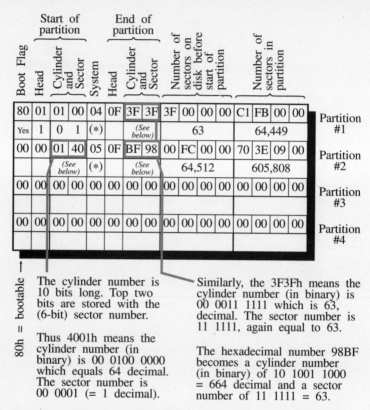

The cylinder number is 10 bits long. Top two bits are stored with the (6-bit) sector number.

Thus 4001h means the cylinder number (in binary) is 00 0100 0000 which equals 64 decimal. The sector number is 00 0001 (= 1 decimal).

Similarly, the 3F3Fh means the cylinder number (in binary) is 00 0011 1111 which is 63, decimal. The sector number is 11 1111, again equal to 63.

The hexadecimal number 98BF becomes a cylinder number (in binary) of 10 1001 1000 = 664 decimal and a sector number of 11 1111 = 63.

(∗) DOS understands the following values for the system byte:

    0 means an unused partition table entry
    1 for a DOS partition using 12-bit FAT entries
    4 for a DOS partition using 16-bit FAT entries
    5 for a DOS Extended Partition
    6 for a "huge" partition (more than 32 MB,
        created using DOS version 4 or later)

Figure 7-3: The structure of the partition table in the Master Boot Sector

TECHNICAL NOTE The sector and cylinder numbers for the start and end of each partition are stored in a way that reinforces the INT 13H limits on the size of those numbers. (INT 13H is the BIOS interrupt that handles reading and writing to the disk. It limits cylinder numbers to the range 0 to 1,023, and sectors from 1 to 63. Also, at least officially, it limits heads to values from 0 to 15.)

Thus, this is one of the places that imposes the 504 MB limit on the maximum size disk that DOS can address (assuming 512 byte sectors). Since head numbers can really be anything up to 255, both in the Partition Table and in INT 13H, this could be an 8 GB limit. Raising the limit this way is only possible by "breaking one of the rules" of the INT 13H BIOS design.

The total number of sectors and the number of sectors from the start of the disk to the start of each partition are stored in 4-byte locations (32 bits each). This is compatible with the convention in DOS 4.0 and later versions for large hard disk partitions. Thirty-two bits for the sector numbers means one could, conceivably, have up to 2^{32} sectors. If they each hold 512 bytes, the disk could then hold 2 TB (terrabytes, or mega-megabytes), or about four thousand times as much as the maximum size disk permitted by the maximum sector, head, and cylinder numbers.

The diagnostic cylinder: The diagnostic cylinder or, as IBM refers to it, the customer engineering cylinder, is one entire cylinder (all heads on one track). Normally, it is the last cylinder, closest to the spindle. IBM included this cylinder in order to have a place to conduct tests without messing up any of the data stored on the rest of the disk.

> **TECHNICAL NOTE** Some controllers do not set aside a diagnostic cylinder. Since such a reserved cylinder was a standard part of the IBM drive design, many utility programs depend on its existence. *SpinRite* will check to see if a particular drive has such a reserved, diagnostic cylinder and will use it if it does. It also correctly notes if that cylinder does not exist and refuses to attempt the operations that would have used it, thus keeping itself from accidentally overwriting any of the data on the drive.

The "secret" cylinder: The last part into which the system may carve up your disk is what might be called the "secret" cylinder. Not all disks have one, but if yours is an autoconfiguring hard disk controller, it may store the drive dimensions in a cylinder that it reserves for just this one purpose. If so, that cylinder typically is even further in toward the spindle than the diagnostic cylinder.

Where files get stored: Of the two, three, or four partitions into which you choose to divide the middle portion of your disk, you can boot from only one. DOS Version 3.2 or earlier ignores all the other partitions. DOS 3.3 or later, once it has booted from one partition,

7

may be able to access data stored in exactly one of the other partitions if you label it as a "DOS Extended Partition." The DOS Extended Partition may not itself be bootable.

TECHNICAL NOTE All versions of DOS before 4.0 could deal only with a partition size of up to 32 MB. That came, you will recall, from the limit on the logical sector number to a 16-bit number (thus less than 65,535) and the sector size of 512 bytes. DOS 3.3 can still deal with only 32-MB partitions, or what are now called "volumes," but it can have more than one of them on a single hard drive.

For each partition, a number stored in the Partition Table says what kind of partition it is. There are four possible values for this number for any partition that DOS can access. The values 1 or 4 say that this is a regular DOS partition — the only kind versions of DOS earlier than 3.3 could create. (The two different values indicate the size of the entries in the FAT table, which we explain in the section "The File Allocation Table" later in this chapter.) The value 5 says this is a DOS Extended Partition, which only Versions 3.3 and later could create. The value 6 is used for a "huge" DOS partition, a bootable partition created by DOS 4.0 or later that exceeds 32 MB.

Some third-party disk partitioning software puts other values into the Partition Table. Only their special installable device driver program can access the partitions those programs create. Without one of those programs, DOS alone cannot get at anything stored in such a partition.

7

DOS extended partition: DOS treats the DOS Extended Partition almost as if it were a separate disk, or a collection of separate disks. Its entries in the Partition Table (in the Master Boot Record) look much like any other partition, but DOS uses them very differently. Since it looks like another disk or disks, you can make the DOS Extended Partition any size you like (up to 504 MB, or perhaps up to 8 GB), even if you are using DOS 3.3. The entries in the Partition Table are pointers to this region.

Normally, the Master Boot Record program goes to the start of the active partition and expects to find a boot sector program there. For a DOS Extended Partition, it goes to the corresponding location, but instead looks for another partition table. This subsidiary partition table shows a further subdivision of the DOS Extended Partition into DOS logical volumes. If you are using DOS 3.3, it is these logical volumes that must be no larger than 32 MB.

The Partition Table at the start of each DOS logical volume within the DOS Extended Partition is just like a Master Boot Record Partition Table, with two exceptions: It doesn't contain the Master Boot Record program; and its data table has only one or two entries. The first entry tells the size of the current DOS accessible subpartition. The second entry points to the start of the next DOS logical volume. (See Figure 7-4.) The third and fourth entries are filled with zeros. The partition table for the last logical volume in the DOS Extended Partition will have zeros for its second entry also.

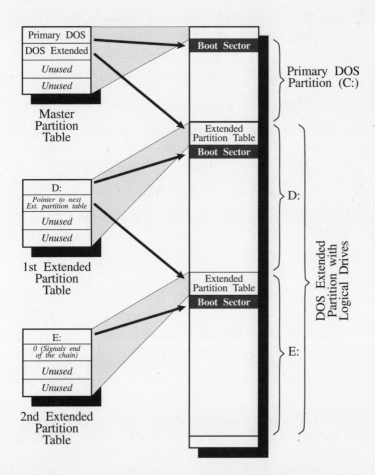

Figure 7-4: How the master and extended partition tables divide up the disk

Filling in the Partition Table

DOS includes FDISK, a program for creating, examining, and altering these partition tables. In addition to working with DOS partitions, FDISK can reserve room for other partitions that other operating systems can later format and use, but it cannot do much with those partitions, since it is designed for use with DOS.

You can also use FDISK to mark any of the four partitions in the Master Boot Record (except the DOS Extended Partition) as the active, or bootable, one. In this way, FDISK can "turn off" DOS and "turn on" Unix, or another operating system residing in one of the other partitions.

 If you use DOS 4.0 or later to create the Partition Table, you can make the partitions as large as you like. However, due to a limitation in Unix, current versions of that operating system cannot use partitions greater than 32 MB.

Whenever you run FDISK on a new disk, you should first ask it to show you what partition information it can find, before authorizing it to make any changes. If the disk is newly low-level formatted, FDISK will not find a Master Boot Record/Partition Table. Then it is appropriate to ask its help in creating one.

 If you are working with a disk that already has a valid Master Boot Record, be very careful. Altering the numbers in its Partition Table will most likely make all the data on the disk seem to disappear. It may be possible to get your data back (or at least most of your data) by restoring the Partition Table values, but only if you know exactly what all of them were.

If you alter these numbers using a program that allows direct disk editing, you will change only the numbers in the Partition Table. Then you can reverse the effect of your work simply by putting back the original numbers. If you use FDISK to alter the Partition Table, it will erase the most critical part of the information in any partition it establishes, precluding any easy way back.

Steps to partitioning a new disk with FDISK: Assuming you don't already have a DOS bootable C drive, you will first have to boot your computer from a DOS disk in the A drive. Keep it handy, as you will find yourself rebooting the computer from that disk several or even many times before it is ready to boot from the hard drive.

If the disk is smaller than 32 MB, the job is simple. First, you run FDISK, allowing it to use all the disk for DOS. You then proceed to the high-level format described a couple of sections further on in this chapter.

> `0110 0110`
> **TECHNICAL NOTE** FDISK, in this case, does several things in one step. First, it creates the Master Boot Record with its Partition Table. Next, it marks the first partition starting and ending points as the beginning and end of the space on the disk (except for the sector or track used for the Master Boot Record and the diagnostic cylinder at the end). FDISK marks that partition as belonging to DOS and makes it the active partition. The other three entries in the partition table are filled with zeros to show that they are unused.

WARNING!

The most insidious thing FDISK does is wipe out the first half dozen cylinders or so of each partition it creates. This is what makes reversing its effect so very difficult.

FDISK does this to make sure that the partition will not appear to be high-level formatted. If all it did was put numbers in the Partition Table, you could easily reverse its effect, but then you also might find yourself with some leftover "junk" in your new partition that could, the DOS designers thought, cause you some trouble sometime.

You could use less than all the disk for DOS, if, for example, you wanted to reserve a portion of the disk for another operating system, the reason partition and FDISK were invented. For such a 32-MB drive, though, this is not very practical. Current versions of most other operating systems require well more than half this much disk space to do anything useful. Further, most DOS users today would find anything less than 16 MB to be a cramped working space for DOS and their DOS applications and data files.

If the disk is larger than 32 MB, there are possible three cases, depending on which DOS version you are using:

1. DOS Version 3.2 or earlier: The only way you can use all of your disk is by using a third-party disk partitioning program. Your only other options are to upgrade to a later version of DOS or simply to ignore all the disk past the first 32 MB. (And who would want to do that?) We discuss third-party disk partitioning software more fully in the next section.

7

2. DOS Version 3.3: This version allows you to use most any size disk you wish, but it does so by breaking up the large disk into several regions, each of which must be smaller than 32 MB.

3. DOS 4.0 or later: You can use any size disk (at least up to 500 MB) as a single large partition, or you may subdivide it. Before you decide whether and how to divide up a large disk under DOS 4, please reread the discussion in the section "Disk Partitions" in the last chapter.

If you choose to make a single large partition under DOS 4, the process is the same as with a small disk (less than 32 MB) under the earlier versions of DOS. Let FDISK "do its thing" (with the default options) and go on to the high-level format.

If you choose to (or need to) subdivide your disk, you must take several steps. First, you run FDISK and ask it to create a partition in some size smaller than the whole disk. DOS 3.3's FDISK will not let you choose a size larger than 32 MB. Next, you must make an Extended Partition, assigning it the rest of the disk if you want to use all the disk for DOS. Do this even if you want to have several smaller partitions eventually.

> **TECHNICAL NOTE** In these steps, FDISK again creates the Master Boot Record and its Partition Table. It fills in the first entry for the DOS partition, whatever size you chose to make that. It marks that partition as belonging to DOS. Then FDISK fills in the second entry of the Partition Table for the DOS Extended Partition. It puts zeros in every location in the last two entries (showing that they are unused).

Now you must "create logical DOS drives" within that DOS Extended Partition, once more using FDISK. DOS 3.3's FDISK will again limit each of these to 32 MB or less. DOS 4 and later will let you set these to any size you choose. You may create as many logical DOS drives as will fit. Any of the DOS Extended Partition you do not allocate to a DOS logical drive will remain unavailable for use by DOS.

> **TECHNICAL NOTE** At this step, FDISK is creating the partition tables within the DOS Extended Partition, one for each subpartition, or "logical DOS disk." Each of these tables has one line for that subpartition, and all but the last one have a second line that points to the next of these extended partition tables. For its size, it shows however much of the total extended partition is still unaccounted

for by this and the previous DOS logical disks. The last two (or for the final subpartition table, the last three) entries are filled with zeros.

Once you have built the Master Boot Record, including its Partition Table, you can format the DOS partition. If you have a DOS Extended Partition, once you have created DOS logical disk drives within it, you can format each of them. To the DOS FORMAT program, each of these partitions or DOS logical disks looks almost exactly like a floppy disk. The only difference is that FORMAT knows it is a non-removable disk and what size it is.

Using third-party disk partitioning software: If you have a disk drive larger than 32 MB and are using DOS Version 3.2 or earlier, you either must upgrade your DOS version, use some third-party disk partitioning software, or ignore the rest of your drive beyond 32 MB.

These third-party programs can manage all three parts of the process: low-level format; partitioning; and high-level format, for which they require a DOS disk.

Since several different vendors produce these programs, we will not detail how any particular one operates. Each is easy to use if you operate it in its default mode. If you wish to have more control, you can follow each package's instructions for working in an interactive mode. The discussion above should help you understand the principles and thus be able to make the necessary choices correctly.

Important reminder: Third-party disk partitioners provide a non-DOS solution to a problem pre-3.3 versions of DOS could not solve, making them inherently incompatible with standard DOS procedures. You must install a device driver through your CONFIG.SYS file to get at all but the very first partition created by these programs (and that one is often very small). Booting from a copy of your DOS distribution disk will not work.

These programs will install the needed device driver for you, but you must make sure you have suitable backup copies for safety purposes somewhere other than on your hard disk. The backups should be bootable, and include any device drivers needed, with configuration files properly modified for a floppy drive. Test the

7

disk once you've created it, to make sure it allows you to access your hard drive.

A recommendation: If you upgrade to DOS 3.3 or later, don't continue to use third-party disk partitioning software. When you install your new version of DOS, upgrade your disk partitions too. To make this change, you must first back up your data.

Next, boot from the new DOS disk, then use the new DOS' version of FDISK, which renders your old data inaccessible. Delete any DOS Extended Partitions and the DOS Partition. Then run FOR-MAT (also from the new DOS). This step will prepare the partition and also install the new DOS on your C drive.

 The needed command is FORMAT C: /S /V. Recent versions of DOS include a command, SELECT, that you can use as well.

Be sure you update all your DOS files (which most likely will be in the C:\DOS subdirectory). Finally, restore all the data.

When you restore your data, you could put it back in the original directories, or you could take advantage of the opportunity to reorganize your hard disk.

Watch out for the lazy system installer, whether it be a dealer or a friend, who may continue to use partitioning software after upgrading your system to DOS 3.3 or higher. Ask whoever put your system together to remove that unnecessary software, or do so yourself.

High-Level Formatting

Once you have given the disk its low-level format and have partitioned it, you are ready for the high-level format. In terms of the parking lot analogy, you have now got the stalls painted (the controller has written the sectors to the disk) and the fences built (the partition table or tables created by FDISK). All that remains is to create the valet parking support structure so cars (files) can be parked for us automatically. DOS FORMAT will create this last structure for us. In this section, we will describe that program's several functions, as well as explain what a disk's FAT (file allocation table) is.

The logical organization of a DOS partition

You have learned about preparing a disk with a low-level format and the division of a disk into a Master Boot Record, one or more partitions (of which only one may be a DOS partition and one a DOS Extended Partition), and a diagnostic cylinder (plus, possibly, a secret cylinder). Next, the DOS FORMAT program must be used to create more divisions within the DOS partition, and within each DOS logical disk inside the extended partition (if any). Only then is the disk ready for DOS to use.

DOS divides every disk into four areas. It divides every DOS partition and every DOS logical volume on a hard disk into the same four areas. They are the boot sector, the file allocation tables (FAT), the root directory, and the data area.

At this high level, DOS looks at all the disk space on each of these drives as a single long list of logical sectors. Only when it gives commands down to the lower levels of DOS and ultimately to the BIOS does that view translate into the real, physical addresses.

The boot record: The boot record in a regular DOS partition and the boot records in each DOS logical volume within any DOS Extended Partition are just like those on DOS disks. They are stored in the very first sector of the partition or logical disk.

 For a disk, the boot record is at the physical address: cylinder 0, head 0, sector 1. On hard disks under DOS 2, the first partition's boot record is at cylinder 0, head 0, sector 2. (The Master Boot Record, aka the Partition Table, occupies cylinder 0, head 0, sector 1.) In later versions of DOS (3.0 and above), the boot record is at cylinder 0, head 1, sector 1. (This means that in the later versions of DOS all but the first sector of the track containing the Master Boot Record goes unused.)

Similarly, in the DOS Extended Partition (which only exists for DOS versions 3.3 and above), each DOS logical volume starts at head 1, sector 1 of the first cylinder of that part of the disk. The extended partition table is at head 0, sector 1 of that cylinder, and the rest of the sectors on that track (head 0, sectors 2 to whatever) are skipped.

The boot record serves two purposes: It is a program that will load the operating system, a step required to boot the computer (hence

7

the name "boot record"); and it contains a data table of critical information about this disk partition.

> **TECHNICAL NOTE** A boot record starts with a jump instruction. Then comes a data table, most of whose values get copied into an area of RAM called the BIOS Parameter Block for this drive. Finally, we have the actual boot program that will use those numbers to find the operating system files in this partition, if it is to boot from there. Of course, only the DOS partition (which will be the C drive) can be bootable. Thus none of the other partitions or logical volumes need that last part. Still, all DOS partitions or logical volumes have the same boot record for simplicity. Later in this chapter, we explain the meaning of the numbers stored in the boot record data table, in the section "Interpreting the boot record data table".

The data area: Though not the next part of the partition, it is useful to consider the data area next, since once you understand how it is used, you can more easily understand why the other two sections exist and how they are constructed.

At one level, DOS keeps track of information a file at a time. At a slightly lower level, it keeps track of it either a character at a time (when the file is coming from or going to a character device) or a sectorful at a time (when it is coming from or going to a block device like a disk drive).

You'd think that since DOS keeps track of data a sector at a time when it is on its way to a disk drive, it would use the same unit to keep track of it once it arrives. It doesn't. Instead it uses another unit, which we call either a *cluster* or an *allocation unit*.

Clusters: A cluster is a small group of sectors. It may have only one sector in it, or it may have two sectors, or four, or any power of 2. How many sectors DOS puts in a cluster depends on two things: the size of the disk drive and the version of DOS. Let us see why we need clusters and how DOS decides how big to make them.

Every place where we can store data on the disk is either available, in use by a file or subdirectory, or damaged and therefore not fit for data storage. DOS must keep track of the status of every sector in the data area of each DOS drive.

Further, DOS must keep track of which file "owns" each place on the disk that is in use. If a file is larger than will fit into one of those places, it will get stored in pieces. DOS has to be able to link together the right pieces to make up the whole file whenever some program requests those data.

The system keeps a permanent record of this information on the disk with the files whose locations it describes. In order to increase its file access time, it also keeps a copy of at least a good deal of this information in RAM for the disk that DOS is currently accessing.

Keeping that information in RAM, however, uses up some significant portion of the precious first 640K of system RAM, so the designers of DOS had to compromise by separating disk file information into two parts — the file directory information, which tells everything about the files but gives us only a snippet about where they reside; and disk space allocation information, which tells everything about the status of every part of the disk data storage area.

In our parking lot analogy, the first is the list of whose car is where and what it looks like. The second is the list of which stalls are occupied, which are vacant, which are damaged, and, for groups of cars, which ones are in each group.

On the disk, some of the file directory information is kept in the *root directory*; the rest is kept in *subdirectories*. The disk space allocation information is kept in a file allocation table (FAT).

When accessing the disk to get a single file, DOS needs to keep in RAM only the file directory information about that one file, or at most about a few files in the same subdirectory. To know where on the disk it may find that file and where it may put additional information for that or a new file, DOS must keep the disk space allocation information for much or all of the disk in RAM.

 If you are only getting information out or putting information into one file, DOS can do so quickly. When it needs to access a new file, it takes just a bit longer, for it must get the directory information about that file off the disk.

By simplifying the disk space allocation information and divorcing it from the lengthy details about the files that are using the space, the designers of DOS made it possible to minimize the RAM used by DOS while it is getting at and creating files. When it needs to know a file's name, size, when it was created, or other facts, it can look that up elsewhere.

Still, even the space allocation information is a lot to hold on to. If DOS tried to keep track of the status of every sector on a very large hard disk individually, it would use all of RAM just for that purpose, leaving no room for your applications. This is where clusters come into the story.

A cluster is some convenient number of consecutively numbered sectors. By dividing the disk space into these larger units, DOS has fewer of them to keep track of. By reducing the maximum value of a cluster number to something much less than the total number of sectors, DOS realizes a second space savings, as you will learn in the section "How Big Is Your FAT?"

> TECHNICAL NOTE DOS Versions 1 and 2 divide the data storage area on any disk into no more than about 4 thousand storage units, or clusters. Each cluster is numbered, starting at 2. (Yes, that's right. For this one purpose DOS numbers things starting not with 0, nor with 1, but with 2.) Starting with DOS Version 3, the number of possible clusters has grown to over 65 thousand. Version 4 of DOS has the same maximum cluster number, but it calls clusters "allocation units."
>
> Only having to keep track of some 4 thousand or even a bit over 65 thousand clusters substantially simplifies the system for DOS, compared to keeping track of every sector. Remember that early versions of DOS (before Version 4) allowed up to 65,536 sectors on one disk drive. With DOS 4 that maximum number has been increased to a whopping 4 billion according to one rule, but only to just over a million by another rule.

The File Allocation Table: DOS puts the status information on all the clusters on a DOS partition or DOS logical drive in the file allocation table (FAT). A FAT is simply a table of numbers, one per cluster, that tells the status of those clusters. One special value designates those clusters that are available for data storage, while another indicates a damaged cluster that the system should not use. A few other values say a file that fits entirely within the cluster is using it, or that a file that overlaps other clusters ends in this one. Any other number points to a cluster where the file contained in this cluster continues.

The FAT contains "chains of clusters" that show where the system has put each file stored on the disk. It also shows available space, which DOS uses when it has new information to record. Finally, the FAT's record of damaged areas on the disk prevents the system from storing data there.

You may have seen the DOS program CHKDSK display the message that it has found "[some number of] lost clusters in [some number of] lost chains." You will learn how a chain may become lost in the section "How Clusters Get 'Lost.'"

> **TECHNICAL NOTE** A couple of extra numbers at the start of the first sector of the FAT mark the beginning of the FAT and show what kind of disk this is. The first of these bytes is called the *media descriptor byte*. The other one or two special bytes are filled with ones (and thus have the hexadecimal value FF).
>
> The media descriptor byte also appears in the boot record's data table. Unfortunately, it does not give much useful information. Still, if it is not F8H, you know the disk is not a hard disk.

FATs come in two types: 12-bit and 16-bit. Prior to DOS Version 3, we had only 12-bit FATs. Later versions use both kinds. This distinction refers to the size of the numbers stored in the FAT for each cluster. For most purposes, you don't need to know what size FAT entries your disk has.

You do need to know the size of your FAT entries if you are upgrading from a 12-bit FAT to a new version of DOS that uses a 16-bit FAT. In this case, you must back up your data before you upgrade or you will lose access to your data.

> **TECHNICAL NOTE** All DOS versions before 3.0 used 12-bit numbers in their FATs exclusively, the source of their limit of no more than about 4 thousand clusters. Raising 2 to the 12-th power yields 4,096. Subtracting the special values that can't be used to point to other clusters, one gets a maximum of 4,078 clusters. All versions of DOS use 12-bit FAT entries for every floppy disk.

When DOS 3 or later is high-level formatting a hard disk, it examines the size of the disk (its total number of sectors). It then decides whether it can get away with only 4 thousand clusters without making the cluster size "too large." If it can, it uses a FAT with 12-bit numbers. If not, it uses 16-bit numbers in the FAT. This larger number for the FAT entries means one can have up to 65,518 clusters.

You may have noticed the vague term "too large" in the previous paragraph. The exact rule that DOS uses to choose the cluster size and which size of FAT entries to use is not well documented. Further, DOS does not provide any way for you to tell it what you would prefer. Its FORMAT program does whatever it was built to do, and you just get to live with it. One thing you can do to influence it, though, is to choose your partition sizes carefully. Any partition over about 16 MB will get a 16-bit FAT and as small a cluster size as possible. Smaller partitions are likely to get a 12-bit FAT; the resulting cluster size may meet DOS's notion of not "too large," but not yours.

Also notice that if you choose to create partitions that are larger than 32 MB, the clusters will necessarily be larger than one sector each. If the partition is very large, the clusters become very large, too. For example, if you have a 260-MB partition, your clusters will be 8K each.

How big is your FAT?: Whatever kind of FAT your disk has, it occupies only a small fraction of the disk that it describes. Since it is so critical to the proper accessing of the files on the disk and it's small, DOS keeps two copies of the FAT on most disks for greater reliability.

TECHNICAL NOTE If you have a 12-bit FAT, then DOS will place two cluster status numbers in every three bytes. This is because three bytes are 3 x 8 = 24 bits. So the size of your FAT under DOS 1 and 2 could be no more than about 6K (4 thousand entries times 1.5 bytes each). For DOS 3, the maximum size of the FAT is larger because you can have more clusters, and thus more entries in the FAT, and because if you have a 16-bit FAT, each cluster number will take up two bytes instead only 1.5 bytes. For DOS 3 and later versions, the maximum FAT size is 128K.

Though it's easy to allocate DOS room in RAM for a copy of a 6K FAT, you couldn't permit it to store all of a 128K FAT there. So, DOS 3 and 4 are a bit more clever about what part of the FAT they must keep in RAM and what they will get from the disk when they need it.

Whenever DOS allocates a new cluster to a file or notices that a cluster has been released (because a file was erased), it updates both copies of the FAT. If DOS gets an error reading the first FAT, it will try to read the second FAT. If that succeeds, DOS will use the information it got, but it may not tell you that it had to use the second FAT and it won't attempt to repair the damaged first FAT.

The DOS program CHKDSK allows you to find out about discrepancies between the two copies of the FAT. Other than these two uses, though, DOS ignores the second FAT. This is one reason why it makes sense to run CHKDSK regularly, to reveal problems if they do arise.

The root directory: The root directory, an orderly table of facts about files, is the final separate region of a DOS partition or logical drive that the FORMAT program creates. It is here that DOS begins to store the file directory information, connecting the file name with its location on the disk.

Each directory entry takes up 32 bytes. The first 11 bytes give the file's name (8 bytes) and extension (3 bytes). The next byte stores the file's attributes. Ten bytes are reserved, which means Microsoft tells us not to use them. Customarily they will be filled with zeros. Then comes the time and date at which a program opened the file with permission to change its contents (2 bytes for the date and 2 for the time). This is followed by the cluster number at which DOS began storing this file's contents (2 bytes). The last 4 bytes store the file's size in bytes.

Notice that the directory entry states only where the file begins, not where the entire file resides. To find the rest of the file, DOS must consult the FAT, starting with the cluster where the file begins (and ends, if it's a small file) and following the chain of clusters till it reaches the file's end.

7

 The attribute byte can store up to 8 yes-or-no facts about a file. So far DOS uses just six of them. Some networking software uses one or the other of the two leftover bits in that byte.

The root directory has a fixed size, which depends on your version of DOS and the size and type of your disk drive. A common number for a hard drive is 512 entries.

Subdirectories: If you have more than 512 files, you have to store their directory information in a subdirectory, a concept introduced with DOS 2. A subdirectory is nothing more than a special file. That is, while it is stored like a file, its contents are interpreted as an extension to the root directory.

The first-level subdirectories are listed as files in the root directory. They contain listings of other files and perhaps other, second-level subdirectories, and so on.

> **TECHNICAL NOTE** The tree of subdirectories can go about as many levels deep as you may wish. The limit is that the path from the root directory to any file must not be more than 64 characters long, including a backslash character (\) to separate each directory name from the next, and one backslash at the end of the path.

The volume label: One other special "file" that may be found in a root directory is the disk's *volume name*, which you can use to store the name you want to associate with this disk partition or logical volume. The system lists this like a file, but it has the special volume attribute bit turned on, and its size and cluster number are both zero.

The purpose of this entry is simply to store some name you want to associate with this disk partition or logical volume. You don't have to give partitions or volumes a name, but it is a good idea. Starting with version 3.2 of DOS, the FORMAT program has a very valuable feature: If you ask it to reformat a hard disk that has a volume name, it will refuse to do the job unless you can tell it what that volume name is. This helps keep you from accidentally wiping out your C drive.

7

At last, we have all the elements on our disk to allow DOS to use it. In terms of our parking lot analogy, the painted stripes on the pavement are like the low-level format. The fences are like the partitions. The valet parking structure is like the FAT and directories. The disk volume label is like a sign over the entrance.

How clusters become "lost": DOS updates the FAT and the directory information independently of each other. Normally DOS updates the FAT every time it adds new information to a file on the disk. It only updates the directory information when it finishes work with that file.

If something interrupts a program while it's writing a file to disk, the FAT entries will reflect where on the disk to find the data for that file, but there won't yet be a directory entry for the file indicating where it starts. We call the clusters marked in the FAT for that file a *lost chain*.

One common way this happens is when a program gets confused and the only way to interrupt it seems to be by rebooting the computer. That stops what it was doing, but it also prevents it from cleaning up after itself. Lost chains are almost an inevitable consequence. This is one reason that it is generally not a good idea to stop programs by rebooting your computer.

The rest of what FORMAT does

The job of the FORMAT program is more than simply to set aside these four areas of the DOS partition or DOS logical drive. It also must initialize their contents, or at least the contents of three of them. Most versions of DOS write nothing to the data area. In the next chapter, in a section titled "Destructive FORMAT Programs," you will learn about some that do (and read a warning about what to do if you have one of them on your PC).

The boot sector receives a copy of the standard DOS boot program and a data table appropriate to this partition or logical volume. The FAT has its first byte set to the media descriptor byte, and the next two or three bytes have all their bits set to ones. The rest of the FAT is filled with zeros.

Next, FORMAT reads the whole of the data space. It records in the FAT any clusters in which it finds one or more bad sectors that either it couldn't read or that the low-level format program marked bad. Finally, FORMAT enters a zero into every location of the root directory. If the disk is to be bootable, it copies the system files to the disk and makes appropriate entries in the root directory and FAT for those files.

Interpreting the boot record data table: Now, at last, you can understand all the numbers contained in the boot record's data table. Thirteen to 25 of these numbers (depending on the version of DOS) get copied to the BIOS Parameter Block for this drive. All of them are available to DOS programs through an interrupt call.

The data area in the boot sector begins with an 8-byte field for the OEM (Original Equipment Manufacturer) name and DOS version number for the FORMAT program that created this boot sector. This does not go into the BIOS Parameter Block.

Next comes the number of bytes per sector (which can be anything at all, up to 65,536 bytes). This is followed by the number of sectors per cluster. So the product of these first two numbers tells how many bytes there are in one cluster.

The "reserved sectors" number is really the number of sectors in this partition before the first FAT begins. Since logical sectors begin at number zero, this is the number of the first sector in the first FAT. The number of FATs and the number of entries in the root directory are self-explanatory.

The next entry, "total number of sectors in volume," is for DOS volumes less than 32 MB in size. Since it is only a 2-byte number, it cannot express the number of sectors in a larger volume (assuming the sector size is the DOS standard value, 512 bytes). For partitions or logical disks over 32 MB, a zero is put here. The actual size for these "huge" partitions is in a later field that only occurs in boot records created by DOS 4 or later versions.

The Media Descriptor Byte comes next, which for any hard disk is simply F8 hexadecimal. The boot sector data table under DOS 2 ends with one more entry giving the number of sectors in each FAT.

DOS 3 added three fields. They give the number of sectors per track, the number of heads, and a number called "hidden sectors." This is the total number of physical sectors on the drive before the start of this partition. (Notice the difference between the reserved sectors and the hidden sectors. The former says how many sectors *within this partition* to skip to get to the beginning of the first FAT. The latter says how many sectors *on the drive* to skip to get the beginning of this partition.)

DOS 4 adds several more fields, the most important of which is the "big total number of sectors," which is the actual number of sectors in any partition over 32 MB. Other fields added by DOS 4 contain a disk serial number, extended boot record signature, volume label, and the BIOS physical address for the disk containing this partition or logical drive. (This last value is 80H for the first disk partition and 81H for the next. DOS then calls these the C and D drives.)

Alternatives to the DOS high-level format

The discussion in this chapter of low-level formatting and partitioning applies to disks used with DOS and those used with other

PC operating systems. The controller lays down the low-level format, so the operating system cannot change it. The BIOS reads the partition table, so it must be the same no matter which operating system you install on your disk. Things can be quite different in the high-level format.

Unix and OS/2 are the other popular operating systems for single PCs. A lot of local-area networks (LANs) use Novell software, which amounts to a special operating system for the file server PC in those LANs. Novell supplies only the file server's operating system; the workstation PCs hooked to the file server run DOS or OS/2.

Since these operating systems understand and use the same partitioning method used by DOS, they can share a disk with DOS in the manner described in the section on "Partitioning" earlier in this chapter. Equally, they could be the only operating system on a PC's disk.

Unix does its high-level format very differently from DOS, making a partition that has been formatted by Unix completely mysterious to DOS.

> **TECHNICAL NOTE**
>
> Here are a few of the ways in which Unix (or Xenix) does things differently from DOS:
>
> It defines areas on the disk in terms of things called blocks and "inodes." These are similar to sectors and clusters, but Unix will check them for ECC errors every time they are read or written. If any errors occur, the data will be moved to some new location automatically. In order for this to work, you must set aside some spare tracks when you format the partition. When you run the Unix format program, it will offer to do this for you and suggest a number of spare tracks to use, based on the size of the partition.
>
> Unix keeps track separately of the disk space occupied by files belonging to each user of the system. Each user is limited to some number of files and number of megabytes of total storage independent of what any other user has taken.
>
> Unix defines more attributes that a file may have, such as various permissions and the notion of linking more than one file name to the same data.

7

Unix defines a "dirty bit" for files. If a file is somehow not correctly written to the disk and its directory entry properly updated, the system will notice this fact and demand that you run the equivalent of CHKDSK the next time you start the system.

OS/2 operates a bit strangely. It can make its disks look just like DOS disks, which lets it share those disks or partitions with DOS. It also can allocate disk space using the high-performance file system (HPFS), a new, improved method that is completely incompatible with the DOS FAT method of disk space allocation. You can make some of your OS/2 drives FAT format and some HPFS format, allowing DOS access to the former when you reboot your PC.

TECHNICAL NOTE DOS descended from both CP/M and Unix, with more of the Unix features included in each new version of DOS. As a child of DOS, OS/2 not surprisingly has much in common with Unix. Here are a few ways in which OS/2 does things in an HPFS partition differently than in a normal DOS partition.

An HPFS partition does not have FAT tables. Directory information is kept closer to the file locations on the disk, meaning there may be less time wasted moving the disk heads between files and the directory entries describing them. The new directory format allows one to use long file names (up to 256 characters).

The HPFS file system allocates disk space directly in sectors (no more multisector clusters with their resulting inefficiency). Unfortunately, it does not automatically test the data integrity and move data to safety.

An HPFS partition can be huge. This is a maximum logical size. Since OS/2 uses the BIOS, INT 13 still limits it to a maximum physical disk size of 504 MB or 8 GB, depending on whether one "cheats" or not.

OS/2 radically extends the notion of file attributes. OS/2's HPFS uses disk caching extensively, including deferred write caching. This is risky, as was explained in Chapter 5. If you turn off power (or power fails) before your information gets written to the disk, your files will not get updated correctly. To help guard against disaster, OS/2 keeps track of the state of its disk cache and will alert you if you should make that mistake (or have that misfortune).

Novell uses a special format for its file servers for a couple of reasons. The format allows Novell to optimize the disk usage for its special needs, and it ensures file security.

Novell provides several barriers to access to files stored on its servers by requiring passwords and permissions. This security would be worthless if one could get at those files by rebooting the file server PC off a DOS floppy disk and then using standard DOS commands to read or copy the hard disk's files. With Novell's unique high-level format for the file server, booting off a DOS disk doesn't let you get at those files.

> **TECHNICAL NOTE**
> Novell is famous for its *COMPSURF* program. The standard Novell installation procedure takes one through all the steps of preparing a hard disk, from low-level to high-level formats, with partitioning in the middle. This has lead some people to think that Novell is doing all the levels of disk preparation in some special way.
>
> That is not really true. Novell simply hides from you most of the steps. Of necessity, it first asks the controller to do the usual low-level format. Next, the *COMPSURF* program tests the disk as an extension of the normal controller tests after doing a low-level format. Conducting many more tests assures Novell it has found all the bad spots on the server's hard disks. In fact, *COMPSURF* does for a Novell partition something very much like what *SpinRite* does for a DOS partition, at least in terms of testing the disk's integrity. The major difference is that it only does so before the data get put on the disk.
>
> After it finishes testing the newly low-level formatted disk, Novell's installation procedure creates a standard partition table, then does the high-level format, which is the part unique to Novell.

Finding and Avoiding "Bad" Spots

During the low-level format process, the disk controller tests each sector, at least superficially. The manufacturers would like you to believe that this assures you the sectors are able to store and retrieve data faithfully. Though the controller will flag bad sectors it finds in their sector header, occasionally a bad sector will pass the controller test and be marked good.

Some controllers only check to see that the sector headers can be read without a CRC error. They don't even check to see that the sector headers contain the right information, and they don't check the data areas of the sectors at all.

The low-level format program also may allow you to enter "bad track" or "bad sector" numbers. It will then set the bad sector flag in all the sectors on those bad tracks or the specified bad sectors, whether or not it found them to be bad.

The DOS high-level format program (FORMAT) retests all of the data area in each DOS partition or DOS logical drive that it is formatting. (This test is a little bit better, but it still is just a read test and will not catch many marginal sectors.) The FORMAT program then records in the FAT a special value for each cluster that contains one or more bad sectors. Notice that whole clusters get marked bad, rendering them unavailable for data storage. This must be so, since DOS cannot keep track of any smaller unit of disk storage than the cluster.

 Another tricky point may have occurred to you. What if the sector I want to read is bad in its header? Then I cannot read which sector it was. How do I know which one is the bad one? The answer is that you only read a sector by asking the controller for it by number. If the controller comes back with an error, you know that the sector whose number you asked for is a bad one.

Any such sector (with a bad sector header) may not be able to receive an appropriate mark in its bad sector flag. Still, FORMAT will catch it, though only after many attempts to read it. That is the source of the grinding noises you may hear when FORMAT is testing a disk after it applies the high-level format.

No other DOS program ever marks clusters bad. Since you normally only format a disk once, if a region goes bad after you have been using it, DOS will not help you find that bad spot, a situation that can have dire consequences. You'll learn more about this in the next chapter.

This completes our discussion of how healthy hard disks work. Next, we move onto how hard disks sometimes die, how to prevent untimely deaths, and how to try to resuscitate expired drives.

Chapter 8

How Hard Disks Die

So far we have focused on how healthy hard disks function. In this chapter, we discuss why and when (it's not a matter of if) your hard disk will die, pointing out the benefits of taking precautions and backing up *regularly*. We also describe ways to revive a failed disk, as well as steps you can take that will help forestall (though not prevent) your hard disk's demise.

Failure Modes

Your hard disk can fail for a number of reasons. Some are a consequence of human error, such as dropping a hard disk, a near guarantee of seriously damaging it. Random hardware failures can also do in your drive, as can external events, such as power surges. Some drives fall victim to a creeping "illness."

Given the degree to which most PC users depend on their hard disks, a disk crash is likely to induce terror and panic, not the best state of mind for troubleshooting a bad drive. The fact that you can often recover your data after a disk failure should dispel some of that fear.

Given that your hard disk is part of a larger sub-system of your PC, a failure of any component in that sub-system will look like a failure of the hard drive. The important hardware parts to consider are these: the controller card; the cables connecting the controller to

8

the drive and the drive to the power supply; and the drive electronic and mechanical parts. You should also consider the format and partitioning information on the drive, and the program and data files on the drive (see Figure 8-1) — data-only failures are more common than you might imagine.

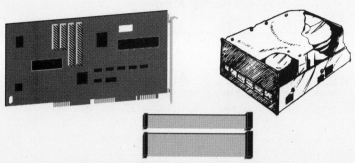

(a) The hardware parts of disk sub-system:
Controller, cables, and drive(s)

In order to access data on the drive at all you need these:

> Low level format must be correct for every sector that is to be read or written.

> Master Boot Record (with its Partition Table) at Cylinder 0, Head 0, and Physical Sector 1 must contain the correct partition data.

> High level (DOS) format in partition must be complete. The boot sector's BIOS Parameter Block data, both FATs, and root and other directory information must be intact.

8

Additionally to boot from the disk you also need:

> Master Boot Record program must be sound. Also boot sector in DOS partition.

> Two hidden files (IBMBIO.COM or IO.SYS and IBMDOS.COM or MSDOS.SYS) and COMMAND.COM must be in right places on disk and from the same version of DOS.

> May also need a proper CONFIG.SYS file and some special driver software.

(a) The information "parts" needed for DOS to use a PC's hard disk sub-system.

Figure 8-1: The hardware and information parts of a disk subsystem.

To help tell which part has failed, you could try some diagnostic test programs. Though it's not sold as a hard disk testing utility, *SpinRite* offers one of the best tests of the hardware and controller electronics.

Many other disk utility programs claim to offer disk testing, but most of them do a much more cursory job. An inexpensive one that does a fair job and is very easy to use is *CheckIt* from Touchstone Software Corporation (2130 Main Street, Suite 250, Huntington Beach, CA 92648-9927; (800) 531-0450, (714) 969-7746).

Distinguishing hardware failures and information pattern failures

If your hard drive is reporting errors such as "Sector not found reading drive C," "Read [or write] error on drive C," or "Cannot find system files," then it is probable that your controller, cables, and hard disk hardware are all fine. Your problem is with the information on the disk, not with the disk. Refreshing the information with *SpinRite* should remedy your problem.

If you get an error message such as "Invalid drive specification" or "General failure reading drive C," on the other hand, that may indicate a more serious, hardware-related problem. Even here, though, the source of the problem might only be some messed up information recorded on the drive's surface. Recalling the steps necessary to prepare a disk for DOS, if any of the patterns recorded during those steps were to become damaged, it could render the disk totally inaccessible until you repaired the damage. When you encounter such problems, it makes sense to try the easiest and least expensive remedies first.

Simple things that sometimes go wrong

Look at your hard disk. Listen to it. Does it sound any different? Does the LED (light emitting diode) light up in normal fashion? Does the drive get as warm as usual? (To test how warm your disk gets, you may have to let your PC run for awhile before opening up the PC's system unit case and feeling the outside of the drive.)

Some Warnings

`0110 0110`
**TECHNICAL
NOTE**   Before you open your PC, be sure to disconnect it from the power line. Don't just flip off the power switch. Unplug the power cord where it enters the PC's chassis. Also unplug the power cord for the monitor and any other peripheral devices you have attached to your PC (or disconnect the data cables that connect your PC to those devices). You can substantiallly damage your PC, and possibly yourself, if you ignore these precautions.

Also, please touch the power supply of the PC before touching anything else inside it. This will make sure you and the PC are at the same voltage. Do this *every* time you reach inside.

Do not move your PC while it is turned on. In particular, do not tilt the case. Your hard drive is spinning all the time your PC is on. That makes it a gyroscope. Tilting a spinning gyroscope puts a terrible strain on its bearings.

After doing some work inside your PC, you may choose to plug it in and operate it for a brief test before you put the cover back on. That is fine. But **never** unplug or plug in any cables inside your PC while it is turned on (*e.g.*, the cables from the power supply to the drive or from the drive to the controller).

Also do not put the cover back on while the PC is turned on. It is too easy to drop a screw inside and short out something. Following these simple precautions can make the difference between safe exploration and utterly destroying your PC.

A disconnected power cable can cause your drive to fail absolutely, preventing the light from coming on and the drive from getting warm. Such an eventuality is easy to overlook but simple to remedy, by just unplugging the power cable and then plugging it firmly back in. The data cables (usually flat, "ribbon" cables) can come loose as well, causing the drive to fail in some way. Again, you should unplug the cables and then plug them back in at each end, the only sure way to diagnose such a problem. If that does not work, replace the cables with new ones.

A Useful Suggestion

`0110 0110`
**TECHNICAL
NOTE**   Before you replace the cables, you should sketch out where and how to hook up the cables. If you hook up the cables incorrectly, you probably will do no damage, but your hard disk sure won't work. You must also be very careful to get the connector

orientations just right. Some cables are "keyed" to prevent them from being plugged in wrong, but most are not.

Unplugging the cables and then plugging them back in again can help because doing so wipes their contacts. The friction can remove oxides or grease that might have been preventing good electrical connection. Since the wiping action is what counts, you can just barely remove the connectors and then replace them, working with only one connector at a time. That way you are less likely to get one connected incorrectly.

Very rarely, the cable will actually be broken. Even a bent connector pin at one end is enough to bring down the cable; replace it. Fortunately, you can often see a damaged cable, and it is one of the cheapest components to replace.

Slow death by growing misalignment

Hard disks are mechanical wonders. They move their heads around by millionths of an inch at a time and expect to get them repositioned precisely where they first were, a difficult chore at best. Over time, a head positioning mechanism in a hard drive may simply not be able to put the heads back exactly where they should go.

From the point of view of the heads, the tracks of information recorded on the platter surface will appear to have slipped a bit to one side. The disk will work adequately as long as the slippage remains small, but as the slippage increases, it can cause the disk subsystem to malfunction.

Remember that your computer puts down the sector header information only when the low-level format is done. As the drive ages and the heads move sideways relative to those recorded sector headers, it will have an increasingly difficult time reading the headers, until one day it delivers the dreaded message, "Sector not found." (See Figure 8-2.)

 If the drive was bumped while you were doing the low-level format, the head might have momentarily swerved to the side a bit. That would make the track it wrote have a wave in it. Depending on which way the head assembly drifts as it ages, this sector will be either the first or the last to show a problem. (See Figure 8-3.)

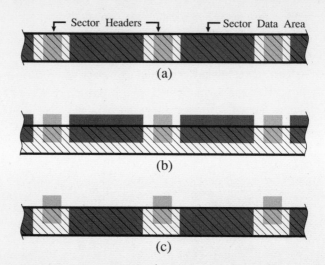

Figure 8-2: How head drift can cause drive malfunction. (a) When track is first recorded it will certainly line up with the head that wrote it. (b) Later if that head drifts to one side it may no longer be able to read information on that track reliably. (c) Rewriting the data aligns it, but not the sector headers, to the new path of head. This can lead to "Sector Not Found" errors. Redoing the low-level format will restore the original perfect alignment.

A "read fault error" can occur if the sector you are trying to read was written to only once, quite some time ago. The magnetic pattern could become weakened over time so that eventually the signals picked up by the head may be too small to decipher correctly. At first the ECC (error correction codes) recorded with the information will suffice to get your data back, but eventually even that may not work.

8

> **0110 0110**
> **TECHNICAL NOTE** The heads themselves are permanently magnetized. If you do not "park" the heads each time your turn off your PC, those permanent magnets will set down on top of some of your valuable data. When the drive starts up, the heads will scrub around a bit, at random, before starting to fly above the surface. This process can weaken, if not reverse, some bits recorded in the surface.

The system writes information into most sectors from time to time. Thus, as the drive alignment drifts, the data portion of the sector will be constantly rewritten under the current location of the heads. This means that gradually a sector that was labelled bad during the low-level format (due perhaps to a pinhole in the magnetic coating on the surface) no longer contains any defect, while a good sector may have in turn inherited the flaw. (See Figure 8-4.)

Figure 8-3: Bumping a hard disk while low-level formatting can lead to a wavy track.

Redoing the low-level format resolves these problems by moving the sector headers and the data portions under the new head location. It is important that you retest the sectors, to make sure you don't put data back into a bad sector.

For the cylinders of a drive that fall inside a DOS partition or DOS logical drive, a program like *SpinRite* provides the most convenient way to refresh the format, test the disk surface, and replace the data. If you run *SpinRite* before your heads drift so far that your data is unreadable, you have a good chance of never encountering such errors. Even if you wait until DOS finds the drive almost unreadable, amazingly *SpinRite* can sometimes recover *all* your data and eliminate the drive's errors.

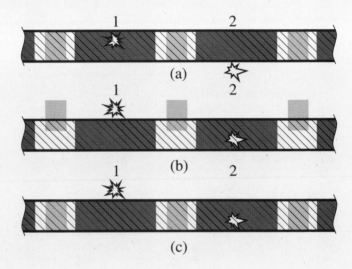

Figure 8-4: (a) Pinhole defect in drive makes sector bad at time of low-level format. (b) Drifting head moves track to one side. (c) Pinhole defect not originally in sector, now makes sector unusable.

8　Data accidents

Some hard drive failures arise due to data accidents, such as when a power surge causes a bit to flip from one to zero or vice versa. The most common human errors that induce drive failure include erasing COMMAND.COM, or copying over it with a different version of the same program; erasing all the files in your root directory; or mistakenly executing the command FORMAT C: despite DOS' warning that you are about to wipe out a fixed disk.

The following PC-DOS 3.2 error messages are typical indicators of a data accident: "Probable Non-DOS disk;" "Bad or missing Command Interpreter;" "Bad or missing xxxx" (where xxxx is some file name mentioned in your CONFIG.SYS file in a DEVICE= line); "Bad Partition Table;" "Disk boot failure;" "Disk error reading FAT x" (where x is 1 or 2); "Error loading operating system;" "Invalid partition table;" or "Missing operating system." Depending on the version of DOS you use and whether it's been customized by a manufacturer, you may get slightly different messages, but their general import will be the same. Happily, some data accidents are transient, vanishing with a simple reboot of your computer. On the other hand, a persistent problem means that you need to find and repair the damaged information.

Fixing damaged data and some popular disk utility packages that make it easier: Of course, if you know you reformatted your hard disk by typing FORMAT C:, then you need to find a way to "unformat" the drive. Paul Mace made his fortune marketing the first program to do this, *Mace Utilities* (now available from Fifth Generation Systems, 10049 Reiger Road, Baton Rouge, LA 70809-4559; (504) 291-7221). The *Norton Utilities* package (Peter Norton Computing, Inc., 100 Wilshire Blvd., 9th Floor, Santa Monica, CA 90401-1104; (213) 319-2000) also includes this capability, as does *PC Tools* (Central Point Software, 15220 Greenbrier Parkway, #200, Beaverton, OR 97006; (503) 690-8090).

If you deleted or copied over the correct version of COMMAND.COM, simply copying it onto your hard disk from your original DOS disk should set things straight. If you deleted all the files in your root directory, you could restore them from backup files. If those don't exist, you could use one of the programs mentioned above to "unerase" the files, a capability Peter Norton pioneered.

If your disk won't boot or has a bad partition table, programs like the *Norton Disk Doctor* or *Disk Editor* (included with recent versions of the *Norton Utilities*) might solve the problem. Another approach is to use KFDISK to repair partition-table damage and the DOS command SYS to refresh the hidden, system DOS files. KFDISK is one of several programs included with HTHF from Kolad Research (1898 Techny Court, Northbrook, IL 60062-5474; (708) 291-1586). Using a commercial program to remedy these problems offers two advantages: such programs operate automatically, and most of them allow you to undo any functions they performed that weren't helpful.

8

If you decide to use only DOS commands to recover, you should seek counsel from an experienced user — there are many wrong ways to use the DOS commands and only one right way.

> **TECHNICAL NOTE** For example, if you decided to try using FDISK to repair partition table damage, you would wipe out the most essential information on your disk. That is because in addition to changing the entries in the partition table, FDISK clears out the first several cylinders whenever it creates a partition.

Destructive FORMAT programs: The FORMAT program completely initializes a floppy disk, doing both a low-level and a high-level format. On a hard disk, in most DOS versions, it initializes only the boot record, FAT, and root directory. This makes it possible, at least partially, to "unformat" the disk.

Some versions of the DOS FORMAT program do a bit more. AT&T's DOS up through Version 3.1, Compaq's DOS up through Version 3.2, and some versions of MS-DOS from Burroughs, for example, have FORMAT programs that supplement the usual functions by initializing the data area of the partition or DOS logical drive. This prevents even an unformatting program like that offered by *Mace* or *Norton Utilities* from recovering the data in that partition or DOS logical drive. To avoid such a catastrophe, you should strongly consider upgrading to a new version of DOS if you are using one of these obsolete versions.

You also may wish to consider replacing your FORMAT program with something like the *Norton Utilities* "Safe Format" program or the *PC Tools* program, PCFORMAT. If a low-level format already exists, these programs will do only the high-level format, even on floppy disks (unless you specifically request a destructive format), allowing an unformat program to recover data.

On the other hand, if you want to sell your computer, you may truly want to erase your hard disk, to protect your privacy. In that case, rather than just deleting your files (using the DOS command DEL or ERASE) or even using the DOS FORMAT command, you should use one of the programs offered by the utility packages: Mace has "DESTROY" and Norton has "WIPEFILE" and "WIPEDISK" or, in their latest version, "WIPEINFO." The *PC Tools* PCSHELL program includes a Clear File command for the same purpose.

Sudden death by drive hardware failure

The most common hard-drive hardware failure occurs when the drive sticks, refusing to turn. (One disk repair depot estimates that 60% of the drives they service have this problem.)

Stiction: This failure mode is called *stiction*, short for *static friction*, which occurs when the heads stick to the platters after you have turned off your PC. When you turn it back on, the drive's motor may not be strong enough to dislodge the heads. If you do break the platter free, the drive may work fine until you power down again.

TECHNICAL NOTE

Something to try, if you are daring

You can sometimes fix this problem, temporarily, by a simple trick. Turn off and unplug your PC. Open the system unit. Remove the hard disk. (*Don't try to open the hard disk's sealed chamber. Doing so will only destroy any remaining usefulness of the drive.* Remember to draw a picture to help you plug in the cables again correctly.)

Lay the disk down with the electronic circuit card on top. (This is upside down from the normal mounting position for the drive.) You will likely see a hole in the card, through which you can see the end of the spindle. (This hole may be covered up with a plastic cover. You can gently pry off the cover.) If you can gently but firmly twist that shaft with a screwdriver or pair of pliers, you may be able to get the disk turning freely again.

If you do, then reconnect the disk to your computer with the cover off. (It is okay to sit the drive upside down on the PC frame if you wish; just be sure the cables are on right. Also, be sure the disk won't slip and fall off the frame. Putting a piece of cardboard between the disk drive and the PC's frame will help insure against short circuits.)

Power up the computer. If all goes well, the hard disk will turn and everything will work as usual, for a while, anyway. You should immediately back up in case the disk fails again.

8

Spindle bearing failure: Sometimes the spindle bearing will completely seize up, preventing the drive from turning. Since manufacturers supposedly lubricate hard drives for life, a spindle-bearing failure means the hard drive's life is over. Approximately fifteen percent of all hard drives meet their end this way. The symptoms for spindle-bearing failure resemble those for stiction, except that you cannot get the spindle to turn at all, making it very difficult to retrieve your data.

The only way to recover data from such a drive is to open it up and somehow get the spindle to turn, definitely *not* something you can do at home. An expensive solution is to take your drive to a data-recovery service. If you have been backing up frequently, you can save a lot of money by just replacing the hard drive and loading your software and data from the backups.

Drive electronics failures: About another twenty percent of drive hardware failures result from failed electronics mounted on the drive. The drive and the heads may still function well, but the electronics might be unable to read or write data to the drive. If the electronics of the drive-motor controller fail, the drive won't turn, or it won't turn at the right speed. To diagnose this problem, you could replace the electronics board with a functioning one from a very similar drive. (A repair facility may have a spare.)

Temperature-related problems: Often a drive will fail when only at a certain temperature. For example, your hard drive may not operate properly until after the power to your PC has been on for a few minutes to an hour, warming it up. The fix may be as simple as running *SpinRite,* or it may require extensive repair.

The drive may be about to fail due to a slow distortion or wear of the mechanical parts, which change shape just enough to function when they warm up. In such cases, you should back up your data and then have the disk either repaired or replaced.

8

If the disk can start the boot process but then has trouble finding the system files, however, your problem lies in the information stored in the DOS partition. Running *SpinRite* may move the data tracks back under the heads and strengthen the recorded information enough to make the drive work correctly.

If that does not work, you should boot your computer from a DOS disk, preferably the same version of DOS that you have on your hard disk. If you can then access your hard disk, the data damage is fairly minor, and *Norton Disk Doctor* can usually repair it.

If the drive can't even begin the boot process, you may have a problem with the readability of information outside the DOS partition, indicated by error messages such as "Invalid partition table," "Error loading operating system," or "Missing operating system." If you have an identically partitioned drive in your system of the same type and size, you could copy the good drive's partition table to the bad drive. (Some popular utility programs allow you to save your hard disk's partition table to a file on a disk. They also give you a simple way to use that disk to repair any damage done to your hard disk's partition table.)

If all else fails, you may have to recover the old-fashioned way: Back up all your data. Do the low-level format as if this were a new drive. Use FDISK to reinstall the partitioning information. Do the high-level format (with the FORMAT program). Reinstall your software.

If your drive works when cold but fails once it warms up, the mechanism may be drifting. If so, the techniques just described may help. On the other hand, your drive may be seriously overheating, due to either a bearing problem (the drive may stop turning after it warms up) or a problem with the electronics.

You need to repair a drive that overheats. One way to retrieve your data before taking the drive in to the shop is to chill it thoroughly. Literally take the drive out of your PC and put it in your refrigerator or freezer for several hours, then hook it up to the PC. Soon after you turn the PC back on, when the drive first starts to function, copy off as much data as you can. Once it overheats, turn off the PC, put the drive back in the freezer for a while, and then try again.

 Put only the drive in the freezer. You don't want the main PC to get cold, as condensation of moisture on it while it warms up could lead to other problems.

Head crashes: Though often mentioned as a cause of disk failure, damaging head crashes rarely occur. Every time you turn off your PC, the heads "softly crash," but thanks to their good design, they rarely do any damage to the magnetic coating on the disk surface as they land.

You can further guard against damage by "parking the heads," which positions these soft crashes in an area in which you do not have any important data stored. *Always* use a park program before powering down a hard drive, unless it is a self-parking drive. (You can use a good park program, like that shipped with *SpinRite*, on any drive. See Chapter 4 for a discussion of safe and unsafe park programs.) You should park the heads if your PC is going to be idle for a while, in case the computer is accidentally bumped or knocked to the floor. *SpinRite's* park program doesn't require you to shut off your PC, as some programs do.

Even with the best of parking habits, your hard disks may some day suffer a damaging head crash. The disk may suddenly flail its heads around violently for no obvious reason, or an earthquake might knock the computer to the floor while it's running. The good news is that the heads are not likely to gouge out more than about twenty percent of the disk surface, allowing you to back up the remaining eighty percent.

The bad news is that the gouged-up magnetic coating goes somewhere else inside the drive. It may clog up the ventilation holes, stick to the read/write heads, or seem safely out of the way for awhile and later come back to haunt you. You may be able to use a disk that has suffered a major head crash, but you shouldn't rely on it for the long term.

Some simple mistakes to avoid

`0110 0110`
TECHNICAL NOTE When installing an electronics card on a hard disk, you should beware of screwing it down too firmly, which can distort the frame. This could then make the disk platters rub against the inside of the sealed housing, preventing them from turning.

Similarly, when mounting the drive back in your PC, be careful not to distort the drive frame or sealed housing. In a PC or XT (and in some ATs), the disk is screwed to the computer's case. Use very short screws, or make sure there is enough space behind the hole so the screw will not bear on the sealed chamber (see Figure 8-5). Don't ever put more than two screws into the frame, and then never from opposite sides.

In most ATs and 386 computers, the hard disks have rails screwed to each side; these rails slide into some channels in the PC's frame. Clips screwed into the front of the computer's case hold the drives from sliding out of those channels. The only worry here is that if you use long screws to fasten the rails to the drive, again you may distort the sealed chamber of the hard drive.

8

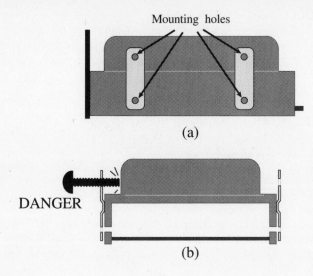

Figure 8-5: Mounting a hard disk: Some errors to avoid.

Controller death

Hard-disk controller boards also rarely fail, but when they do, it can be dramatic. For example, your PC may return a message along the lines of "Invalid drive," "General failure reading drive C," or "Drive not ready" when you execute a command that requires access to the hard disk. If unplugging the cables connecting the hard disk to its controller and plugging them in again doesn't resolve the problem, you could try removing the controller card from the PC and then putting it back. It might be a good idea to clean off the contacts where the card plugs in while you have the card out of the PC. (Again, remember to turn off the PC and unplug it before you open the case.) If this doesn't work either, you may have a failed controller card or disk, or you might have suffered a data accident.

Diagnostic programs can help you decide whether your drive or your controller has failed. Sometimes they even get it right! You could also try replacing one or the other to see if that eliminates your problem.

> ```
> 0110 0110
> ```
> **TECHNICAL NOTE**
>
> ### A Caution
> Your hard disk must have just the right patterns of information recorded on it for your controller to read and write data to it. Remember that each controller is likely to put down its low-level format information in a slightly different way. If you replace your controller with a new one, you very likely will have lost access to all the data on your hard disk, even if the disk itself has not been damaged. The one exception is if you use a new controller that is the same model and revision level as the old controller, which should let you get at your data.
>
> Only replace your controller as a last option. Also hope you have a good, current set of backups. You are likely to need them.

This ends our description of the many ways in which your hard disk can die. Before we leave this topic, let's consider a misleading symptom that may make you erroneously conclude your disk is dying.

A form of degradation that does *not* signal impending hard disk death

When you first use a hard disk it will seem wonderfully fast, particularly when compared to a floppy disk. If, after some months or years of use, you notice that it has slowed down appreciably, the culprit most likely is file fragmentation.

File fragmentation: Whenever you write a file to your hard disk, DOS first looks in the FAT (file allocation table) for available clusters. If the first file takes ten clusters, DOS will assign it the first ten on the disk. If the next file takes six, it gets the next six, and so on. If all you ever did was write new files to the disk, sequential files would reside in adjacent clusters. Of course, most users also remove files and add to existing ones. Let's look at how each of those actions affects a file's placement on the disk.

If after putting several files on the disk you remove the third file, it will leave a hole. If you then write a new file to the disk that is larger than that third file, DOS will allocate part of the new file to that hole and place the rest of it far away, *fragmenting* the file in two. You could also fragment a file by adding data to it, if there isn't enough room for the data between that file and the one just beyond it.

8

When DOS goes to retrieve a file from the disk, it looks in the directory to locate the first cluster of the file's information, and then it consults the FAT to track down the rest of that file's information. If all the clusters for that file are close together, the controller can read them quickly. The more scattered the clusters are, the longer it will take to read them.

> **0110 0110**
> **TECHNICAL NOTE**
>
> When DOS 3.0 came out, much was made of a special built-in feature that was supposed to help reduce file fragmentation and overwriting of deleted files. This simply was a pointer that DOS maintains that says where in the FAT it last found an available cluster. When DOS wants another cluster, it will begin its search through the FAT right after that point. If the disk is fairly full, this does help DOS find a new cluster more quickly. It also will tend to prevent putting a new file into the holes left behind after a file is erased.
>
> It cannot do anything to prevent file fragmentation that comes from adding to an existing file. It also does less than you might imagine to prevent fragmentation of new files. Since DOS keeps this pointer in memory, it must return to the beginning of the FAT each time you reboot your computer. Serious file fragmentation builds up over months or years despite this feature of DOS.

After months of use, most of a hard disk's data files and many of its program files commonly are fragmented. This process will continue to reduce your disk's efficiency and over time may even make your hard disk slower than your floppy disks, but it does not signal incipient data loss or disk failure. Unlike the creeping misalignment problem, no matter how fragmented your files become, you will always be able to access your data, albeit slowly. The extra head motion needed to access fragmented files, however, will hasten your hard disk's demise.

8

The obvious solution to this creeping inefficiency is to unfragment your files. You could do it the hard way by copying your files to floppies, erasing them from the hard disk or formatting the partition, and then restoring the files to the hard disk. Or, you could use a special file-unfragmenting program.

All the popular disk utilities mentioned in the section "Fixing Data Accidents and Some Popular Disk Utility Packages That Make It Easier" include such a program. Another very good file unfragmenter is *PC-Kwik Power Disk* from Multisoft Corporation

(15100 SW Koll Parkway, Beaverton, OR 97006; (800) 274-5945, (503) 644-5644).

Data Recovery

Anyone who has lost data wishes for a way to recover it. You can sometimes resurrect lost data from a hard drive, but it is not always feasible.

The hope versus the reality

A lot depends on how you lost your data. If you had a minor data accident, it may be simple to recover. If one of your drive cables came loose or you need to remove and reinsert your controller card in the slot connector on your PC's motherboard, attending to that will take just a few minutes. If, on the other hand, a destructive head crash gouged off some of the magnetic coating on the platters, the data stored in that part of the coating are irretrievable.

An in-between case is when the spindle bearing seizes, so that it won't turn. Your data is there, but you can't read it. Someone who has the necessary equipment and knowledge (and a clean room) may be able to coax the drive into working again, allowing you to reach your data, but the process can be expensive, sometimes costing much more than the drive itself. (This is one case where the *possible* may very well not be *feasible*. That depends on the value of your data, and perhaps on the age of your backups.) One company that offers this sort of data recovery service is Workman and Associates (1925 East Mountain St., Pasadena, CA 91104; (818) 791-7979).

8

A far simpler way to lose data is by mistakenly erasing files. It may be possible to unerase them, but the task may turn out to be infeasibly difficult and complex. (Some utility programs, if used in advance, can make unerasing files much more feasible: These include the *Mace Utilities'* RXBAK program; the *Norton Utilities'* FR/SAVE or, in the newest version of the *Norton Utilities*, the IMAGE program; and *PC Tools'* MIRROR program.)

An even tougher situation arises when you overwrite as well as delete valuable files. A mere unerase program cannot help you in this case — you will have to resort to some very specialized (and again, expensive) data-recovery services. This presents another strong argument for implementing a regular backup strategy.

What is a good backup strategy?

To be good, a backup strategy must first of all be one you will use — regularly. Almost any approach is fine *if* you use it; still, some are better than others.

How often should you back up?: How often should you back up? Here is a simple rule of thumb: If the pain of recreating the data that would be lost if your computer failed in the next few minutes exceeds the pain of making a backup, then make a backup. For some people this means doing an incremental backup every day; for others, it means backing up every hour. You should still make occasional total backups, to make it quicker and easier to restore files, but you can do it a lot less often with complete safety. You might also want to keep a spare set of your incremental and total backups in another building, but you can do it more rarely since the hazards of theft, fire, or flood are less likely than data corruption.

A good backup strategy: So, how do we define a good backup strategy? The combined total and incremental backups should work well for most offices. You could perform the total backups every quarter or six months, storing a spare set elsewhere. You should add to the incremental backups at least every day or so.

Once you fill an incremental disk or tape, catalog it and make it read-only. For easy access, you could store the incremental backups close to the PC, or you could lock them up for greater security. Don't rerecord on these backup media — once filled, use them only to restore files when needed. One way to enforce this policy is to use WORM drives (Write Once, Read Mostly optical disk drives). Since you cannot rewrite the disks in these drives, they provide permanent, unalterable copies of your files at each stage of their evolution.

8

Another use for good backups

Most people make backups to protect their data against the possibility of a disk failure, but backups can be very useful for other reasons. If you catalog your backup disks or tapes and keep them forever, you can quickly find the backup copy of a file you have long since deleted from your hard drive. Occasionally, that can be even more important than restoring a hard drive after a crash.

One good program to use for disk cataloging is Rick Hillier's *CATDISK*, a shareware program. You may find it on a local BBS, or you can contact Mr. Hillier at 405 Barrington Lane, Waterloo, ONTARIO, Canada N2T 1H9; (519) 888-6763.

That's it. All you really need to know about how hard disks work and why they die — and then some. I hope you enjoyed reading it, as I did researching and writing it.

8

Appendix A

Who Is Steve Gibson? The Genesis of *SpinRite*

"If you have drive — and I was lucky enough to be born with incredible drive and focus — you soon learn that you can teach yourself anything. Then you try anything. And you find you can do almost anything." That is Steve Gibson's explanation of how he got to be what he is today.

It helps to be born into a supportive family. Steve's father was educated as a mechanical engineer. He shared with his son a love for how things go together and how they work. Once Gibson discovered electronics, at age five, he felt a "deep need" to understand that field. For a decade, he immersed himself in it, disassembling surplus radar gear and later reading every book or magazine he could find on the subject.

From this and similar experiences, he gained a deep understanding of how things are assembled and how they really function. He calls this understanding essential to his ability to create innovative products.

The next major influence on Gibson was Harold Fearon, his electronics teacher at Aragon High School in San Mateo, CA. In addition to teaching Steve many lessons, Mr. Fearon gave him the opportunity to create

A

and teach two years of advanced electronics classes. Also while in high school, Gibson found physics and computers — discoveries, he said, that "opened up my world."

During the next several years, Gibson found many more mentors and role models, mainly at the Stanford Artificial Intelligence Laboratory, where he worked on some cutting-edge projects in computer design, including the very first interface to the world's first laser printer.

He enrolled at the University of California. Though he did very well in his studies, in his sophomore year he learned that if he tried to patent a novel processor he had invented, the Regents of the University of California would own all the rights to it, since he was a student at a tax-supported institution. Gibson thought this unfair and, with financial difficulties at home and a summer employer wanting him to stay on, he left formal education.

He continues a life-long habit of "paying close attention to things and being intensely interested in them." Gibson credits this habit with his ability to learn the many skills he has needed in his diverse jobs. He has served as a software and hardware designer, marketing director, and in many other roles in several companies. He created his own advertising agency, but he finally found his niche as a creator of products for personal computers.

When Gibson bought his first Apple II computer, he missed the light pen he had used at the Stanford AI Lab. In 1982, there wasn't one available for microcomputers. That presented a business opportunity he could not resist. He created the *Gibson LPS-II* (Light Pen System for Apple II computers). Acclaimed by reviewers, the LPS-II sold very well.

One thing Gibson learned early in his business career was what he calls the "lesson of margin:" If you have a good profit margin on your products, "you can eat well, drive whatever car you want, and generally have a lot of fun." Pursuing this aim has been a key part of his thinking in choosing all his product innovations.

To make and market the *LPS-II*, Gibson created Gibson Laboratories. Although this was a very successful company, he did not enjoy the experience of managing it. When he got the chance, he sold it, after which he immediately sought another need he could fill with yet another innovative product.

Gibson began using an IBM-PC with both a monochrome and a color graphics display. Horrified by the CGA's poor visual quality, he saw his next opportunity. He wrote a "terminate and stay resident," or TSR, program called *FlickerFree* that would remain "resident" in the PC's memory to improve the CGA display's performance. Though not the first TSR program, it was one of the early ones. Creating it was no simple task.

Rather than establishing a large company again (and take on the resultant management headaches), Gibson produced and sold *FlickerFree* from his home with the help of only one employee. His product was very well received. He sold it to local dealers, at swap meets, and to computer user groups, soon saturating the regional market.

He asked the editor and publisher of *InfoWorld* (a weekly PC computer magazine) to let him write a weekly column in exchange for a free quarter-page advertisement in each issue. They agreed. Thanks to the success of both the column and the advertisement, the arrangement continues today, many years later. Gibson's "Tech Talk" remains one of the most popular and widely read columns in *InfoWorld*.

With *FlickerFree* selling very well, Gibson looked for a product to follow it. He thought he might create a simple hard disk reinterleaving program, a project that he initially thought would take perhaps two weeks. It was not to be quite as simple a task as he thought. After more than a year of hard work, he released *SpinRite*, Version 1.0 — a much more comprehensive disk utility program than he had initially imagined.

With the success of *SpinRite*, Gibson and his one assistant were unable to keep up with the telephone calls, let alone do all the other work of a small business. So Gibson Research acquired an office-warehouse and several more employees. As this book goes to press, Steve Gibson and his small band are hard at work preparing more wonders for our benefit and enjoyment.

Index

I

I

I

I

I

I

I

John M. Goodman

John Goodman has always been a teacher. The thrill of understanding something and the joy of seeing someone else understand it have been central to his motivation.

In choosing what to study and later share, he decided early in life that things were easier to understand than people. Following that notion, he got an undergraduate and a doctoral degree in physics. His graduate minors were mathematics and the history of science.

He has taught in diverse venues, from colleges to preschools, as a classroom teacher and as a museum exhibit designer. Currently, he specializes in seminars on personal computer upgrading and repair throughout the U.S. and Canada.

An active member in the PC user group community, he has served the Orange Coast IBM PC User Group in Southern California in many roles, from newsletter editor to President.

All of the art in this book was created by the author using Corel Draw. The book was typeset in New Caledonia using an Apple Macintosh and Aldus PageMaker.

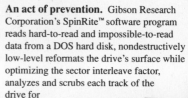

More from the New World of Computer Books...
IDG Books Worldwide

Other Valuable Guides from the New World of Computer Books...IDG Books Worldwide

Finally--a practical guide to portable computing!

Portable Computing Official Laptop Field Manual

▲ A complete, take-it-with-you-on-the-road-manual:
with printer codes, software keystroke references, on-line access phone numbers, individual hardware references, DOS summaries, and more

▲ Leave your manuals at home--everything you need is in this one handy-sized book!

▲ From Portable Computing Magazine--the mobile professional's monthly bible

$14.95

by Sebastian Rupley, with a foreword by Jim McBrian, Publisher, *Portable Computing* Magazine
1-878058-10-X, 224 pp., 5 1/2 x 8 1/2"

The powerful programming tool you need for Paradox 3.5!

PC World Paradox 3.5 Power Programming Techniques

▲With hundreds of programming tips and techniques not found in any other book

▲ Definitive coverage of the Paradox engine, PAL, and SQL Link

▲ Includes one 3 1/2" disk of valuable software, including a ready-to-run accounting system, an advanced program editor, and utility scripts--fully customizable and worth $$ hundreds!

$39.95, includes one 3 1/2"disk with over 2 Mb of program code, condensed onto a 1.44Mb disk

by Greg Salcedo & Martin Rudy, with a foreword by Richard Swartz, Borland International
1-878058-02-9, 750 pp., 7 3/8 x 9 1/4"

IDG Books Worldwide Registration Card -The Official SpinRite II & Hard Disk Companion

Please take the time to fill this out—and you'll be sure to hear about updates to this book and new information about other IDG Books Worldwide products. Thanks!

Name _____

Company/Title _____

Address _____

City/State/Zip _____

What is the single most important reason you bought this book? _____

_____

Where did you buy this book?
- ❏ Bookstore (Name _____)
- ❏ Electronics/Software Store (Name _____)
- ❏ Advertisement (If magazine, which? _____)
- ❏ Mail Order
- ❏ Other:

How did you hear about this book?
- ❏ Book review in: _____
- ❏ Advertisement in: _____
- ❏ Catalog
- ❏ Found in store
- ❏ Other: _____

How many computer books do you purchase a year?
- ❏ 1
- ❏ 2-5
- ❏ 6-10
- ❏ More than 10

How would you rate the overall content of this book?
- ❏ Very good
- ❏ Good
- ❏ Satisfactory
- ❏ Poor

Why? _____

What chapters did you find most valuable? _____

What did you find least useful? _____

What kind of chapter or topic would you add to future editions of this book?

_____

Please give us any additional comments. _____

_____

❏ Check here if you need additional infomation on SpinRite/Gibson Research products. Add specifics: _____

Thank you for your help.

❏ I liked this book! By checking this box, I give you permission to use my name and quote me in

Fold Here

Place
stamp
here

IDG Books Worldwide, Inc.
155 Bovet Road, Ste. 730
San Mateo, CA 94402

Attn: Reader Response